BREAKING THE SILENCE ON THE RETURN OF TOTALITARIANISIM

BY EDDIE HOBBS

PUBLISHED BY

104 publishing

Praise for 'Breaking The Silence'

"This book uncovers in stark reality the truth behin• the Covi• pan•emic an• the Climate change scam. E••ie Hobbs uncovers that throughout history, human societies an• governments have trie• to rule by enforcing the greater goo• for the population. It is in fact roote• in feu•alism with a ruling entitle• elite trying to control the population coercing them to swap Free•om for Safety.
Safety involves inventing external enemies to invoke more an• more control which gives rise to totalitarianism an• the silencing of opposition. You have seen it before, think Hitler an• Stalin an• the effects lai• bare in '1984', 'Animal Farm' an• 'Brave New Worl•'.
However, the vast majority of the western thinking population have misse• its gross resurgence with the planne• an• exaggerate• covi• pan•emic an• the oh so obvious global warming cause• by Human pro•uce• CO2 scam. These are the start an• it will get worse with the banking system eventual collapse. (If you want to survive it then you must rea• this book!)
Hopefully, everyone who rea•s this remarkably well researche• book will imme•iately spot what is going on an• the attempts to reset your lives everywhere, then challenge it an• sen• it back to the •ark ages from whence it came!"

Professor Angus Dalgleish, Professor of Oncology at St Georges Hospital Medical School, London.

"We are •eeply embe•••e• in an information war, in which myria• geopolitical forces are manipulating the global public. Time-honore• totalitarian tactics are being •eploye• with impressive effect in our mo•ern population, exploiting technology to enhance the outcomes. In this superb book E••ie Hobbs eloquently reveals these metho•s an• processes, so that the average person can maintain an in•epen•ent min•. An• more importantly...be well prepare• for the challenges that lie ahea•."

Ivor Cummins, Biochemical Engineer and Metabolic Science Author, www.TheFatEmperor.com

"E••ie Hobbs has successfully summarize• the key issues of our time in a way that is both compelling an• rea•ily accessible. Fearlessly calling out problems at societal, national, an• international levels, he invites rea•ers to critically examine the psychological an• societal mechanisms that enable control an• manipulation in our •igital age. This book is an excellent starting point for anyone seeking to un•erstan• an• challenge these forces."

Dr Clare Craig BM BCh FRCPath, Diagnostic Pathologist, Co-Chair HART, www.hartgroup.org

In 'Breaking Totalitarianism' E••ie Hobbs , much like Solzhenitsyn, Aren•t an• Desmet before him •elivers a thoughtful an• well researche• Tour •e Force •etailing the latest coming of Totalitarianism in our Digital age. As shoots of resistance emerge across the Western Worl• in 2024 Hobbs invites us to carefully stu•y both through his own awakening an• experiences, as well as through the testimony of the important thinkers of our time who are also raising the alarm. Much as sunlight is the best •isinfectant, Hobbs luminously exposes the What, Who, an• Why behin• the latest form of Totalitarianism. Consistent with his positive outlook an• hopefulness, he ultimately •escribes the tools all aroun• us, with which we can confront an• ultimately overcome this threat, an• usher in a new age of free•om, critical thinking, an• •ecentralise• prosperity.

Dr. Alan Farrell, MB BCh BAO BA MSc, expert in Preventative Medicine/High Performance Medicine, and founder of www.cdx-p.com

First published in 2024 by 104 Publishing.
Cover design by Andrew Walsh.
Editing and typesetting by Abby Wynne.
Published by Abby Wynne & Mark Attwood (104publishing.com).

ISBN
Paperback Edition 978-1-7385735-3-0
Ebook Edition 978-1-7385735-4-7
Hardback Edition 978-1-7385735-5-4

IF YOU WANT THE AUDIO VERSION OF THIS BOOK...

If you would like to buy the audiobook,
gain access to exclusive interviews and more;
use the Qr code below, or type our web address into a browser:

https://bit.ly/EddieHobbs

A NOTE OF GRATITUDE

This note of gratitude I write in July 2024, to everyone who helped guide me to this moment and especially to all those who quietly approached me after open public speeches to offer their prayers. I never thought I'd write that, convinced, perhaps like you, in the age of rationality, liberal democracy and a functioning media. I've humbly learnt that I knew little of the world outside that fed us and that I had stopped listening to my soul.

It is very challenging to accept that you've been duped; I get that fully because I fought against it for nearly four years. I contested what my research, discussions, and experiences laid out as the truth insofar as I could discern it, the truth of the big lie.

The Covid 19 response is not what it seems; it was a very carefully contrived fraud delivered with military knowledge of psyops and ubiquitous resources with a deep reach into the media we consume for the purposes of birthing 21st century totalitarian control over humanity. It is not over. It is in open sight. What is in deficit is enough of us to push past our cognitive dissonance to see it and call it out. This is happening.

We are being tested. Are we to accept that our destiny is a mechanised future where humans are controlled from the centre, digitalised, parsed, and tracked with forensic surveillance over our carbon limits, vaccination compliance, spending on food, and what we say and write? This is the grand plan of those in powerful positions to deliver it, but only with our compliance, our permission, and our fear.

I want to thank the many who contributed to the writing of this wake-up call, all those who volunteered for interviews on Counterpoint on YouTube, engaged in exchanges on X and TikTok and emailed privately. Most of all, I want to thank the large numbers who showed up at public events and who offered their energy. I felt it, profoundly. It is a fire.

In particular, I want to thank those who continue to help me figure all this out behind the scenes, and that is where they will remain to protect them from those who might cause them harm. I've had occasion to meet and get to know many experts who were first to carry the load in defending humanity even when misunderstood, mislabelled and ostracised for doing so. These are remarkable people, some of whom I touch upon in this book, others I've interviewed, more of whom I've yet to meet.

It is not over. We are in a contest across multiple fronts and face an impulse to herd us into a sterile, mechanistic near future, where we convince ourselves that we are not of God. This is where the Killarney Declaration comes into play. You will find it in Appendix I. It addresses the interconnections; it could have been delivered anywhere from Reykjavík to Hobart. There is hope now; a pivot point has been reached as more and more people awaken to the real and present danger of totalitarianism. It will be defeated by the numbers who wake up and are still waking. I wrote Breaking the Silence because I was compelled to help people.

I dedicate this book to the champion of free will, Archangel Michael.

TABLE OF CONTENTS

PREFACE

We police ourselves. Our own words have become weaponised. As technology has advanced, we have become alienated and atomised. Nobody answers the phone anymore. Nobody likes to be quoted on their true thoughts about a variety of social and political matters that are important to them. It is forbidden. Journalism is dying - what remains is a husk of what it once was. We revere the new restrictions, the ever-expanding micro-rules and regulations that govern the professions, our food, our consumption, and our content creation. There is no safe forum for public debate to achieve collective consensus and decisions. The simplest technology, fire, could achieve what our advanced phones cannot. Gathered around campfires, our ancestors could achieve a higher degree of humanity by sharing stories, directly responding to each other and coming to collective wisdom.

This, however, is a surface explanation; peel away at the layers fearlessly long enough, and you will see a different truth emerging. Here's as good a summary as you'll find, by Nick

Hudson, Actuary and Chairman of PANDA, a global independent group of multi-disciplinary professionals, data scientists, lawyers, engineers, economists and businesspeople focused on individual sovereignty, free exchange of ideas and decentralised innovation.

> *"Let's just take a step back, the general rule of thumb that I believe everybody should adopt is that if any problem is being presented as a global crisis then it is a scam. The pattern that we are confronted with is really the fabrication of global crisis, the presentation either of non existent problems or small local problems as being general global crises. That fabrication followed by the assertion that the only solutions that are permissible are global ones, that require a global authority and global control is the general pattern that we are up against.*
>
> *The Covid policy response was one of those, look at what happened to countries like Sweden or Tanzania who tried to push back against the orthodoxy. The climate change crisis is another example where we are told that the biggest threat to the world is this molecule CO2 and that an increase in the level of this molecule will cause an increase in temperature and that that temperature increase will be bad for us and that the only thing we can do is consume fewer fossil fuels fuels and less energy. That is fitting the pattern exactly.*
>
> *The other things you can observe is instead of presenting science as an ongoing evolving activity, it is presented in terms of static knowledge consensus and you see the cancellation and censorship of dissident voices rather than engagement with them. These patterns are proof of a scam that is what people need to understand whenever something is presented as the science as a consensus, it is a scam. You do not have to go and get engaged in all of the minutiae of the scientific principles and the models and the*

> *measurements, at all you can know with absolute certainty is that you are dealing with a scam when dissent is suppressed."*

The problem is that what is happening is organised. It is not happenstance nor purely motivated by simple greed. It is driven by a global oligarchy, the robber baron dynasties old and new, using a weapon created and managed by them, the Deep State, which has followed them globally. Their objective is total control of the masses; this is totalitarianism, a state of captivity through which total power, profit and self-preservation can be attained. It doesn't happen overnight but is built in increments presented for our own good, until it is too late. This is the key to understanding the current resurgence, totalitarian control isn't just the ultimate model for an oligarchical class to make super profits and eliminate competition, it is the only way they perceive through which family dynasties can survive the inevitable rise of the masses.

During the pandemic, freedom was sacrificed for a simple illusion: a false sense of safety. This happened on a global level. How is any of this even possible? Social science has offered many explanations, but we have been slow in accepting them. We prefer not to talk about the human propensity to embrace herd mentality and flock together and how psychological operations (psyops) can manipulate that. All too easily, we begin to murmurate like starlings, moving mindlessly in a mass formation to adore a new deity and sacrifice our freedoms in the hopes of receiving safety from artificially manufactured crises.

Since the shock of Italy's lockdown in March 2020, I've spent much of the intervening years attempting to make sense of all the irrational thinking and denial of data and science that accompanied it. Finally, in 2023, I discovered a large part of the answer, but I am still learning. It is why I started the Counterpoint interview series on YouTube, which inspired me to write this book. The truth, when you stumble on it, rings like a bell across frosty meadows on a still winter morning. It wakes even the heaviest sleeper. However, not everyone will rise at the same time. Many will stay in denial, deep in cognitive dissonance.

The totalitarian tendency that wreaked havoc on the European population in the 20th century has returned, if it ever went away. It's camouflaged and prepared – disguised in a benign and caring guise. It cannot be wholly formed and directed by a secretive and centralised cabal, that is too simple, but for it to take root, it has to be invited in as part of us, our culture and everyday behaviour. In short, we have to give it our permission.

Totalitarianism has never been a simple social phenomenon; its causes are many and complex. Whether consciously or unconsciously, we are all contributing to its resurgence. It is not a political ideology; it is a mechanical, rule-bound model for humanity that ultimately aims for its masters to become a superior transhuman class, its victim's slaves, captive within digitalised walls and the excess baggage, the useless underclass eventually targeted for eugenics. The impulse itself, at its essence, is a denial of God.

Totalitarianism was implemented by Stalinists in the Soviet Union and the National Socialist Party in Germany, both of which promised utopia. Eventually, it annihilated large parts of their respective populations after vilifying and dehumanising them. Totalitarianism, unlike dictatorships governed by leaders who consolidate power once in charge, requires additional fuel for the pyres; it must continue to crush and eradicate obstacles that obstruct the route to utopia, and all that is required is a violation of an arbitrary rule or an accusation of intent to do so.

When faced with no opponents, totalitarians turn inward on their managerial class, seeking new victims to burn. Totalitarianism has no real values or ideals except its own survival.

Ultimately, it didn't matter if the totalitarian authorities lied and were caught doing so. As Hannah Arendt remarked:

> *"The totalitarian mass leaders based their propaganda on the correct psychological assumption that, under such conditions, one could make people believe the most fantastic statements one day, and trust that if the next day they were given irrefutable proof of their falsehood, they would take refuge in cynicism; Instead of deserting the leaders who had lied to them, they would protest that they had known all along that the statement was a lie and would admire the leaders for their superior tactical cleverness".*[1]

Totalitarianism can undermine our most basic sense of reality and our values. It aims to transcend humanity, to attain something higher, yet it leads us to lower levels of our animal nature. In this primitive state, truth is of no value, and might makes right.

Aleksandr Solzhenitsyn fingers the dry tinder that fuelled Soviet totalitarianism and, in doing so, makes this harrowing observation in his book, *The Gulag Archipelago*:

1. *The Origins of Totalitarianism*, p. 382

> *"If only there were more evil people somewhere insidiously committing evil deeds, it were necessary only to separate them from the rest of us and destroy them. But the line dividing good and evil cuts through the heart of every human being, and who was willing to destroy a piece of his own heart?"*[2]

Solzhenitsyn observed how regular people engaged and aided in the institution of totalitarianism in Russia. There is nothing inherently totalitarian in Russian, German, or Italian culture and character. Totalitarianism is a universal plight of humanity. It is not wholly foreign or new to human nature. It exploits our deepest flaws and appeals to our basest fears and desires.

But surely humanity has learned from the carnage of the 20th century, and there are no equivalent monsters now? It seems that the monsters have grown only more cunning and have embraced new technologies. As the impulse towards mass formation during the pandemic has dramatically shown, totalitarianism has set down roots. It is spreading thanks to the desire to reduce perceived risks and anxieties by micromanaging all aspects of life, by passing the power over us to centralised technological bureaucracies run by banal and anonymous officials. Evil, real evil, should not be ignored or downplayed. However, totalitarianism needs much more involvement and cooperation to function. The mass formation during the pandemic was led chiefly by banal bureaucrats with good intentions, banal people like oil salesman Adolf Eichmann who joined the SS and Nazi party in 1932 and whose 1961 TV trial in Jerusalem was studied closely by Arendt. In the

2. *The Gulag Archipelago* Volume I, p. 168

introduction to *Eichmann in Jerusalem,* Amos Elon sums up Arendt's account of evil in the following way:

> *"Evil comes from a failure to think. It defies thought for as soon as thought tries to engage itself with evil and examine the premises and principles from which it originates, it is frustrated because it finds nothing there. That is the banality of evil."*[3]

Without banal people like Eichmann, truly evil individuals, like Hitler certainly was, could not get into power and use it destructively. Psychopathic individuals are not a serious threat to society if they cannot count on the corruptibility and banality of others. As dangerous as they might be, there are never enough psychopaths to run a whole totalitarian system. They always rely on the assistance of flawed but still humane individuals.

For a mass psychosis to take root and be sustained, it requires a two-way street. Totalitarianism is ultimately a mass formation it triggers and finds its fuel from us, from the masses, because it promises the illusion of a future that addresses the object of our anxiety. The actual leaders don't matter that much once this process takes root. Again, as Arendt noted:

> *"In substance, the totalitarian leader is nothing more nor less than the functionary of the masses he leads; he is not a power-hungry individual imposing a tyrannical and arbitrary will upon his subjects. Being a mere functionary, he can be replaced at any time, and he depends just as much on the "will" of the masses he embodies as the masses depend upon him."*[4]

---

3. *Eichmann in Jerusalem*, p. *xiv*
4. *The Origins of Totalitarianism*, p. 325

We may single out Stalin, Hitler and Mussolini as uniquely guilty for the crimes of totalitarianism, but they were not the only ones responsible. Behind them was a whole apparatus and oligarchy, and behind it, an entire population undergoing a mass formation.

The identification of the unvaccinated among us as carriers of Covid and their vilification based on the false science that jabs would stop transmission maps closely to the early process of mass formation in Germany and Russia where Jews, White Russians and Kulaks were, through consistent propaganda, presented as the objects of mass anxiety and fear. The masses had their scapegoat. Only through the slaughter of the scapegoat is the village made pure again, and its people brought to catharsis. Between the Nazis and Communists, tens of millions were exterminated or marched to Gulags, where most died. Their deaths were seen as necessary and justified. How else would the past humiliation be overcome and utopia come about?

The Stalinists and Nazis didn't corner the market in death by the government; let us not forget the Chinese Communists, who are responsible for an even larger number of killings. In his 1994 book, *Death by Government*, R. J. Rummel puts the total killed intentionally by the Chinese government by 1987 at 35 million. In his book, Rummel also discusses democides in Japan, Cambodia, Yugoslavia, Turkey, Poland and Pakistan and other areas of suspected genocide in North Korea, Mexico and feudal Russia. He concludes that more than 169 million people have been victims of democide or death by the government. Not all of the responsible regimes were strictly totalitarian, but there is a clear conclusion: authoritarian governments kill, totalitarian regimes kill much more.

But surely, Covid policies or those associated with climate change and moves to create programmable central bank currencies cannot be put in the same category as these extreme outcomes from the 20th century? Not yet, but our current trajectory poses a real and present danger of 21st century totalitarianism, this time on a global scale. What would society have devolved into by now if our human immune systems had not dealt with the coronavirus? The pandemic should be seen as a warning and a rehearsal for future crises and solutions. The beginnings of technocratic totalitarianism are all around us in science, politics and culture. But there is hope; it lies in the great numbers of people awakening to the forces unleashed, seeing its omnipresence and calling it out fearlessly.

We may, by definition, know very little about the surveillance by security agencies eavesdropping on the internet, except that, under the guise of covertly protecting us, it is rampant. But we do openly see a surveillance society well underway through the introduction of centralised digital currencies, which when programmable, may give unelected bureaucrats the most powerful means to thwart individual freedoms. Although this process has been slowly underway, regulating our spending, consumption and travel, Covid has given it a considerable boost. Covid was accompanied by digital passports without which access to international travel, local restaurants, hotels, cafes and bars – the very fabric of social life – was denied. In many countries access to basic shopping and healthcare facilities was precluded from those who did not have the digital passport. Political leaders in many countries excoriated the unvaccinated and the vaccine-hesitant, urging citizens to inform on organisations and individuals who did not follow the rules.

It doesn't take much imagination to connect the dots and see the trend. Things like programmable currency, vaccine mandates and personal carbon limits work together to undermine basic freedoms in favour of more control, surveillance and, supposedly, security. With the groundwork already laid by Covid, future mass formations are ready to seal the deal and make total control official. The WHO declaring Monkey Pox as a Public Health Emergency of International Concern (PHEIC) in 2024 was the next testing of the waters. For the next big pandemic, the WHO intends to be in full control of public health policy in your country, bounded by an international treaty with the power to decide what is a pandemic, what rules apply, and which jabs are approved. The elites and technocrats learn from their previous projects and mistakes; they are not afraid to change course or adopt new tactics if it means achieving final victory.

In early June 2024, the governing body of the WHO, the World Health Assembly (WHA), met in Geneva and attempted to get a treaty over the line. During discussions, they'd relabelled it as an agreement to misdirect its impact on national sovereignty. This would have established an unelected global technocracy with complete discretion to declare health emergencies, both local and international, across human, plant and animal health and, clearly linked to climate change, it also covered ecosystems. It failed to make the agenda and was withdrawn a week before the assembly. Instead, The WHA concentrated on amending the 2005 International Health Regulations (IHR), where they proposed deleting the term 'non-binding' over 160 times. This failed but only by a whisker.

Due to activism worldwide led in Japan and the USA, leaders are ahead of the game in grasping what happened during the 'pandemic'. Those behind establishing the WHO and UN, both of which are in strategic alliance with the World Economic Forum (WEF), experienced a setback, but all of them want to establish global technocracies and plan to come back as early as 2025 to have another go. By the Autumn of 2024, the agents behind the WHO, noting the failure to land their technocracy in Geneva mid-year, plot to come through the back door, through the UN.

On April 25th 2024, I called a free and open public meeting, '*Breaking the Silence*', held in Cork in the south of Ireland at a conference centre. It was jammed with up to a thousand people travelling from all over Ireland to listen to the arc of the story, my findings from studying the pandemic years and studying the works from the writers outlined in this book. To put the meeting attendance into USA numbers, multiply it sixtyfold. The Irish media ignored it despite the relative scale and reach of the event on social media, where the live stream and recording garnered over a quarter of a million views on X.

The Breaking the Silence lecture talk is available on my YouTube channel, Counterpoint[5]. A few weeks later I read the Killarney Declaration outside the 5-star Europe Hotel in Killarney, which was holding a Global Economic Summit opened by the WHO Director General. The declaration reading is on Counterpoint on YouTube and also available at 1215Tribes.com if you'd like to add to its seven thousand signatures. It is replicated in the Appendix of this book. On May 30th 2024, on the eve of the WHA meeting in Geneva, I read out the Killarney Declaration on the exact spot where Padraig Pearse read out the 1916 Rising Declaration outside the GPO on O'Connell Street. In mid-October 2024 I interviewed a panel of five UK medical experts in Dublin for *The People's*

5. https://www.youtube.com/@RealEddieHobbs

Vaccine Enquiry for Ireland, published on X, it was instantly deleted by YouTube. Censorship is real, it is here and, it is the enemy of critical thinking and public discourse.

In the early stages of the global pandemic in March 2020, I noticed something very odd happening in Ireland. Government officials and bureaucrats seemed to be leaking advanced notices of Covid policy to run as speculative front-page Irish Times headlines, which RTE then picked up to set the day's national news agenda to generate feedback for the politburo. My media background led me to suspect we were being manipulated; this was not journalism, it was propaganda. To test the hypothesis I contacted an insider in a pivotal position within the RTE sphere and learned that several of the senior presenters had been brought into a meeting and told how the Covid policy was going to go down; in short, they were to follow orders.

Alarmed by the global plans to go into lockdown, accompanied by a vast amount of money printing, qualitatively different from all the money printing that followed the global financial crisis, I submitted an essay to the *Irish Examiner,* which it published in April 2020. In it, I warned that there will be an outbreak of high inflation as well as waves of defaults, personal, business and sovereign from lockdowns. The inflation dynamic first took root in Irish data from October 2020, and by the time of writing in 2024, the total losses in real money purchasing power, affecting all cash deposits and incomes in the population, will have totalled 20%, which means the value of one Euro in every five has been lost permanently. Inflation had a big impact on the seismic shift in US politics November 5th 2024 as President Donald Trump and his Republican party garnered a clear cut mandate within which the impact of inflation on the basic cost of living appears to have driven marginal voters in high numbers to his core message. It isn't the only driver, the Republican leadership has also pushed back on the globalist agenda as represented by the WHO, UN and WEF including the indoctrination of children in schools into critical theory including gender ideology, censorship of free speech and net zero, meanwhile Robert F Kennedy Jnr whose work features in this book is set to tackle public health and the captivity of health regulators by the powerful pharmaceutical lobby. It comes not a moment too soon and represents the first major push back against the underlying totalitarian impulse and objectives, blind to Irish mainstream media still mired in the woke swamp.

In the early part of 2020 and whilst I had a reasonably good grasp of the financial and economic implications of what was happening, I knew little or nothing about the complex social, psychological and medical aspects of the pandemic. Each evening in the Spring of 2020, along with millions of fellow Irish citizens, I too sat down to listen to reports from breathless RTE journalists emerging from the latest Covid updates. Sleep wasn't coming easy, but I couldn't explain why. I now know that I had free-floating anxiety, a general sense of unease without any identifiable targets. Eventually, I stopped engaging with mainstream media altogether. That helped considerably. I redirected my energy into writing a novel set safely in the early 14th century while also working on e-commerce innovation and running my financial firm.

A short time later, I was asked to chair a discussion in a private home led by scientists and doctors I did not know, talking about subjects I knew very little about. When I arrived I was astonished that no one was wearing a mask; everybody was shaking hands, even hugging, while their kids ran about playing. There was no social distancing; it was as if the virus didn't exist. I remember feeling anxious and uncomfortable. These people had no fear, whereas I was still rattled by it even though I'd unplugged from RTE. That was the moment I realised that I'd been under a spell, that I'd been hypnotised.

The discussion that unfolded over the next couple of hours changed my life. I woke up. I could no longer unsee what I had only begun to see. From that point I started to explore the counter and alternative science, psychology, laws, policies, politics, media and public behaviour surrounding this massive global event.

On Twitter, now X, I campaigned against the vaccination of healthy children, because they were more at risk from the potential side effects of the vaccine than to the virus itself. I also campaigned against vaccine passports, which were supposed to stop transmission. Now we know there was no science to support the nonsense they blatantly told us. It was simple lies, effective at the time. My campaign also included publicly criticising the Irish President's decision not to challenge new legislation that gave effect to the yellow pass, which I warned would lead to the media to demonise fellow citizens and promote a new kind of apartheid and division. I did all this even though I was vaccinated myself. It didn't take long for things to escalate.

Shortly after the vaccine passports, I published a letter from Beaumont Hospital in Dublin on X, telling patients waiting on the transplant list that a lack of vaccination would exclude them from getting a lifesaving organ. For days I was attacked online, accused of faking the letter. I messaged senior people in the mainstream media, including Jon Williams, the Director of News for both TV and Radio at RTE, imploring him to put this out as the lead RTE news item. Within minutes, a message with the State broadcaster's refusal to carry the story landed in my WhatsApp. Jon Williams messaged that he was too busy trying to get two Afghan journalists out of Afghanistan. Only when a newspaper finally published the story, after it first trended online, was the Beaumont decision rescinded.

Over three years, such was the media lockout on op-eds, I took to broadcasting warnings in ads on Newstalk radio, warning about inbound inflation because not a single Irish economic professor, institution or commentator spoke against the narrative. Throughout 2021, central banks, led by the Fed and mimicked by the ECB and the Central Bank of Ireland, told us that the surge of inflation was *transitory*, and then the blame was put on Putin the following year. It was an orchestrated misdirection; anyone who has studied inflation could see it coming after the massive injection of excessive money creation that accompanied lockdown, qualitatively and quantitatively different to every episode since the Global Financial Crisis. This wall of money went straight into the veins of the economy, into consumer bank accounts, creating a massive increase in the supply of money. Inflation was to head towards double digits before the Fed came clean over the New Year's holiday in 2022 to admit that inflation needed to be tackled with a rate hiking cycle; then, weeks later, the Russian army invaded Ukraine.

It wasn't until 2023, after reading the *Psychology of Totalitarianism,* by Professor of Clinical Psychology Mattias Desmet, and later reading the *War for Technocracy* and *Wall*

Street and the Nazis, by Professor David Hughes, that I finally found frameworks that made sense of what was happening. It helped that these frameworks are solidly grounded in research and in historic mass formation events that occurred among the populations of the former Russian Empire and Germany in the early part of the 20th century. It also helped that Desmet was familiar with and relied upon the works of Hannah Arendt. This does not diminish the clear findings in science, economics and finance that point to the playing out of agendas administered through supranational institutions like the World Economic Forum. These agendas are no conspiracy, they are openly implemented with little ideological coating. However, that is not the main topic of this book. I'm more interested in what is not in plain sight, about a deficiency in critical thinking—a cultural virus that has spread widely among us.

Total silence is the soundtrack of totalitarianism. The totalitarian culture of docility accepts self-surveillance and micro-rules and even begins to venerate them. The current digital environment is also a tipping point for widespread loneliness, alienation from social bonds, free-floating anxiety and unvented aggression. We have created the perfect petri dish where mass formation can run loose. This can be triggered by unrelenting propaganda and reinforced through social media feedback loops. This has happened and continues to happen. It has led to a significant diminution in critical thinking, which is the main antidote to the effects of mass formation. Professor Hughes, a senior lecturer in International Relations whom I interviewed in 2024 on Counterpoint and who conducted a detailed academic study over three years, takes it further and deeper, concluding that the events were preplanned, with military-level psychological operations and a distinct agenda.

Also on Counterpoint is a detailed interview in July 2024 with Professor Francis Boyle of the University of Illinois in Chicago. What makes his work fascinating and deeply concerning is that as a respected international human rights lawyer, he drafted the USA Bioweapons Anti-Terrorism Act 1989, which was signed into law by President George Bush Snr on 22nd May 1990. He knows the US military and industrial complex inside out. In January 2020, he described Covid 19 as a bioweapon for which he was castigated, which carried across over 60,000 publications globally because he dared challenge the narrative of its zoonic origin. In his Counterpoint interview, Professor Boyle draws a parallel to the anthrax vaccine injected into half a million US troops in the Gulf War, causing, he believes, the Gulf War Syndrome that gave permanent health damage to 100,000 and caused the deaths of 11,000 army personnel. Chillingly, Professor Boyle believes that the anthrax vax harm is the baseline for what is unfolding after lockdowns and jabs into over 5.5bn people worldwide. If he is correct, the legal actions underway between 10% of all US States and Pfizer over non-disclosures is a drop in the bucket compared to the fury to come.

The impact of the three years to the end of 2023 can be studied by looking at the data for the excess deaths - that is, deaths above the normal trend. These deaths can be attributed to biological excess from lockdown stresses, non-Covid vaccine interventions and the vaccines themselves. In a study released on 19th July 2024 by Ottawa-based not-for-profit Correlation Research covering 35% of the global population across 125 countries, that's 2.7bn people, the all-cause excess death rate in 93 countries with sufficient data is 0.392% over the three years to end 2023. The study by Rancourt, Hickey and Linard estimates all ages deaths for the vaccine at greater than 0.1% per year.

By August 2024, the WHO declared another Public Health Emergency of International Concern (PHEIC); this time, it was Monkeypox. The WHO seems to be setting up an assembly line of PHEICs to reward those who finance it. There is too much money to be made, too much power to control and too much long-term planning and resources invested to deliver an unaccountable global technocracy to stop it from doing so. This is the WHO's prime objective. Its sister, the UN, has its own parallel objectives and has created its own bogeyman to create fear—climate change. Both are interconnected.

Climate change is a multi-trillion Dollar industry as promulgated by the UN IPCC and has morphed into a science-for-sale industry since its obscure origins in the early 90's. Both are dealt with in this book and on Counterpoint, along with an examination of the impulse to implement a version of 21st century totalitarianism. Those who advocate for their vision of centralised surveillance and control don't use the term totalitarianism to describe their policies. They prefer to use different names for apparently disconnected objectives like bio-microchipping, programmable digital currency and personal carbon limits linked to digital wallets, lab-grown meat, insects, chicken culls and fifteen-minute cities. All for the betterment of mankind, but they are all connected. Critical thinking starts when we refuse dogmatically to accept the first explanation. This is a mechanistic, authoritarian vision of human society, one that we must reject. The easiest way to begin is to call it out and use what it most fears: derision, satire and the laughter of the crowd. Eric Clapton has said of mass formation, *"Once I kind of started to look for it, I saw it everywhere."*

My hope is that you too, will begin to see totalitarian creep everywhere and be able to laugh at it out loud. Totalitarianism *must be* invited in, however, refusing it permission destroys it, and we must do it en-masse before it becomes unstoppable.

INTRODUCTION

In the councils of government, we must guard against the acquisition of unwarranted influence, whether sought or unsought, by the military-industrial complex. The potential for the disastrous rise of misplaced power exists and will persist. We must never let the weight of this combination endanger our liberties or democratic processes. We should take nothing for granted. Only an alert and knowledgeable citizenry can compel the proper meshing of the huge industrial and military machinery of defence with our peaceful methods and goals, so that security and liberty may prosper together.

— PRESIDENT DWIGHT D. EISENHOWER

This quote comes from President Dwight D. Eisenhower's January 17, 1961 farewell address. In this speech, Eisenhower warned the American public about the potential dangers posed by the close relationship between the country's military and defence industry, an unholy union he famously termed the military-industrial complex. Eisenhower cautioned against the undue influence that the military-industrial complex could acquire in the near future. He noted that this influence might be actively pursued or arise naturally from the system. If left unchecked, this means that the mere existence of a large military and defence industry could distort policy and governance. Such a complex would entail the misplacing of power into the hands of unelected, unknown and unchecked elites. The concentration of power in the hands of the military-industrial complex would lead to potential conflicts of interest, unnecessary military engagements, and a diversion of resources from other critical areas such as education, healthcare, and infrastructure. These worries, although completely reasonable, pale in comparison to the totalitarian tendencies arising from within the military-industrial complex.

Eisenhower rightfully identified the unchecked power of the military-industrial complex as a threat to American freedoms and democratic governance. A democracy relies on transparency, accountability, and the rule of law. A powerful military-industrial complex automatically undermined these principles, leading to a less open and less democratic society where decisions are made behind closed doors. To counteract these dangers, Eisenhower called for vigilance and an informed citizenry. He believed that only a population that is aware and knowledgeable about the workings of the military-industrial complex can ensure that its power is properly balanced and integrated with the nation's overall democratic values. Citizens should be engaged, questioning, and proactive in their civic duties.

Eisenhower's farewell message stressed the importance of balance. He acknowledged the necessity of a strong defence but stressed that it should not come at the cost of liberty and democratic values. In this, he was perhaps too generous. However, the Cold War was well underway. No one, especially not a retired general, could deny the revitalised importance of the military. Eisenhower advocated for a harmonious compromise where the nation's security apparatus works alongside a civic commitment to peace, freedom, and democracy. Even if we accept that an inflated military-industrial complex was necessary in order to win the Cold War and prevent the spread of Communism, we should not accept its continuing expansion and influence.

Eisenhower's warning remains relevant today, more so than in 1961. The defence budget of the United States is the highest in the world and its defence industry continues to wield significant influence in Washington, D.C. The issues he highlighted—such as the potential for conflicts of interest, the risk of perpetual warfare, and the strain on democratic processes—are still pertinent and more than apparent. In the modern context, this also extends to the influence of technology companies and private contractors in defence and intelligence operations.

Even though the military has undergone privatisation, it has become even less transparent and accountable. It is no wonder that the Pentagon cannot account for more than 60% of its $3.8 trillion budget. Eisenhower's farewell address was supposed to be a reminder of the importance of vigilance, transparency, and balance in the relationship between national defence and democratic governance. It is clear that America has largely failed to remember that democracy is a continual fight. The military-industrial complex, unopposed by any major political force, has established itself as the core of the *deep state*. The deep state is no shadowy organisation or malevolent cabal; it is simply a group of people and organisations that wield significant power. Importantly, they are oblivious to democracy. Their power is not mandated by any constitution or law; they are not elected or appointed by the people. Presidents, senators and congresspeople come and go, but the deep state persists.

The growing power of the deep state was made clear after the assassination of JFK on 22nd November 1963. The Warren Commission was established seven days later to investigate the assassination and the holes in the official narrative. Its conclusion that Lee Harvey Oswald acted alone faced significant scepticism, leading to various alternative theories about the assassination's details. A document, CIA Dispatch 1035-960, released internally coinciding with the Warren Commission, was revealed through a Freedom of Information Act (FOIA) request by the New York Times in 1976 and outlined strategies for countering criticisms of the Warren Commission. It highlights how the CIA sought to manage public perception and undermine conspiracy theories surrounding JFK's assassination. The CIA ingeniously inverted the term critical thinker into conspiracy theorist and pushed an agenda to make it stick. It worked.

Critics of the Warren Commission were portrayed as narcissists, more interested in self-promotion than uncovering the truth. It was suggested that critics had ulterior political motives, and the CIA aimed to discredit them as biased and not unobjective. Charges of sensationalism and profiteering also undermined the sincerity and integrity of the critics.

The dispatch advised using media outlets and journalists sympathetic to the CIA to disseminate counterarguments and criticisms of conspiracy theories. This method leverages established credibility to challenge the theorists indirectly. The counternarratives were attacked in the usual and familiar ways. They were dismissed as rehashed or outdated storied, *old news*, to minimise their relevance and impact. Additionally, they were seen as irresponsible speculation. Labelled as such, they were naturally seen as harmful distractions rather than legitimate lines of inquiry. Eyewitness reports were also undermined. Any firsthand testimonies that might contradict the official narrative were scrutinised and promptly dismissed.

A line of logic was developed to disprove even the possibility of a larger conspiracy. We can call it the *too-big-to-succeed* argument. This argument hinges on the idea that large-scale conspiracies are inherently unfeasible because someone would inevitably leak the information before or after wrongdoing. It appeals to common sense, making it an effective tool to sow doubt about complex conspiracy theories. However, this argument fails to acknowledge that conspiracies are rarely 100% successful. After all, we are talking about it. Information does leak, or is public from the start, but this does not automatically undermine the conspiracy. Real conspiracies endure, as is clear from the deep state, despite constant leaks.

The strategies outlined in CIA Dispatch 1035-960 have significant implications for contemporary public discourse. Delegitimisation, control and marginalisation continue to be tactics used by the mainstream in order to control public opinion. The framing of critics as self-serving individuals or politically motivated actors delegitimises their arguments, making it harder for the public to take their claims seriously. Who would believe a narcissist or fanatical partisan? Media sources in bed with government agencies are used to shape the narrative and maintain control over public opinion. Leaks by agencies are blindly accepted by the media and published as pieces of investigative journalism. Supposed news outlets become nothing more than the mouth through which the government dictates *The Truth*.

At the same time, alternative theories and counternarratives are marginalised as old news or irresponsible speculation. Their claims suffer a loss of visibility and perceived credibility. They are not disproven but made out to be impossible and incomprehensible. In the historical example, the CIA reinforced trust in the official version of events by emphasising the improbability of large conspiracies remaining secret. The probability of large conspiracies was deemed to be insignificant. To posit a conspiracy theory was, therefore, illogical. The dispatch also suggests the use of the label *conspiracy theorist* for what it perceives to be critical thinkers.

The tactics described in CIA Dispatch 1035-960 reflect broader strategies used by powerful entities to manage dissent and protect their interests. These methods are not confined to the JFK assassination but can be applied in various contexts where official narratives are questioned. The fine line between critical thinking and conspiracy theorising often hinges on public perception. The willingness to question official accounts does not include the propensity to see patterns where there are none. The CIA's efforts to label critics as conspiracy theorists highlight the secretive nature of power. Critical thinking would not go near conspiracy theorising if power was transparent.

Professor David Hughes, writing in *The War for Technocracy*, references *Mein Kampf* where Adolf Hitler emphasised the power of the big lie within which he foresaw:

> *...a certain force of credibility; because the broad masses of a nation are always more easily corrupted in the deeper strata of their*

> *emotional nature than consciously or voluntarily; and thus in the primitive simplicity of their minds they more readily fall victims to the big lie than the small lie, since they themselves often tell small lies in little matters but would be ashamed to resort to large-scale falsehoods. It would never come into their heads to fabricate colossal untruths, and they would not believe that others could have the impudence to distort the truth so infamously.*"

Yuval Harari, described as the protégé of WEF founder Klaus Schwab, is quoted by Professor Hughes echoing the Nazi leader. "*If you repeat a lie often enough people will think it the truth. And the bigger the lie, the better, because people won't even think about how something so big can be a lie.*" In the *Origins of Totalitarianism,* published in 1962, Hannah Arendt identified the "*possibility that gigantic lies and monstrous falsehoods can eventually be established as unquestioned facts*" when pressed with enough repetition, guile and force.

In a broad sense, critical thinking means questioning and scrutinising information based on evidence and logic. It is an active approach to reality. Conspiracy theorising often involves drawing connections and forming conclusions that may not be supported by robust evidence. However, it is also an active approach to reality, as it does not accept the mainstream narrative. We should not automatically accept the dogma that critical thinking cannot have anything to do with conspiracy theorising in a neutral sense. A conspiracy theory can be a critical conclusion based on evidence and logic. It can also be the opposite: a fanciful fabrication that conveniently connects distant points of information. We must also remember that our evidence and logic are not complete and infallible. The CIA, just like other government agencies, has both censored and fabricated evidence. The same is true for logic, as the *too big to succeed* argument shows. The truth is that power will distort both empirical evidence and common sense in order to shape public perception. Conspiracy theorising can be based on the available evidence and follow logic; it *can* be critical.

The CIA switcheroo shows how legitimate scepticism can be reframed as irrational conspiracy theorising through strategic and systematic discrediting. The CIA Dispatch 1035-960 is a historical example of how intelligence agencies and other powerful entities can influence public perception and manage dissent, emphasising the need for vigilance and critical evaluation of official narratives and alternative theories. Intelligence agencies like the CIA are experts in psyops warfare, in manipulating and nudging public mood up to and including regime change. Deploying such power in secrecy makes its use inevitable and prevalent, especially when the 4th Estate has reached its docility and Governments take the power to decide what information the public consumes. It is why X is constantly under attack by the EU. When the evidence eventually surfaces, conspiracy theories will be either proven or disproven. As part of our critical stance towards power, we should treat them as tools, something to be used and eventually discarded.

When discussing the military-industrial complex, the deep state, the elite and the powerful, we must not be too vague. We must ask, "*Who Runs the West?*" and try to answer concretely. This is by no means an easy task, but even an outline will suffice. The West is still influenced by an enduring ideology rooted in aristocratic and imperialist mindsets, which shapes Western nations' power structures and geopolitical strategies. This complex and often disguised ideology of control works through economic and financial imperialism to maintain a modern *soft* empire that continues to influence the affairs of the whole world. In simple political speech, we can note that control is both extensive (*global*) and intensive (*totalitarian*). Admitting that control and the use of power are inherent in society and that we cannot live a civilised life without states does not mean that we accept global totalitarianism. Control must be counterbalanced with democracy, transparency and responsibility. The ideology of control is hostile to these and any other checks and balances.

Although it may be useful to delve into the history and development of this mindset, a simple outline of its origins will suffice for now. The notion of aristocratic control dates back to European feudalism, where a few elite families held significant power and influence over vast numbers of landed peasants. Power was sanctified by religion and upheld through brutal military suppression. Feudalism was an improvement compared to ancient slave economies, but not by much. Serfs were still legally bound to agricultural land, and that land was the legal property of lords. This hierarchical state of mind, rooted in the belief of inherent superiority and entitlement, persists in modern forms. The modern manifestations of this mindset are visible in the power dynamics and concentration of the global elite, who maintain control through economic and political means rather than through direct hereditary rule. As is increasingly the case, these *masters of the universe* live by rent and taxation, not through classical profit. They are increasingly parasitic and decreasingly productive. This return to feudal practices has been called *neofeudalism* or *technofeudalism* by some.

The globalisation of control has been achieved through trade and political agreements, but in the banking system, the apex of power is at the top. Banks generate assets by lending money upon which they charge a 'rent'. Whoever controls the top end of international banking through the Bank for International Settlements (BIS) is at the fulcrum of real-world power. These do particularly well at a time of extensive loan issuance, namely during wars and financing both sides, is as old as banking itself and sitting at the apex, behind these structures lie family dynasties, as they see themselves.

Their prime objective is the survival of multi-generation dynasties, which requires stealth, a very low profile and the accumulation of power, a type of power that is very different to representative democracy and its structures. Their biggest fear is exposure to revolution against their concentration of wealth, that eventually the masses will come for them, as has happened in grossly unequalised societies throughout history. It is the story of humanity itself and is the best explanation of the lunge for totalitarian controls to maximise the vice grip of surveillance and technologies. It is, in essence, a counter-revolution to stave off a revolution of the working and middle classes. Know dynastic self-preservation impulse for what it is, for it will help you understand much of what works behind supranational agencies and structures, including national governments.

Economic dominance is achieved in parallel through creating interdependent trade relationships, which bind nations together in a web of financial obligations and dependencies running through the international banking system. Unlike classical imperialism, which relied on territorial conquest, modern imperialism operates through economic mechanisms —trade agreements, multinational corporations, and global financial institutions. Compared to violent colonial wars, this seemingly more civilised and *soft* approach has also been much more effective than previous strategies.

After World War I, the British Empire, facing the decline of its traditional land-based empire, supported the creation of the League of Nations. This was seen as a move towards a new form of influence—global governance through international institutions. The once strong and harsh (to put it mildly) empire now adopted a soft approach. The term *soft empire* refers to control exerted not through direct political domination but through economic influence and international norms established by institutions. In the case of Britain, the key conduits for this transformation were the Council for Foreign Relations (CFR) in New York and the Royal Institute of International Affairs (RIIA) in London, also known as Chatham House. The CFR and RIIA (Chatham House) are think tanks that play a lead role in shaping foreign policy and international relations.

These institutions are by no means unique in promoting the interests of the global dynasties. In general, these think tanks work as high-grade propaganda producers. They either produce or co-opt (one might say seduce) a class of intellectuals whose job is to promote the political agenda of the powerful. These organisations disseminate ideas and strategies that favour economic interdependency and global governance among policymakers and influential leaders. The *seduction* refers to the allure of joining the global elite, offering individuals and nations a share in power and wealth in exchange for aligning with the globalist agenda. This can be anything ranging from scholarships, university positions, research grants, book promotions and paid trips. Although not formally part of the elite, these intellectuals, leaders and policymakers are seduced into working for it. In general, this involves undermining national sovereignty and democratic processes, favouring a more centralised global governance structure that can better resolve the issues of the day.

In broad strokes, the steps to global unification involve trade agreements and political unions. Free interdependent trade agreements reduce trade barriers, creating economic interdependence among nations. Although they seem like economic agreements meant to foster mutual prosperity, which they certainly can be, trade agreements have a political function. Trade was identified as a political weapon long ago. There is nothing inherently mutual about trade. If we look at the British empire, we can see it engaged in trade with nations it had defeated, conquered and occupied. Modern trade agreements skip this nasty first step and jump straight to interdependence. Usually this means competition for the masses and collaboration for the dynastic upper classes.

The next step is the formation of regional unions (e.g., the European Union), which consolidate the economic and political power of the elites within a region. These regional unions can offer some benefits to their member states and populations (stability, peace, freedom of movement). However, the cost of regional unions cannot be underestimated. The loss of sovereignty is multifaceted, as nations lose control over their borders, currency and environmental policy. In June 2024, the Irish Government voted to opt voluntarily into the EU Migration and Asylum Pact, passing border control to faceless bureaucrats in Brussels involving a minimum acceptance of over 30,000 mostly undocumented refugees annually from outside the EU, mainly from North Africa.

The ultimate goal is the formation of global governance, where regional unions further integrate into a unified global political entity. Organisations like the United Nations and the World

Health Organization are vehicles for implementing this globalist agenda, promoting international norms and policies. These institutions help establish frameworks for global cooperation at the explicit expense of national sovereignty and identity. With global governance, the ideology of control reaches its full extent. The next step is full intensity of control: totalitarianism.

The unified global elite views ordinary people as mere tools to serve their agenda, reminiscent of feudal times when serfs were bound to serve the aristocracy. The best thing a lowborn can strive to be is a good and useful servant. This is what the intellectual class is. This elitist mindset has led to policies that prioritise the interests of the elite over the well-being of the general population, including economic exploitation and population control measures. That the whole of humanity is becoming enslaved, or *enserfed,* is not surprising given the political structures at work. The masters of the universe are no masters unless they have a mass of serfs at their command, ideally one that can be commoditised and traded on exchanges.

To conclude, there has been an unbroken historical continuity of aristocratic and imperialist ideologies, manifesting in modern forms of economic and financial control. The role of influential organisations and international institutions cannot be ignored in promoting a globalist agenda. The risks of elitism and the erosion of democratic values are perhaps the most obvious consequences of this takeover. A new and reinvigorated critical examination of power structures and the motives behind global governance initiatives is necessary.

Most recently, this ideology has taken a keen interest in our health. Their agenda includes promoting certain pharmaceutical interventions while discrediting alternative approaches and dissenting opinions. An atmosphere of fear, anxiety, and paranoia is being fostered in order to promote drastic measures. The fearmongering about the threat of a new imminent pandemic involves drastic exaggeration about the severity and immediacy of the risk. This creates a heightened state of fear and urgency among the public and policymakers.

In the recent pandemic we saw the tendency to focus on a specific pathogen as the primary threat, overstate the infection rates and the potential impact of mutant strains to amplify fear and ensure that the public perceives the situation as dire, necessitating immediate and drastic action. The response to the pandemic was a giant disruption in normalcy that left the public off balance due to continual broadcasted *responsible lifestyle changes* (e.g., lockdowns, mask mandates). All of this kept the public and politicians uncertain and dependent on official guidance. We were stuck in a state of perpetual mobilisation.

First, the bar on the definition of a pandemic was lowered in 2009 by the WHO to remove high fatality and morbidity rates, so the focus became infectability rates. Then, the use of methods such as high-cycle PCR tests grossly overestimated the number of infectious cases, creating a phantom pandemic. The data was further overestimated by lax attribution of deaths, with no attention to comorbidities, to the virus. This made the situation appear worse than it actually was to justify stringent measures and interventions. Not everyone was fooled or agreed to this malpractice. This is why it was necessary to create a monolithic narrative that discourages public debate and scrutiny. Dismissing and discrediting alternative scientific opinions and approaches, such as those presented in the Great

Barrington Declaration, a document which today has been [1] signed by more than nine hundred and forty thousand professionals in over 44 different languages across the globe, offering alternative methods to deal with the Covid-19 pandemic, became standard practice[2]. The practice of labelling dissenters as conspiracy theorists to undermine their credibility was also given new life.

The medical result was a loss of informed consent and focus on one solution. The traditional doctor-patient relationship and informed consent process were undermined. Patient autonomy and choice in healthcare were quickly sacrificed. Additionally, the vaccine was offered to us as the only viable solution. Alternative treatments were discredited and vilified. Drugs that have been repurposed for treatment (e.g., Ivermectin) and other health measures (e.g., vitamin D, fitness) were either completely rejected by the mainstream or downplayed.

Corresponding with the authorisation for the Pfizer vaccine called Comirnaty, on 23rd of August 2021, the US Food and Drug Administrator (FDA), the regulator, attacked Ivermectin. "*You are not a horse. You are not a cow. Seriously y'all. Stop it*". By July 2024, 10% of the US states had filed lawsuits against Pfizer, attempting to breach its federal indemnity on the grounds that it misled the public by stating that it had a '*safe and effective*' Covid-19 vaccine, alleging that Pfizer knew and concealed the extent to which the vaccine caused failed pregnancies, myocarditis, pericarditis and deaths, Texas, Utah, Kansas, Mississippi and Louisiana.

The mainstream media and commercialised science ensured

1. https://gbdeclaration.org/
2. https://reclaimthenet.org/facebook-deletes-epidemiologists-behind-the-great-barrington-declaration

that these alternatives did not detract from the primary narrative or reduce reliance on new, profitable drugs. We cannot ignore the imperative of profit during a crisis. Massive amounts of funding and resources were directed towards new pharmaceuticals, regardless of their safety and efficacy. This sort of funding is mainly done by the state, meaning your taxes subsidised or directly funded the development of the vaccines. Financial gain, not public health, was the priority. If it was actually about public health, there would have been no Emergency Use Authorization (EUA), which expedited the approval and distribution of new vaccines and treatments. Facilitating rapid deployment of new and potentially unsafe drugs is not something you do if you care about public health.

It is much easier to speak of these matters today. The Covid storm is over and the damage can be seen. Even during the pandemic, brave and perceptive individuals spoke out against the carnage. As in every situation, the powers that be suppress every hint of rebellion. Experts who support the official narrative were the only ones given any attention while concealing any conflicts of interest they may have. The goal was to present a unified and authoritative front to the public. Those who spoke out were ignored at best, and at worst, they were ridiculed, marginalised from their communities and fired from their positions. Through constant repetition, the official narrative was reinforced and reshaped. The public was forced to internalise the message through consistent and pervasive propaganda. Health is one of those topics where we instinctively trust experts the most. However, we did not properly hear what the experts themselves had to say during the pandemic. Instead, it was the global elite who had the loudest voice.

Challenge propaganda with science or a credible counternarrative, and immediately, you will be branded a conspiracy theorist. The objective is clear - to shut you down by undermining your credibility with an easy trope. So, let's talk about conspiracy theory properly, then.

1

THE NATURE OF CONSPIRACY THEORY

IDEALLY IN OPEN PUBLIC DEBATE, farfetched conspiracy theories that are without concrete evidence or, are plainly ludicrous, are killed off or, relegated to the sidelines. Parsing out what remains is not easy. It is made more difficult by the prevalence of cognitive dissonance and learned ignorance, which is often the deliberate result of covert and sustained propaganda masquerading as current affairs in popular media. This is plainly seen on social media by the refusal to engage in substantive debate. Instead, uncomfortable information is greeted with ad hominem tropes to attack the messenger and deflect the message. These are everywhere; you will see them in phrases such as “tinfoil hat”, “down a rabbit hole”, “settled science”, “scientific consensus”, and, of course, “conspiracy theorist”.

Real conspiracies do occur; conspiracy theories try to explain them. Humans have a need to create meaning and understand predictable patterns in the world, but many social, economic and psychological factors influence the demand acceptability, and spread of conspiracy theories. Real conspiracies can be complex social phenomena with economic, political and sometimes religious dimensions.

A conspiracy theory is the belief that a group of actors secretly conspire to achieve a harmful goal. Conspiracy theories are social: they are formed, shared and improved collectively. According to various studies, conspiracy theories are prevalent in all cultures and countries around the world. In 2019, 47% of the US population declared that they believed Lee Harvey Oswald did not act alone in assassinating President Kennedy. Some 23% believed that the US government planned the attack on the Twin Towers (9/11) and 11% believed that the 1969 moon landing was staged. On July 13th 2024, the internet lit up with content, videos and commentary about the attempted assassination of President Trump at a rally in Butler, Pennsylvania, by 20-year-old Thomas Mathew Crook using an assault rifle from a distance of only 120 metres. Instant conspiracy theories ranged from an inside job by US security services to a staged event by Donald Trump to garner public sympathy, even though the man was shot and nearly killed on live TV.

Although we call them conspiracy *theories*, care is needed to emphasise that such claims do not correspond to either the philosophical or scientific definition of theory - they can also be dogmas, suspicions, and speculations about conspiracy. In philosophy, a theory is a system of knowledge or understanding about a phenomenon or group of phenomena based on the observation of their essential regularity. Science is different, every scientific hypothesis, if confirmed by new empirical facts predicted by it, becomes a theory.

Many conspiracy theories resist falsification and rely on circular reasoning: both evidence against the conspiracy and lack of evidence for it are taken as evidence of its truth, making the conspiracy more a matter of faith than something that can be proven or refuted. Real conspiracies, even very simple ones, are difficult to conceal and routinely encounter unexpected problems. They are secretive for a reason. The more members they have, the more difficult it is to keep them a secret.

Conspiracies also tend to compound; they engage in continual conspiratorial activity in order to maintain their secrecy. Conspiracy theories tend to depict conspiracy as unrealistically successful, competent, and secret. The causes of events or situations are simplified to exclude complex factors or interacting causes, as well as the role of chance and unintended consequences.

In essence, conspiracy theories are elaborate socially constructed narratives that explain important events resulting from hidden, sometimes hostile, acts by powerful individuals or organisations. These ideas usually deviate from common sense and accepted wisdom and are defined by a profound distrust of established explanations or authorities because, at their core, they fulfil a range of psychological, social, and cultural goals. They help to instil a sense of authority or control in people who feel powerless, anxious and uncertain and allow individuals to assume they have a deeper understanding of the world.

It is necessary, nevertheless, to approach conspiracy theories in a fair and balanced manner. While some may contain truth or raise important issues about power dynamics, an equal amount are founded on misinformation, logical fallacies, or outright fabrications. This is why it is necessary to examine them critically and establish standards that allow us to judge them properly, as they can foster paranoia, polarisation, hopelessness and mistrust within society. So, in what context do they originate?

Social turmoil, economic insecurity, and political unrest all contribute to the creation and spread of conspiracy theories. Humans need to understand their environment, and conspiracy theories are one way of understanding the world. In today's networked society, the rapid spread of information, which is usually unregulated or unverified, can bolster conspiracy theories and make them appear more credible, but equally strong is the threat of actual conspiracies that are also bolstered by the same technologies. Technology is a double-edged sword; we have yet to grapple with its consequences in framing public discourse to support collective wisdom without falling into the trap of "big brother" type regulation that sanitises open public discourse and destroys critical thinking.

The internet and social media platforms have contributed significantly to the propagation of misinformation, forming echo chambers in which like-minded people reinforce each other's beliefs while blocking out opposing viewpoints. This digital ecology makes it difficult to battle misinformation but at the same time, promote critical thinking. It is also important to refer to conspiracy theorists as rational people, addressing their underlying concerns without using ridicule or dogmatic acceptance.

While conspiracy theories might provide alternative explanations for complex events, they typically lack the rigorous proof required to back up their claims, however, this is not always the case. The influence of poor-quality conspiracy theories can be lessened by critically evaluating facts, fostering open discussion and cultivating a culture of scepticism. Attacking the phenomenon with government control, leaving banal bureaucrats to decide what is disinformation and misinformation, is a stepping stone towards enforced docility and totalitarianism.

I believe that we should allow people to believe in a variety of absurd conspiracies, because, in the absence of convincing proof or logical reasoning, it causes little harm. Here are a few of some of the major conspiracy theories of our time:

Flat Earth theory: the Earth is a flat, disc-shaped object rather than a spherical globe. Despite substantial scientific evidence to the contrary, including satellite images, space exploration, and centuries of astronomical observation, some people still believe this.

Moon landing hoax: NASA and the United States government fabricated the Apollo moon landings as a Cold War propaganda tool. The legendary film director Stanley Kubrick is often credited as the main producer of the fake moon landing videos. Even the rocks brought back from the moon's surface are dismissed as fakes.

Reptilian Elite: A species of shape-shifting reptile aliens masquerading as humans secretly control global governments, financial institutions and media organisations. Believers frequently cite supposed evidence such as anomalies in prominent persons' appearances or rumoured secret societies; however, there is no solid evidence to back up these assertions.

These conspiracy theories are fantastical and contribute nothing to our analysis of and fight against totalitarianism. At best, they are irrelevant. At worst, they can be used to discredit well-founded claims which ought to be rigorously evaluated and based on actual data and rational analysis rather than unsubstantiated guesswork.

We ought to acknowledge that conspiracy theories might result from cynicism towards official narratives and offer a healthy distrust of authority, originating in response to actual cases of corruption, cover-ups, or power imbalances in society. These provide a platform for marginalised or disenfranchised people to challenge prevailing narratives and question established norms and, during the course of history, they have helped to uncover actual wrongdoing or sparked crucial discussions about responsibility and openness.

Addressing the underlying problems that feed beliefs and encouraging open discourse, can help us to bridge the gap between conspiracy theorists and mainstream culture. The mainstream itself is not without its own conspiracy theories, including the zoonic origin of Covid-19 or the accuracy of PCR tests in mapping infection rates.

While many conspiracy theories are not objectively true, they frequently arise from genuine social tensions and serve as a form of resistance to perceived injustices. Acknowledging and addressing the legitimate issues that underpin conspiracy theories through constructive debate fosters a more inclusive and understanding society. For instance, we could reject the extreme conspiracy theory that the elites who run the globe are reptiles but acknowledge that this belief stems from a genuine concern about globalisation and world governance. The narrative can be fantastical, but the message is clear: beware of unchecked power.

Real, recorded conspiracies are instances in which people or organisations conspired to perform illegal or unethical acts, frequently with serious consequences. These conspiracies are not just speculative beliefs; they are supported by credible evidence, official investigations, and legal processes. Here are just a few of them:

Watergate scandal: In the early 1970s, officials of President Richard Nixon's administration plotted to conceal their role in the break-in at the Democratic National Committee headquarters in the Watergate complex. This conspiracy eventually resulted in Nixon's resignation and criminal convictions for numerous of his associates.

The Iran-Contra affair: In the mid-1980s, senior Reagan administration officials covertly authorised the transfer of arms to Iran despite an embargo, using the funds to pay Contra guerrillas in Nicaragua. This covert operation violated both US laws and foreign policy objectives, prompting congressional inquiries and criminal charges against some participants.

Tuskegee Syphilis Study: From 1932 until 1972, the United States Public Health Service carried out an unethical experiment on African American males at Tuskegee, Alabama, withholding syphilis treatment long after penicillin became available. This study, which meant to examine the evolution of the disease, deliberately caused unnecessary agony and death among participants.

Operation Northwoods: In the early 1960s, the US Department of Defence presented a plan called Operation Northwoods, which involved conducting false-flag terrorist operations to justify military intervention in Cuba. While the plan was never carried out, its existence was declassified and recognised by government officials.

Genuine conspiracies do occur and can have far-reaching implications, but to discern between true conspiracies and spurious speculation, all must be approached with scepticism and properly evaluated evidence. Conspiracies can sometimes serve a positive purpose, even if unintentionally, and act as a catalyst for change.

Conspiracy theories involving the discovery of corrupt or unlawful activity within governments, corporations, or other institutions can result in accountability and more transparency. Whistleblowers who uncover conspiracies may launch investigations, legal processes, or policy changes to address systemic concerns and avoid future abuses of power. An abundance of conspiracy theories around centres of power can be seen as a signal of actual corruption and not some accidental public reaction. Exploring conspiracy theories can lead people to challenge official narratives, scrutinise information sources, and improve their critical thinking abilities. While not all conspiracy theories are valid, the act of analysing data and questioning assumptions can foster a healthy distrust of authority and inspire independent investigation.

Some conspiracy theories, even if unfounded, can attract attention to underlying systemic issues or imbalances in power relations in society. The prevalence of conspiracy theories in contemporary society shows there is immense distrust in governments and institutions. It is important to distinguish between healthy scepticism, *bad faith* scepticism and unfounded speculation. Healthy scepticism means spending time analysing and checking the claims of conspiracy theories but not everyone has the time or capacity to examine claims that are possibly, and probably, false. Healthy scepticism, nevertheless, is an ideal to uphold and we all should cultivate habits towards it. Bad faith scepticism, on the other hand, is unhealthy; it involves disbelieving claims that have solid evidence to support them as a way of deflecting theories and facts that may be uncomfortable. Unfounded speculation, on the other hand, has no use for scepticism; it goes beyond any evidence and rationality.

TOTALITARIAN REGIMES REGULATE the flow of information and manipulate narratives in order to maintain power and suppress criticism. This manipulation may include spreading conspiracy theories that demonise political opponents, blame minority opposition groups, so they can justify authoritarian practices. Totalitarians seek to cause confusion, weaken faith in alternative sources of information, and solidify their own power over society by spreading incorrect or misleading information. Even when they have assumed complete control, the totalitarian will blame someone else, and depict them as a cunning enemy.

Totalitarian leaders like Kim Jong Un build a cult of personality, portraying themselves as omniscient and infallible beings who are uniquely able to protect the country from perceived threats. Conspiracy theories can help strengthen the cult by confirming the leader's story of victimhood, persecution, and heroic struggle against hidden foes. Totalitarian governments strive to instil loyalty, obedience, and unquestioned devotion among their people by spreading conspiracy theories that praise the leader while vilifying dissenters. 21st century totalitarianism, however, is far less apparent than the relic of hard communism that is the North Korean regime; it is instead ubiquitous, powerful and growing, residing in open sight across supranational institutions, government agencies and a corporate elite that crave the ultimate in dominance, power without consequences.

Historic totalitarian regimes have used widespread monitoring, censorship, and repression to retain control over society. They instilled fear and distrust, resulting in increased repression of perceived dissidents, further corroding social bonds and atomising individuals. These regimes justify harsh measures to suppress dissent and enforce ideological conformity deploying conspiracy theories to vilify marginalised groups, including ethnic or religious minorities, political dissidents, and perceived "foreign enemies."

The targets of such conspiracy theories are chosen wisely, usually among those who cannot fight back, resulting in mass discrimination, violence and genocide in a series of escalating steps. Nazi Germany, for example, promoted anti-Semitic conspiracy theories to legitimise the Holocaust and demonise Jews as a danger to Aryan dominance. Similarly, Soviet authorities exploited conspiracy theories to portray the Kulaks, political dissidents, intellectuals, and alleged Western agents as threats to the socialist project.

This book is more concerned with the 21st century forces of totalitarianism growing within the West and threatening to subjugate representative democracy and personal freedoms. Recognising this impulse requires critical thinking to look through the tropes and see the truth before it is too late. It is why we need to look at conspiracy theories from all angles.

In ancient civilisations such as Egypt, Greece, and Rome, conspiracy was important in politics and power struggles. Perhaps the most famous conspiracy ended in Julius Caesar's assassination on March 15th, 44 BCE, when a group of senators conspired against the emperor. Later, the Pisonian conspiracy, led by Gaius Calpurnius Piso in 65 CE, failed to depose Roman Emperor Nero, who, 3 years later ordered his private secretary to kill him.

After Alexander the Great died in 323 BCE, speculation arose about the possibility of foul play by his generals and successors. While historical accounts ascribe Alexander's death to sickness, contemporary conspiracy theories claim that he was slain by rivals or betrayed by his generals to prevent him from gaining further power.

Conspiracy remained common during the Middle Ages and Renaissance frequently linked to religious and dynastic conflicts. In the Templar conspiracy, the French King, Philip the Fair, on the basis of a controversial confession by a Templar insider, accused the order of worshipping a false god, renouncing Christ, and engaging in licentious practices and ordered its destruction and confiscation of its assets on Friday, October 13^{th,} 1307.

The French Revolution of 1789-1799 sparked worries of subversion and conspiracy, resulting in the Reign of Terror and the creation of secret groups like the Jacobins. Due to its abrupt and violent nature, many saw it as a conspiracy by foreign powers against the French monarchy. This period also saw the establishment of secret societies like the Illuminati and Freemasons. These groups were secret due to their illegal and radical nature, but their goals and achievements were likely to be much more modest than we give them credit for.

In the 20th century, events such as Archduke Franz Ferdinand's assassination in 1914, which precipitated World War I, and the Russian Revolution in 1917 spurred conspiracy beliefs about secret forces directing world events. The conspirators involved could not have predicted the wide-reaching effects of their actions. Conspiracy theories proliferated throughout the Cold War, spurred by geopolitical tensions, espionage and ideological strife. The McCarthy era in the United States, which was marked by anti-communist paranoia and the search for "hidden enemies" within, is one famous example.

President John F. Kennedy's assassination in 1963 and the Watergate crisis in the 1970s increased public suspicion of political institutions and fostered conspiracy theories.

Conspiracy theories have grown more accessible and ubiquitous than ever before because of the internet and social media platforms. The attempted assassination of US President Donald Trump on live television in July 2024 ignited a fresh crop of conspiracy theories supported by a blizzard of video clips and Tik Tok commentary from security experts and veteran US Army snipers.

The digital era has fostered the rapid spread of conspiracy theories ~~allowing~~ as it herds like-minded people together, resulting in the strengthening of their convictions. In a way, this has made the spread of genuine concerns and plausible interpretations easier. The internet, however, tends to make everything more accessible at the cost of lower quality. Throughout history, it is clear that conspiracy theories have frequently mirrored underlying societal concerns, political tensions, and cultural shifts. This fact still holds and is well documented.

Richard Hofstadter, a prominent American historian and public intellectual, wrote an essay called *The Paranoid Style in American Politics,* which offers insights into the role of conspiracy theories in shaping political discourse. It is perhaps the most accessible historical work on conspiracies. *Voodoo Histories: The Role of the Conspiracy Theory in Shaping Modern History,* by David Aaronovitch, examines conspiracy theories throughout history, from the *Protocols of the Elders of Zion* to theories surrounding the September 11 attacks and explores their impact on public discourse and historical narratives. Jesse Walker, in *The United States of Paranoia: A Conspiracy Theory,* traces the history of conspiracy theories in the United States, exploring how they have influenced politics, culture, and society throughout the nation's history.

Jim Marrs delves into the old chestnut in *The Illuminati: The Secret Society That Hijacked the World,* plumbing the history and mythology of a secret society believed by some to wield immense influence over global affairs. Robert Alan Goldberg's book *Enemies Within: The Culture of Conspiracy in Modern America,* examines the historical roots of conspiracy thinking in the United States. *A Culture of Conspiracy: Apocalyptic Visions in Contemporary America,* by Michael Barkun, analyses the cultural and psychological factors contributing to the popularity of conspiracy theories in the United States. He has also studied religious, millenarian and utopian movements and their use of terrorism as a political instrument.

The sociology of conspiracy theories aims to explain why people are driven to conspiracy theories, how these beliefs are formed and spread, and how they affect individuals and societies. Sociologists investigate how conspiracy theories are socially produced in various cultural, historical, and political situations – and how social institutions, the media and collective memory shape conspiracy narratives and influence public opinion. These can arise and propagate among social groups or communities with similar views, values, or experiences. Conspiracy theories contain suspicions of powerful individuals or institutions engaged in covert or malicious acts to reveal underlying power dynamics, inequities, and distrust of authority in society. What makes them interesting to sociologists, is that they are social indicators regardless of their veracity.

Equally as important as the sociology of real conspiracies, is the study of how real conspiracies are created. Georg Simmel's work is worth examining. Simmel, a notable German sociologist, is most famous for his essay *The Secret and the Secret Society*, in which he examines the significance of secrecy in social interactions and group formation. He believes secrecy is an essential component of social life and can foster intimacy and exclusivity among those who share sensitive information, resulting in trust and agreement. At the same time, secrecy can breed suspicion and distrust among those barred from privileged knowledge, resulting in societal tensions and conflicts.

Simmel stresses the power dynamics inherent in secrecy, pointing out that persons with secret knowledge frequently exercise influence and control over others. Secret societies, in particular, demonstrate this dynamic by building hierarchies based on the transmission of secret teachings or rites. Members of these societies achieve social rank and authority by participating in secret rituals, ceremonies, or knowledge exchange. Secret societies frequently use secrecy as a symbolic tactic to distinguish themselves from the larger societal order. They can identify members of their group in public, without it being obvious to non-members. By maintaining an atmosphere of secrecy and exclusivity, these groups foster a sense of belonging and identity amongst their members. The concealing of hidden knowledge or practices gives them a deeper sense of meaning and worth, fostering community connection and solidarity. The *knowledge* shared does not have to be true or useful in any way. The important thing is that it fosters exclusivity through its secrecy.

Secret societies can also serve as means for societal control or resistance to dominant power structures. These groups may strive to undermine established hierarchies or pursue alternative agendas by acting covertly and opposing traditional norms or authorities. This was the goal of the original Illuminati, to bring the Enlightenment to Germany, but because the objective was the overthrowing of the aristocracy and church, their gatherings had to be secret. However, Simmel concedes that such societies' opacity can render them vulnerable to external infiltration or repression. Simmel's study of secrecy and secret societies provides insights into the complicated interplay between concealment, power, and social dynamics in human civilisations and continues to have an impact on sociological studies on these themes.

Suspicious Minds: Why We Believe Conspiracy Theories, by Rob Brotherton, provides a balanced and accessible overview of conspiracism and delves into the psychological and cultural factors that make conspiracy theories appealing to certain people, including cognitive biases, social influences, and emotional needs. Edited by Joseph E. Uscinski and Joseph M. Parent, *American Conspiracy Theories* gives a comprehensive analysis of conspiracy theories in American history, covering topics such as the JFK assassination, the moon landing hoax, and contemporary conspiracy movements. Karen Douglas a social psychologist who investigates the social and cognitive processes that impact conspiracy beliefs, believes that conspiracy theories frequently emerge as a way for people to make sense of unclear or ambiguous occurrences, especially those that elicit feelings of fear, anxiety, or distrust. These beliefs give a framework for interpreting complex events and assigning causality to hidden or malicious forces, giving people a sense of control or understanding in the face of uncertainty. This is an important discovery, so what more can psychologists add to our understanding?

The psychology of conspiracy is the study of the cognitive, emotional, and social aspects that influence the creation, acceptance, and spread of conspiracy ideas and looks into how these ideas are sustained and reinforced, and what psychological purposes they serve. Research indicates that cognitive biases and mental shortcuts in problem-solving, also known as heuristics, play an important part in conspiracy thinking. Individuals may engage in pattern-seeking behaviour, confirmation bias (looking for information that confirms preexisting beliefs), proportionality bias (attributing extraordinary events to extraordinary causes), and illusory pattern perception. When examining conspiracy theories we can frequently participate in motivated reasoning, which involves selectively interpreting facts in accordance with our preexisting ideas, values, or worldview. This tendency causes us to disregard contradicting data or rationalise clear flaws in our conspiracy theories.

Unsurprisingly, a general suspicion of authority, institutions, or mainstream sources of information is fuel for conspiracy theories. Those who feel marginalised, disenfranchised, or alienated from society are more likely to support conspiracy as a means of expressing autonomy or opposing dominant narratives. According to Social Identity Theory, group memberships provide individuals with a sense of belonging and identity, and conspiracy ideas can be used to indicate ingroup affiliation. Group dynamics, such as in-group favouritism and out-group derogation, strengthen conspiracy theories and creates echo chambers in which opposing viewpoints are disregarded or reviled. The important takeaway is that understanding the psychology of conspiracy is vital for combating misinformation, boosting critical thinking abilities, and encouraging constructive debate in society.

This understanding of the cognitive, emotional, and social components that contribute to conspiracy theories allow professionals in the field to devise more effective techniques for countering misinformation and encouraging evidence-based reasoning, without resorting to the hammer blows of state regulation which drives the human behaviour underground, adding to any theory's mythological power.

Perhaps the most interesting research findings in psychological studies of conspiracy theories is that even mutually conflicting views, such as Princess Diana faking her own death and being killed, are both believed. Believing in two mutually exclusive ideas is illogical, but not uncommon. Even if we cannot empirically determine the veracity of a conspiracy theory, we can at least logically infer that its opposite cannot be true as well. Cognitive dissonance (the state of holding inconsistent attitudes, thoughts and beliefs), is not exclusive to paranoia and conspiratorial thinking, and it appears to be a widespread phenomenon. In the case of conspiracy theories, cognitive dissonance seems to arise from a certain contrarianism, meaning some conspiracy theories are accepted simply because they contradict the mainstream narrative.

Researchers also discovered that people who believe in conspiracy theories are more likely to engage in preventive behaviours such as purchasing items before they run out of stock, or managing their finances in advance of an economic crisis. The learning point here is that conspiracy theories are unlikely to constitute cognitive errors or indicators of poor reasoning but rather an evolved strategy for recognising and avoiding potential difficulties that threaten our well-being. The reason we are likely to believe conspiracy theories is that conspiracies are likely to happen. Not often, but often enough.

It's also feasible that conspiracy theories have a social purpose, fostering an *us vs. them* mentality by labelling specific groups as enemies or threats, thereby enhancing group cohesion and unity. They can also instil a sense of meaning and purpose in a chaotic world. According to existential psychology, a fear of mortality can lead to a search for meaning and a desire to feel important. Unfalsifiable and fantastic conspiracy theories are especially useful for this because they can never be overturned or proven. They are forever stuck in a state of limbo, fulfilling their social role without pointing to any actual conspiracy. It is important to note that the examples of real conspiracies do not neatly correspond to this description. Accurate conspiracy theories are often chaotic, messy and unclear, they do not establish a clear *us vs them* dichotomy because they show the banality behind significant events.

Although people are generally receptive to conspiracy theories under specific circumstances, some may be more vulnerable than others. For example, studies have found that those with poor trust in authority leaders and institutions are more inclined to believe in conspiracy theories, possibly because they are naturally more sceptical of official answers and prepared to consider alternative theories. Similarly, persons with a higher need for cognitive closure—that is, a desire for certainty and closure in their thinking—are more prone to believe in conspiracy theories. This is echoed in the work of Mattias Desmet speaking on mass formation; those who feel out of control in their life may be more inclined to believe in conspiracy theories, which provide a sense of control and understanding in an unpredictable environment, including people who feel marginalised or disenfranchised.

Conspiracy theories are integral to human psychology and social life and represent normal psychological and social behaviour. The phenomenon should not be seen as pathological, so understanding it at this level elevates the field for more common study. *The Psychology of Conspiracy Theories*, a short paper by Karen M. Douglas, Robbie M. Sutton, and Aleksandra Cichocka, goes over the existential and social motivations behind conspiracy theories. It is an approachable piece by leading scholars in the field. *Conspiracy Theories and the Paranoid Style(s) of Mass Opinion,* is an academic article written by J. Eric Oliver and Thomas J. Wood. The researchers show that half of the American population regularly supports at least one conspiracy theory and that many popular conspiracy theories differ along ideological dimensions. They conclude that conspiracism is not caused by increased authoritarianism, ignorance, or political conservatism but by a belief in invisible, intentional forces and an affinity for black-and-white thinking.

The economics of conspiracy theories is a relatively niche area of study that draws on behavioural economics, information economics and political economy. It offers a more realistic image of *homo economicus* and highlights our irrationalities and deficiencies. In the economics of information, conspiracy theories can be seen as a result of imperfect or asymmetric information. Individuals may lack access to accurate information or may be influenced by misinformation and disinformation. This can lead to the formation and spread of conspiracy theories as an attempt to counter deficiencies in knowledge. More recent approaches, like social network analysis and game theory, also make interesting observations and points. Understanding the social networks through which conspiracies arise and conspiracy theories spread can provide valuable insights. Game theory can be applied to analyse strategic interactions between actors involved in the creation and propagation of conspiracies to find key players in a network who might be interested in spreading conspiracy theories.

Researchers look for structural patterns that point to the formation of a plot. For example, cliques or groups that are very closely connected within a network may indicate that people are working together to further their interests.

People may weigh the pros and cons of joining a plot against the possible consequences, such as being caught or being punished. Putting together social network analysis and game theory can help economists learn more about how plots and conspiracy theories start, spread, and last. No one discipline adequately covers the complexities of conspiracy theory, which is why multi-disciplinary approaches provide for a more comprehensive understanding, which is still evolving.

ONLINE PLATFORMS ARE DRIVEN by algorithms and designed to maximise engagement, by default amplify conspiracy theories due to their sensational nature. This phenomenon is often referred to as the "Attention Economy"; where content that generates clicks and views is prioritised over accuracy or credibility. This is the same mechanism that values negative content and emotions such as fear, hatred and anxiety. Algorithms modify each user's digital experience based on their preferences, habits, and previous interactions. From the outside, this appears advantageous. Content tailored to consumers' interests ensures a seamless and enjoyable online experience. However, beneath this surface lies a more worrisome fact. When algorithms provide users with content that is relevant to their own interests and viewpoints, they unintentionally create echo chambers. These are closed online groups in which participants are rarely exposed to opposing or divergent points of view in a fair and balanced way. Rather, their prejudices and informational horizons are restricted, and their pre-existing ideas are constantly reinforced. Social media platforms and online communities play a significant role in shaping beliefs and norms, with echo chambers and filter bubbles reinforcing existing beliefs and facilitating the spread of conspiracy theories.

Follow the money. Powerful influencers, groups and lobbies may have financial incentives to promote conspiracy theories. This could include selling books, merchandise, supplements or advertising space on websites and social media platforms that encourage conspiracy content. These conspiracies can be purely sensational and fantastical; they are often not serious attempts at describing reality. Belief in conspiracy theories can undermine public goods provision and collective action. If individuals distrust government institutions or perceive them to be part of a conspiracy, they may be less willing to support public policies or contribute to public goods provision, such as infrastructure, healthcare, or education.

Trust is essential for economic transactions and the functioning of everyday society, but widespread belief in conspiracy theories erodes trust in institutions, experts, and even fellow citizens. This loss can have economic consequences, such as decreased consumer confidence, increased political polarisation, and reduced cooperation in social and economic endeavours. Malicious agents promote conspiracy theories for exactly these reasons. But mistrust is not always illegitimate. Trust is valuable, but it should not come at any cost. It has to be earned by states, organisations, corporations and individuals alike.

When we consider the potential of bad actors to establish deep states, to infiltrate supranational organisations, and even to manipulate national intelligence powers, we must, in the first instance, rely on criminology. Criminologists study real-world examples of criminal conspiracies, ranging from organised crime syndicates to corporate fraud schemes. This includes their paying attention to the social construction of conspiracy theories—how they emerge, spread, and influence behaviour. It involves examining factors such as social distrust, political polarisation, media influence, and cognitive biases that contribute to the formation and acceptance of conspiracy beliefs.

Criminologists also explore why certain individuals or groups are more susceptible to conspiracy theories and the consequences of widespread belief in unfounded conspiratorial narratives, particularly how conspiracy beliefs shape public attitudes towards law enforcement, government institutions, and legal proceedings.

Cartels and criminal collusion are of significant interest as they involve concerted efforts by individuals or organisations to manipulate markets, engage in illegal activities and undermine competition. Criminology defines cartels as agreements or arrangements between competing firms or entities within an industry to coordinate their actions, typically to fix prices, limit production, allocate markets, or otherwise manipulate market conditions to their advantage. Cartels can avoid competition and artificially raise prices, harming other potential competitors and consumers. Criminal collusion can be much darker, including assassinations, subterfuge, bid-rigging, bribery, extortion, or other forms of corruption.

Conspiracies are not all fabrications of paranoid minds; they are legal categories that happen all the time. The motives and reasons behind them are not unknowable, and criminology does a good job of demystifying them, but what it does less well is examine the potential for crime at the very apex of power. Criminologists look at the organisational dynamics of cartels and collusive networks, exploring the structures, strategies, and cultures that facilitate illegal cooperation among participants. This involves analysing the roles of key actors, such as cartel leaders, enforcers, and facilitators, and the mechanisms of communication, coordination, and control employed within criminal enterprises. Conspiratorial networks have hierarchies and roles. Understanding these dynamics helps develop strategies to disrupt and dismantle cartels and collusion schemes, including acknowledging the globalisation of cartels and criminal collusion. Cartels and collusive networks can operate across multiple jurisdictions, exploiting regulatory gaps, jurisdictional complexities, and international trade channels to evade detection and prosecution. They use their power to maintain secrecy and continue functioning. Conspiracies are secretive for a reason-they are criminal by nature. If they are not actively trying to hide, then they have already subverted the legal system and do not fear justice, a matter that has not escaped a number of writers.

In *The Power Elite,* C. Wright Mills discusses the interconnectedness of political, corporate, and military elites and their potential for conspiratorial behaviours. His work is a classic of American social science, although it was—and remains—controversial due to its highly critical analysis. Mills does a great job of presenting the inherent criminality and conspiracies in America's elite circles.

Gary Webb, in *Dark Alliance: The CIA, the Contras, and the Crack Cocaine Explosion,* investigates allegations of a conspiracy involving the CIA, drug trafficking, and the Nicaraguan Contras. The book claims the CIA may have supported Contra supporters and contributed to the crack cocaine epidemic in impoverished African American communities. Despite criticism from mainstream media and government officials, his work sparked public debate on the government's role in drug trafficking and social justice issues, prompting calls for further investigation into the CIA's activities.

Although often linked to false beliefs and misleading information, conspiracy theories can also help people think more critically by making them question authorities, investigate claims, be conscious of power dynamics and develop a critical culture. Healthy scepticism towards the media, the government, and other strong institutions can make society more accountable and open. The actual content and merit of any one theory might not always be important, yet it's the very act of taking an interest in conspiracy theories that makes for more curiosity and care about sources of information, available data, and different explanations, ultimately improving a person's analytical and critical thinking skills.

People who believe in conspiracy theories often form groups that can sometimes make echo chambers and polarisation worse. Still, they can also bring people together and help them work together to become more involved in activism, advocacy, and social movements that try to fix systemic problems. Media literacy is a necessary part of the skill set; knowing how to evaluate sources, spot bias, and tell the difference between reliable and false information is vital. By developing better interpretative skills, people can become smarter information users, better able to handle the complicated world of the digital age, and less likely to be swayed by propaganda and disinformation campaigns, including those of the State and supranational organisations to which States report, such as the UN and the WHO, which are a nexus in strategic alliance with the WEF which boasts of infiltrating Governments throughout the world with WEF trained members, a boast that includes Prime Ministers like Ardern, Trudeau and Varadkar.

All conspiracy theories should be treated with care and scepticism, but recognising that they can make us think critically and help us to be socially aware can help us understand their larger cultural and social meaning. The important thing to keep in mind is that conspiracy theories should not be judged, accepted, or rejected before their actual content has been examined.

Totalitarianism involves conspiratorial activity and the cunning use of conspiracy theories, which is crucial for actors who know their schemes are hostile to public interests and the law. The element of secrecy has taken on additional value in the digital age. There is a strong and growing totalitarian trend to make the individual and public space fully transparent whilst making the elites private and anonymous. Secrecy has always been a privilege of the elites to hide behind tall walls whilst the commoners are exposed. This is unchanged, and the internet and contemporary culture wars have only made it worse.

Social media, tracking devices, malware, telephones and cameras have made privacy near impossible and enforced a dystopian transparency. But this is hardly true for the elites. They have the power to defend their privacy and facelessness. Although you can see many wealthy people flaunting their wealth on social media, those people are not the ultrawealthy elite who understand the real value of secrecy across generations.

When humans simply have no idea what the elites are up to, it is no wonder, then, that we turn to conspiracy theories to explain the social world and the behaviour of powerful actors. They are not subject to the same level of transparency and visibility as the rest of us, they are protected by a phalanx of lawyers, tax experts, and security contractors and freely travel in and out of countries on private planes. Digital firewalls and superior technology have replaced their castle walls. The elite has no use for conspiracy theories. They do not have to theorise when they can easily spy on us, legally or illegally.

Consumer information is crucial for companies to develop targeted marketing. You may not know you need another coffee machine or more fresh groceries, but Amazon does. Government officials and politicians also benefit from data on voter behaviour and preferences. They don't simply ask; they buy the data from brokers and use it for propaganda. Most of this data is given away by people who blindly sign it away to use a product. In general, if you generate private data on a device, app or site, it is no longer yours; it belongs to the owner of the device, app or site – who then gets to sell it to the highest bidder. Social media platforms like Facebook, Instagram and X did not become multi-billion companies through advertisement alone. Their business model is based on the exploitation of privacy. If you aren't paying, then you are probably the product.

Totalitarianism has historically enforced and perfected the concentration of secrecy for the people at the top and its elimination for those at the bottom. The further away you are from the seat of power, the more exposed you become to the powers that be. Totalitarian regimes have used secret services to collect data on their citizens whilst keeping secret the often luxurious and opulent lifestyles of the ruling elites. It is not difficult to imagine a society where the ruling elites know through internet data analysis, wearables and implants exactly what kind of macronutrients you are lacking, what kind of shows you like and if you are exercising enough. All of this without you or your fellow commoners knowing exactly who the people are who rule over you. This is how we should imagine 21st-century totalitarianism: a rigid hierarchy with a darkened top and brightly lit base. The lower down the hierarchy you are, the less you know and the more you are *known*.

The issue is not purely technological. Contemporary culture does not value privacy enough, nor does it bind power to responsibility and transparency. We are all too eager to overshare and post details about ourselves online. Giving away personal information online has become normal. Sharing information, thoughts, and experiences on social media sites is not only encouraged but sometimes required. Many people base their self-worth on how many likes, comments, and fans they have. This has created a culture of validation through online presence. Because of this, people feel they need to share more about their lives online to stay relevant and raise their social status.

We easily sign away our privacy if it means accessing features of an app or security which companies and states are eager to exploit for profit and for control. The rise of *influencer culture* has made it harder to tell the difference between private and public life. Influencers appear to use their personal experiences to make money by turning themselves into material that other people consume. This voluntary exposure, bolstered by apparent financial and psychological rewards, has made us forget the value of privacy.

We are more likely to share private information without fully thinking about the long-term consequences. Online exposure is a way of garnering attention and validation, and, if done correctly, it can even become a business. Social media platforms *are* designed to take advantage of the human need for communication, participation, recognition, validation and attention. Features such as comments, shares, and likes cause dopamine, the happiness chemical, to be released, which starts a cycle of praise and reinforcement. So, users are more likely to share more personal information in order to get approval from their online friends.

The false sense of privacy some social media sites offer creates an environment where people share too much of themselves. Many people think wrongly that their posts are private and that only a small group of friends can see them. However, social media sites still collect and sell this information about their users, 'private' or not, which means that third parties can use it for their own ends. Millions of Facebook users' private information was taken without their permission and used to build psychological profiles as exposed in the Cambridge Analytica scandal. The internet was created to allow information to flow freely, which often means people's privacy is ignored, and breaches of privacy are easy to orchestrate. In this day and age, data breaches, hacking, and spying are all very common. Companies in the tech industry constantly gather, analyse, and sell personal information about their users, often without their knowledge or permission. These technological instruments and practices are primarily used for profit and political goals, but they are never far away from totalitarian implementation. Even if CEOs and politicians personally oppose totalitarianism, the algorithms they created and perfected through usage do not care about their values. They are ideal for totalitarian ends.

This cultural and technological environment is perfect for the flourishing of both conspiracies and conspiracy theories. As privacy becomes exclusive to the ruling elite, conspiratorial activity has become routine and banal. Only when totalitarian control is completely secured will privacy become redundant, as the rulers will have nothing to fear. Likewise, the more secretive the power elites become, the more paranoid and curious the rest of us will become. Privacy should be an individual right, one that is eroded only if that individual is a criminal or a politician. It is the responsibility of the populace and culture to enforce transparency in positions of power and to defend its own right to privacy. These matters are not completely settled and should be discussed in public spaces. Humans must be able to decide where the borders between transparency and privacy, knowledge and ignorance, should be drawn, but this is largely left out of political discourse.

2

RULE BY THE FEW: NOTHING NEW UNDER THE SUN

RULE BY THE FEW IS, at least, as old as human history. Across many civilisations and periods in history, powerful families and individuals have ruled through oligarchies, aristocracies, and authoritarian regimes, the governance model shaped by social, political, military and economic forces. Other forms of government, such as dictatorships and monarchies, should not be seen as somehow any different. Even if authority is officially nested in one person, it is usually an extended elite that holds power. In general, oligarchies developed to preserve authority over resources and unite a small number of elites around a common cause.

Oligarchy relies on an elitist solidarity that clearly distinguishes the privileged rulers from the ruled. Comparably, authoritarian governments frequently emerge in reaction to unstable or crisis-ridden times, with a clique formed around a leader imposing its will through repression and force. As such, authoritarian regimes are extreme responses to dire political situations. They are also inherently unstable as they are either ousted from inside or outside, or because they succeed in reestablishing political order and are slowly replaced.

A tiny elite solidified around the kings and pharaohs in ancient Mesopotamia and Egypt. In Mesopotamia, rulers who depended on noble councils often controlled city-states. Similar support came from a noble and priestly class for Egyptian pharaohs. Because these kingdoms frequently concentrated resources and power among the ruling class, a clear social hierarchy was established through religion, law and violence. Kings would often claim they had a divine right to justify their power and their hold over resources. Control of the political and spiritual domains was ensured by their religious leaders' frequent exercise of considerable power, which combined political governance with religious spectacles. By their religious teachings and rites, the priestly classes were essential in preserving social order and stability. Additionally, they frequently acted as mediums for the gods and the kings, legitimising and strengthening their positions of authority in the community.

Noble families dominated early Greek city-states such as Athens, Corinth, Thebes and Sparta. While some, like Athens, eventually adopted more democratic structures, others, like Sparta, solidified as oligarchies. Political leaders and reformers like Solon and Cleisthenes sought to give the ordinary people more power, and had an impact on Athens' transition to a democratic system. This change signalled a dramatic break from the control of a small number of aristocratic families and opened the door for a more democratic governance. These political reforms did not last long, but they left their mark on subsequent history. Emphasising a tight hierarchical society and military discipline, Sparta was ruled by a select group of elders and two kings.

Sparta's oligarchic system, which put stability and order above individual freedoms, was maintained in part by its concentration on military might and rigid social structure. The different ways that Athens and Sparta handled government demonstrate the variety of political structures in ancient Greece and their enduring influence on Western civilisation. Although both were some forms of oligarchy for most of their existence, the democratic experiment and thriving culture of Athens ensured its longevity.

Rome's aristocratic patrician class constituted the Senate, which exercised oligarchic control during the Roman Republic. Even though the Roman Republic had democratic features, such as The Assembly, a small number of powerful families frequently held the majority of the power. Rome had periods of peace and prosperity due to this system of government, which allowed for a balance between aristocratic authority and popular engagement. Ultimately, though, the Roman Republic fell because of the growing concentration of power among a small number of political and military leaders, such as Julius Caesar.

The Roman Empire signalled a change to a more authoritarian government, with emperors exercising almost total authority while preserving the facade of republican structures. Though it resulted in more effective decision-making and centralised authority, the emperors' consolidation of power also cost Roman citizens their political freedoms. Rome's history for many centuries was shaped by the final change from republic to monarchy brought about by the transfer to imperial power.

The decaying Roman Empire served as the foundation for feudalism. Feudalism is a broad term that is used to describe the political and economic organisation of Medieval Europe.

Local lords dominated their estates and vassals with considerable authority. Although the real power was usually in the hands of the high nobility, it was the kings who had the formal authority. When the central authority of the Roman Empire collapsed, feudalism arose as a form of government that gave more local autonomy and prioritised allegiance to individual lords. More flexibility in government was made possible by this decentralised system, but it also meant that nobles striving for power would frequently engage in battles with each other. Medieval Europe was plagued by feuds, conquests and takeovers – and *actual* plagues.

Nobles ruled large estates and legally owned important resources during the Middle Ages. They had near complete control over their serfs and were able to sway, bribe or influence other rulers. Their aristocratic influence shaped the social structure and affected social life at all levels. The feudal system also emphasised the value of interpersonal connections and alliances in preserving peace and order in societies. Marriages were a way to form alliances to keep the wealth inside the family. The exchange of hostages, or *wards,* was also commonplace.

Although emperors were at the head of a highly complex system of government in both the Holy Roman Empire and the Byzantine Empire, their power was not always upheld. In the provinces especially, the local bureaucracy and aristocracy had a big say. Political intrigue and power struggles inside the empires resulted from the emperor's authority being frequently questioned by strong noble families and high-ranking bureaucrats. Local elites were essential in running their particular domains and preserving stability despite the emperor's centralised power. We can refer to the city-states of Medieval Europe as oligarchies, due to their republican nature, however, it is clear that the kingdoms and empires of this period did not work too differently. There was always a group of people in charge, even if power was officially in the hands of a single monarch. One person cannot rule alone.

Even in the late Medieval era, the elite survived and prospered as monarchies solidified. Louis XIV (1638-1715), is a prime example of a king who consolidated absolute power in the French monarchy, although he did so in the early modern era. Before him, there was Louis XI (1461–1483), called the *Spider King* because of his cunning political manoeuvres and successful schemes. His consolidation of administrative authority, economic growth, and subduing of disobedient nobles laid the foundation for French absolutism. In England, Henry VII (1485–1509), made significant moves to solidify his authority after ascending to the throne by winning the Wars of the Roses. Setting the basis for future absolute control, he weakened the power of the aristocracy, instituted a robust economic strategy, and fortified the monarchy's institutions.

On the Iberian Peninsula, the two Catholic monarchs, Isabella I of Castile (1474–1504) and Ferdinand II of Aragon (1479–1516), attempted to unify Spain together. They reformed the government, limited the influence of the nobles, and instituted the Spanish Inquisition to uphold religious unity and strengthen royal authority. The future absolute and colonial control of the Spanish Empire was made possible by their marriage and policies. However, these kings always relied on the nobles and newly formed bureaucratic classes. The emergence of absolute monarchy signalled an unseen centralisation of power and control. These absolute monarchs proclaimed supremacy over formerly autonomous areas and newly discovered lands. To assist in the management of the enormous areas under their control, complex bureaucracies and court systems were also developed during this time. Although absolute monarchies weakened the aristocracy, they also produced a new elite within the state. The absolute monarch was never alone.

Medieval European city-states ruled by oligarchies included Venice, Genoa and Florence in Italy. The city's Leading families made up the Great Council, which governed the Venetian Republic, for example. These oligarchies often dominated political authority and decision-making, resulting in social stratification and restricted public participation in government. The conflicts and alliances among the governing families determined the stability and prosperity of these city-states. The merchant classes were not immune to the infighting and feuds among the aristocratic elites.

Like in Venice, a group of established merchant families controlled Genoa. Through their Grand Council and other assemblies, the affluent and powerful inhabitants of Genoa divided political authority with the Doge, who was elected by them and given a limited mandate. The Flemish cities of Bruges, Ghent, and Ypres worked in a similar way. Affluent merchants and guild leaders constituted councils that oversaw the cities. Particularly in issues pertaining to trade and municipal administration, these councils enjoyed considerable autonomy and authority. Oligarchies ruled some Swiss cantons, including Bern and Zurich. A few privileged families dominated the local councils and the decision-making process. With great autonomy, these cantons ran their affairs apart from feudal lords or monarchs. A tiny number of *boyars*, or nobles, and affluent merchants ruled the oligarchic Novgorod Republic in what is now Russia. The *Veche*, the council that ran the city, elected the *Posadnik*, the highest official, from among the aristocrats.

Political power was intimately related to economic power in many mediaeval oligarchies. Because of their economic power, affluent merchant families and guilds frequently dominated the governmental institutions. The general populace was usually kept out of meaningful governance by this elite group holding political power. To maintain the concentration of power, these oligarchies frequently filled leadership posts with elections or appointments from within the elite group. High degrees of autonomy were enjoyed by several oligarchic cities and regions, which ran their own affairs free from major interference by feudal lords or monarchs. Even when they swore fealty to a monarch, they could buy their freedom and reject interference.

Much changed in Europe with the advent of industrialisation, but not everything. New economic elites, bankers and industrialists emerged with the growth of industrialisation and possessed considerable power over established political regimes. At the expense of workers and the environment, these oligarchies influenced laws to benefit their own financial and industrial interests. Social inequality was made worse, and working-class unrest was prevalent during this period. Many of the feudal laws and customs were gone; serfdom was abolished, and most people were becoming industrial workers. Their freedoms and protections had to be established through new laws. These attempts, however, were hindered by the new and influential industrial elite. This new elite oversaw an unprecedented rise in wealth, alongside rapid social change and unrest. It is no wonder that this age gave birth to the early forms of socialism, anarchism and communism. The industrial and financial elites also created ideologies of control. They did not have the benefit of tradition and custom that the aristocracy did, nor their armies. Their new supremacy had to be defended by new means.

Authoritarian governments arose all over Europe in the 20th century. Most notably, they included Soviet Russia, Nazi Germany, and fascist Italy. There were many others. Arguably, all states in this period went through dire political changes and were authoritarian to some degree. Concentration of authority, repression of opposition, and exclusive leadership or one-party control—often backed by a devoted elite—were hallmarks of these regimes. Mass violence, propaganda, censorship and political repression were necessary to keep control over the citizenry. Additionally, impeding economic growth and innovation were the autocratic characteristics of these regimes, which suppressed creativity and muffled opposing voices. Intellectuals who experienced the barbarism of these regimes described them as more than authoritarian; they were totalitarian. Total control, total mobilisation and total war on a national scale were never seen before. The distinction is important, as authoritarian regimes arose after these totalitarian ones that did not match their intensity or extent.

For instance, authoritarian governments dominated by a small number of military commanders and their followers were frequently formed by military coups throughout Latin America, Africa, and portions of Asia. Many times, these military dictatorships used violence to stifle dissent and opposition, ruling by intimidation and terror. Notwithstanding their claims to bring security and order, their lack of responsibility and contempt for human rights often resulted in corruption, economic stagnation, and social unrest. Although a formidable enemy to democracy and popular governance on their own, they did not have the goals or means of totalitarianism. Part of it is that these regimes were completely militaristic and could never attain the needed popular support through indoctrination. As Arendt noted, the internal security apparatus – the secret police – was the crucial component of totalitarian control, not the military.

The terms *authoritarian* and *oligarchic* are clear pejoratives in the West today. This means we only use them to describe our enemies, never ourselves. For instance, it is easy to identify post-Soviet oligarchies. Following the collapse of the Soviet Union, oligarchs—many of whom were closely associated with political leaders—rose to considerable wealth and power in nations such as Russia, Ukraine, Georgia and Kazakhstan. Inequality and corruption proliferated because these oligarchs could control the political system to serve their own agendas. Both economic growth and democratic advancement in these nations have been hampered by the concentration of power in the hands of a small number of oligarchs, alongside their families and networks. Although the West is formally against such oligarchs, they are free to enjoy Western luxuries, own mansions and apartments in the largest Western cities, and dock their yachts wherever they please. Money is the universal language.

Certain modern governments combine elements of oligarchies and democracies, creating a hybrid regime. Their democratic institutions exist in the public eye, yet a tiny, frequently economically elite group still controls the actual power. Examples of this are found in Asia and Africa, and in transitioning regimes in Eastern Europe. It is challenging for people to hold their leaders responsible in these hybrid regimes since the appearance of democracy can conceal the reality of oligarchic power. For most people, this translates into restricted political freedoms and economic prospects. An interesting example is Singapore, which has successfully implemented capitalism and created an authoritarian but safe and stable country, that enjoys popular support.

We should not think of the West as somehow immune to these historic and global trends. Technocrats and business executives frequently have a big say in modern policy decisions, occasionally raising questions about corporate oligarchy or plutocracy in supposedly democratic countries. These big players can influence laws to suit their own interests. Their money and connections allow them to weaken democratic institutions from the inside. Lobbying is a form of legalised corruption. It affects democratic systems at their core, as it changes the rule *One person, one vote,* to *One dollar, one vote.* It is not surprising, then, that in the United States, the will of the corporations and their lobbyists becomes law.

AUTHORITARIAN, aristocratic, and oligarchic regimes have developed throughout history in reaction to social, political, and economic circumstances. Even if the few have ruled in different ways—from ancient aristocracies and monarchs to contemporary industrial and corporate oligarchies—the concentration of power in the hands of a small minority is nevertheless a recurrent feature of global governance. Understanding our own modern political systems and their own shifts is easier when we are aware of these historical trends. Understanding this history of authoritarian and oligarchic regimes can help us better comprehend the difficulties democracies now face. The enemy is not new. Totalitarianism, although we distinguish it from simple authoritarianism, arose – and rises again – from the same source. Rule by the few, regardless of how we call it or what mask it wears, has always been a threat to democratic systems and popular governance. Elite rule persists, it ensures its own survival and responds to threats through many institutions, organisations and agencies. The totalitarianism of the 21st century is both an attempt to further solidify elite rule and to eliminate the threat of 21st century democracy.

In general, elite rule is a political, economic, or social system in which a small, chosen number of people or families—often referred to as the elite—concentrates power and makes all the important decisions. This elite group greatly influences major institutions in the government, economy, education and culture. The American sociologist Charles R. Mills referred to *the power elite* and showed how it is composed of the tops of the political, economic and military spheres; the power elite is not exclusive to American society, as the short history provided shows. Additionally, it is not static, as different spheres, most notably science and technology, are incorporated into it.

The elite gains most from the policies and laws enacted under its rule. It is not always against the populace, and rarely is it malevolent, but it systematically harms civil society. Although it is helpful to be precise and talk about individual perpetrators and culprits, we must keep in mind that the idea of elite rule is rotten. Individuals can be identified and made liable, even expelled from the elite and imprisoned – but this does not solve the underlying issue. A new elite can always come along and continue the process.

Frequently, this power elite shapes public policy and opinion by exerting considerable influence on institutions like the media, education, and the courts. Often, members of the power elite are owners of their own media networks, social media platforms, magazines, websites and other factories of propaganda. It becomes more difficult for all of us to question the status quo when the elite maintains control over these institutions and public places where debates and cooperation occur. With systems in place to safeguard their interests and preserve their position, the power elite becomes less answerable to the people. A decisive step, discussed later, is the veiling or *anonymisation* of the power elite.

Not only do the elites not answer to us, we do not know who they are. Ignorance is a tool of power, just like knowledge. The age of mass data and information is highly paradoxical; we can easily look up trivial things like the distance between Dublin and Beijing (8,277 km) or the nutritive profile of a snack, but we find it much more difficult to find out who rules us.

Previous ruling elites took pride in their exalted positions of power and sought glory. The noble families and notable kings who ruled ancient Greece and Rome are still known to us. They wanted to live on and attain a semblance of immortality through their wealth and great deeds. We know them through sculptures, temples, epics and other works of art that they sponsored. Today's power elite is much more cautious. Times have changed; to be a master among slaves is no longer seen as admirable. Many rich people flaunt their wealth on social media and in public, but their wealth is insignificant compared to the wealth of the power elite. It is our lack of imagination and laziness in wording that makes us call both millionaires and billionaires wealthy, even though the latter are a thousand times wealthier than the former. A billion dollars is, however, not the ceiling.

Although the modern power elite is cautious and values anonymity, it still promotes an elitist ideology and culture. Elitism is the belief or attitude that an elite should run society as the elite are better and more competent to run a country than the common people. Elitism can appear in many aspects of regular social life and academic political philosophy. In general terms, it is an unwise tolerance of undeserved power. Elitism is present even in democratic countries and liberal cultures. The foundation of most elitism is the idea that the elite are better suited to rule because they have higher levels of knowledge, education, or moral character. Elitism entails a contempt for populism and the people's capacity to make wise judgements or run a government. This kind of thinking causes many to become more resentful and distrustful of the ruling class and their demands.

Today debates on elitism and elite control frequently centre on the power of technocrats, political dynasties, and business executives. In discussions of political lobbying, wealth inequality, and the function of money in politics, elite influence is a common topic of concern. Power concentration and the conviction in the intrinsic superiority of a chosen group are reflected in elite rule and elitism. Though these ideas have existed throughout history, they nevertheless influence modern political and social environments and raise significant concerns about justice, equality, and democracy. This is particularly so through the agency of the WEF, who hold its annual meeting in Davos, Switzerland. The WEF's stated objectives include stakeholder capitalism, which requires the diminution of power in representative democracy and the growth in power of Non-Governmental Organisations (NGOs) and Trade Unions.

The German sociologist Robert Michels wrote about the "Iron Law of Oligarchy" in his 1911 book *Political Parties*. His theory proposes that all organisations, no matter how democratic or egalitarian they may be at first, will eventually turn into oligarchies. Michels claimed that organisations need a more structured type of leadership to function well as they get bigger and more complicated. Because of the need to organise and work together, a leadership class is formed. Over time, this group of leaders gains more power and often turns into an entrenched elite that is hard to remove. Bureaucracy and specialisation become necessary for large groups to function efficiently, whether they are political parties, labour unions, or corporations. There is a hierarchy in this bureaucratic structure, and decisions are made by a small group of leaders who possess the relevant knowledge, control information, and centralise power.

Elites in an organisation often have their own goals, which are different from those of the general membership. To preserve their privileged position, these elites put their own interests ahead of the organisation's goals, interests and ideals. To protect their power, they may keep information under lock and key, change the rules, or try to stop people from disagreeing. Michels first conceived his theory in terms of political parties, especially those that say they are democratic and speak for the working class. He pointed out that even parties such as the socialist and labour parties, which espoused the values of egalitarianism and democracy, tended to become oligarchic. The party leaders would become more conservative and self-centred and would often pull away from the people they claimed they represented.

Even though the goal of labour unions is to look out for the interests of workers, they can also succumb to the iron law of oligarchy. Once they are in charge, union leaders put their own jobs and negotiations with management ahead of the more radical demands or changes that union members want. There are also times when big businesses and nonprofits act in an oligarchic way. Executives and board members have power over how the company runs and what policies it follows. They often make choices to improve the situation for themselves and their peers, rather than for the company's employees or other stakeholders.

Michels' theory is too general; not all kinds of organisations eventually become oligarchic. There are examples of organisations and organisational practices that actively fight oligarchic tendencies and stick to more democratic practices such as term limits, openness, and widespread participation. The Iron Law of Oligarchy puts too much weight on structural factors and does not give people and groups enough credit for their ability to fight back and challenge power monopolisation. However, the fact that not all organisations succumb to this iron law does not mean its alarming implications are to be ignored.

The Iron Law of Oligarchy is a useful tool when discussing how power works in societies and organisations today. We should carefully and critically examine this theory because it shows how power can get concentrated in the hands of the few, even in areas that try to achieve democratic participation. It explains how important it is for organisations to be alert, open, and have ways to check and balance power. By being aware of our oligarchic tendency, all members of a society can better push for structures and practices that encourage accountability, participation, and democratic governance. After all, there are always counter tendencies that can outmatch the tendency towards oligarchy. There are "iron laws" that work in the opposite direction; like the human distrust in overwhelming power and our need for liberty. We can fight, and we often do so without knowing it is because of the inevitable rise of oligarchy. Many strive to uphold the egalitarian values that their organisations were founded upon.

Regardless of how democratic an organisation aspires to be, it certainly can become more oligarchic over time. This is true in politics, businesses, labour unions, and even digital platforms.

The Democratic Party and the Republican Party, the two main political parties in the United States, both have oligarchical traits. The party leadership and its philanthropists have the most power over policy decisions and choosing candidates. For example, during the 2016 presidential primaries, the Democratic National Committee (DNC) was criticised for supporting Hillary Clinton over Bernie Sanders, even though Sanders had much more support from regular voters. In the same way, the Republican Party has seen a rise in power of key figures and big donors which have changed the party's direction and priorities. The centre-right base of the Republican Party has almost entirely eroded away, and it has morphed into a political cult around President Donald Trump who spectacularly won his second term of presidency in November 2024, taking the popular vote with massive poll numbers. People often say that Russia's government is an oligarchy because most of the power is held by a small group of elites who are close to President Vladimir Putin. This group of oligarchs controls important businesses and political groups, which stop real democracy from working while keeping power tight. While it *is* true that Russia is a classic example of oligarchy, it is not unique in this respect.

In the business world, tech giants like Google, Facebook (now Meta), and Amazon show exactly how the Iron Law of Oligarchy works in business. These businesses began with creative and sometimes egalitarian ideas, but they've grown into immense organisations with a strong and centralised leadership. Executives like Jeff Bezos at Amazon and Mark Zuckerberg at Meta have enormous power over the policies and strategies of their companies. These business leaders have so much money and power that they can change industry standards, laws, and even world politics.

The financial crisis of 2008 made the oligarchic tendencies in the banking sector clear. Only a small group of executives and board members run the big banks like Goldman Sachs and JPMorgan Chase. They make important choices that affect the global economy. The crisis exposed how these leaders put money-making at an unimaginable scale and put taking extreme risks ahead of keeping the economy stable and prosperous for all. The subsequent bailouts and lack of criminal accountability made it clear that financial elites have power over government policies.

Labour unions such as United Auto Workers (UAW) are corrupt and controlled by a small group of wealthy people. In the past few years, several high-level UAW officials have been found guilty of stealing money and taking bribes. These actions broke the trust of union members and showed how union leaders care more about personal gain and staying in power than looking out for the interests of workers. The National Education Association (NEA) and the American Federation of Teachers (AFT), two teachers' unions, also showed similar oligarchic tendencies. Their position on important issues like school reform and teacher evaluations are often shaped by the interests of their leaders. These unions fight for the rights of teachers, but there can be problems between regular members and the elite leadership, especially when decisions are made that go against the wishes of the members.

Technology, in general, has not been immune to this tendency towards oligarchy. Social media sites like Twitter and Facebook have centralised ways of making decisions about how to moderate content and enforce rules. Executives and small groups within these companies have power over what content is allowed and not allowed, which affects political movements and the overall culture. You can see how much power the people in charge of these platforms have when they block people like former President Donald Trump from Twitter and Facebook.

Even though the cryptocurrency industry is often praised for being decentralised, it also has its own oligarchical tendencies. Some of the biggest players in the market are Bitcoin miners, cryptocurrency exchanges, and people who make blockchain protocols. These important players and their choices can have a significant impact on the ecosystem as a whole, showing that even technologies that are supposed to be decentralised can become centralised over time.

It's not just big international NGOs like Amnesty International and the World Wildlife Fund (WWF) that have to deal with problems caused by the Iron Law of Oligarchy. The people in charge of these groups often make strategic choices that are different from the grassroots movements they want to support. When decisions are made in the boardroom, it can cause problems between the leadership and local chapters or activists, making their work less effective and less focused.

Wherever we find social organisation and power structures, there appears to be a strong trend towards oligarchy. As the examples and situations above show, this trend is universal and not bound to strictly political institutions.

The Iron Law of Oligarchy remains a powerful way to examine how power works in modern society. It is an overlooked fact that a small group of people hold most of the power in political parties, businesses, labour unions, digital platforms, and nonprofits. This power continues to shape how decisions are made, and what happens as a result. But there are solutions, and we need to encourage accountability, openness, and democratic practices in all kinds of organisations.

An essential aspect of both oligarchy and totalitarianism is that power is centralised. The need for efficiency and expertise justifies putting most of the power in the hands of a small elite as an organisation grows. As we have seen, this concentration of power makes it easy for totalitarian leaders to take over and keep control by using centralised structures in their favour. Even if the Iron Law of Oligarchy does not directly or necessarily lead to totalitarianism, it is clear that oligarchy can easily transition into totalitarianism. During political and economic crises, oligarchy leads to more authoritarian solutions than democratic ones. When the power of the oligarchs is threatened, they will naturally seek preservation in increased centralisation of power. Totalitarianism becomes the logical solution for oligarchies that are in danger.

We have seen throughout history where the elites cut themselves off from the rest of the population and undermine society in order to maintain autocratic rule. In the Soviet Union, for example, Joseph Stalin was able to get rid of his political rivals and set up a totalitarian government. He created a cult of personality and used the party's centralised power to carry out widespread purges and surveil every aspect of life. The Soviet Union was oligarchic from the beginning, with the Communist Party officials controlling all important institutions, so it was natural for it to transition into a one-man totalitarian regime. After Stalin's death, the regime made several important reforms that undermined his cult of personality and political legacy, but the Soviet Union remained a totalitarian oligarchy.

Totalitarian governments use media propaganda to control and sway public opinion and to keep the ruling class in power. The Iron Law of Oligarchy sets it all up, as people put all the power over communication channels into one, easily controllable, place. The Ministry of Public Enlightenment and Propaganda in Nazi Germany, which Joseph Goebbels ran, had control over the press, literature, music, theatre, films, and radio. This ensured the Nazi story was told everywhere and that people who disagreed with it were shut down. When public spaces and means of communication are decentralised and dispersed, it becomes much more difficult for elites to spread their narrative. When totalitarian ideology fails to persuade and pacify the population, totalitarians resort to more nefarious and violent means, including surveillance and punishment. The Communist Party in modern China controls its people by using advanced surveillance technology and a social credit system. This ensures everyone follows their rules, and it stops people from speaking out against the government. Facial recognition, internet censorship, and data monitoring are all used on a large scale in similar societies. In Italy, before World War II, Mussolini's Fascist Party destroyed democratic institutions and opposition parties in a systematic and planned way. They did this by using a centralised party structure to gain loyalty and stop people from protesting. The same is true for China, other parties besides the Communist Party do exist, but are not granted any real authority by the centralised government.

To gain power, totalitarian leaders often work with existing elites, ensuring they will support and help by including them in the government. Elites have a tendency to side with the dominant power in order to keep their status and influence, Vladimir Putin has used oligarchs and influential politicians to stay in power in Russia, balancing the needs of the state with those of the elite. The Iron Law of Oligarchy states that anyone who tries to challenge the powerful elite will be met with resistance or be incorporated into the oligarchy. In totalitarian regimes, this usually means putting down any opposition with brutal force. Using state tools like the secret police, a centralised power structure can eliminate people who are against the government quickly and decisively. NKVD (People's Commissariat for Internal Affairs) arrested, executed, and deported anyone they thought were a threat during the Stalinist era in the Soviet Union. Stalin was a ruthless yet insecure, leader who saw criticism and minor disagreements equally as threatening as assassination attempts.

As power gets concentrated regular citizens and members lose the ability to work together and fight back. Totalitarian regimes take advantage of the fact that groups don't always work well together, to stay in power. North Korea's government tightly controls information and punishes people harshly who speak out against the regime, so there is no effective resistance. Digital surveillance technologies have made it easier for regimes to keep power in the 21st century. Yet the dynastic elite that still rules North Korea today, comes from the descendants of the original elite that formed during the resistance period and later war with America.

An often overlooked aspect of totalitarianism is its connection to war. War has often been the origin of totalitarianism and a mechanism of its preservation and spread. Interestingly, war has also been the usual conclusion of same such totalitarian regimes.

The Iron Law of Oligarchy is a classical sociological theory that explains a major political trend, and elucidates the widespread occurrences of oligarchy. However, there is a common prejudice in Western societies that sees the West as immune to this trend. This prejudice is theoretically incoherent and has become a potential danger to democracy. Western societies, especially the United States of America, have many established oligarchic structures and powerful elites. This is not a new or radical claim, but rather a well-established and documented sociological fact. This is the topic of the next section.

Charles Wright Mills was a famous and important American sociologist who lived from 1916 to 1962. In his lifetime he was known for his critical analysis of power and how it shaped American society. Today, he is mostly known for his work on the sociological imagination, which is a concept that helps individuals learn how their own experiences and larger social forces affect each other. Mills made important contributions to the field of political sociology, especially through his studies.

In his 1951 book, *White Collar: The American Middle Classes,* Mills looks at how the American middle class has changed, and how the rise of white-collar workers has affected social stratification and power dynamics. This book dispelled the myth of "The Classless Society" and gave a nuanced and empirical account of "class". His most famous book, *The Sociological Imagination* (1959), stresses how important it is to understand how personal experiences are connected to overarching social and historical forces. Mills proposed the sociological imagination as a tool to help people see how the problems they encounter in everyday life are connected to the rest of society. Mills helped people understand how complicated social life is, and how important historical and structural factors are, in shaping people's lives. The most relevant book in the context of analysing totalitarianism, is *The Power Elite,* published in 1956. It is one of his most famous works and describes how a small group of military, business, and political leaders hold most of the power in the United States. Mills describes in theoretical and empirical detail how this small group of powerful people historically attained control over national and international policies, which, as he points out, is not too good for American democracy. Mills' idea of the "power elite" is still one of the most important ideas in political sociology. The power elite has a disproportionate amount of power in society, yet it makes decisions that affect millions of people.

His analysis disagreed with the pluralist view of the time, that power is spread out vertically and horizontally in developed democratic societies. Instead, it suggested that real power is held by a concentrated group among the American elites. Mills also thought that intellectuals were very important to society because they questioned power and worked to make things better. He was upset about the rise of "celebrity intellectuals" and the decline of the real and independent intellectual class. Celebrity intellectuals, as he describes them, are more interested in keeping their status and power than in fighting injustices and working for social change. They are unreliable in real political struggles as they are unlikely to properly call out threatening concentrations and abuses of power. Instead, celebrity intellectuals promote seemingly radical and important causes that do not challenge the seat of power in any meaningful way. Mills outlined a clear and simple task for intellectuals: to question power and fight for justice. Modern academia has seemingly abandoned this ideal; we are left with false experts and scholarly fraudsters.

Mills, like Arendt, also criticised the emerging mass society and the passive, conformist behaviour he thought it encouraged. Chapter 13 of *The Power Elite* is dedicated to an analysis of mass society in America. He made the case that the media and bureaucratic structures create a sense of helplessness and cuts people off from the bigger political and economic forces that affect their lives. We echo his arguments when we discuss media bias, consumer culture, and political apathy. Mill's criticism of the role of mass media in shaping public opinion and encouraging conformity is especially relevant in the age of 24/7 news cycles and popular social media platforms. His descriptions of powerlessness and political disengagement, (made in the 50s of the last century), are still apt for our age - with the weakening of democratic norms and the continual erosion of freedoms. The relevance of his sociological work has only increased in the 21st century; it has become essential studying for understanding the politics of today. More and more people are becoming increasingly worried about the wealth and influence that is being concentrated in the hands of an increasingly shrinking elite. The danger we experience at the present time comes no longer from the threat of a national power elite, but from a global one.

In *The Power Elite*, Mills points out that the military, big businesses and the federal government are the three most powerful institutions in the United States. The members of the power elite hold key positions in all of these institutions, and, as we have seen in the examples already discussed, they make important decisions affecting millions of souls. These people in power are not isolated individuals; they are closely linked through professional, social, and educational networks. They often have similar social backgrounds, attend the same top schools, and are part of the same exclusive groups and clubs. This interconnectedness helps them stay in charge and makes it easier for them to work together and gain power. In other words, the power elite exhibits a remarkable degree of solidarity. Its members know who their friends and enemies are. They may occasionally squabble with each other, but their true ire is reserved for the commoners, who usually have no say in the matter or any occasion to watch over the process..

The concept of institutions plays a crucial role in the Mill's analysis . A modern power elite is only possible because of large and complicated modern institutions. The power elite is not the product of sheer oligarchic will or collusion, like every other social phenomenon it is the product of complex technological, social and cultural developments. It is the rise of powerful institutions that makes a power elite possible, although not inevitable. According to Mills, the main institutional orders—political, military, and economic—have all become centralised, interconnected systems. Technological progress has caused each of these sectors to grow in size, administrative complexity, and decision-making centralisation.

The economy used to consist of many tiny, independent producing units, but a few hundred massive, mostly international, corporations now control it. What was once the norm, small and local business, is now the exception. These mega-corporations make important economic decisions with their overwhelming economic might, as well as having ties with the political system and administration. The political system has evolved into a powerful, centralised executive establishment from a once decentralised conglomerate of states with little central authority. Previously distributed powers have been absorbed by this centralisation, impacting every facet of the social system. It is foolish to think of the United States of America as a federation of free states. Its military has developed into the most significant and expensive sector of the government, from a tiny, mistrusted establishment that depended on state militias. Though it maintains a marvellous public image, it is no more than an inefficient bureaucratic organisation.

Mills highlights that these institutions now possess far more power due to tighter administrative procedures and expanded central executive authority. Each institution now has much more influence thanks to intimate links with the rest of society. Corporate decisions, for instance, influence worldwide military and political events; military decisions influence political life and economic activity; and political decisions influence both military and economic initiatives. Mills concludes that there is no longer a conventional division between military, political and economic institutions. Instead, there is one highly integrated political economy (also called the military-industrial complex by Eisenhower) that combines the major political, military, and economic institutions. Understanding this "triangle of power," created by the interlocking of once different power institutions, is essential to comprehending the history of the current social reality.

Mills talked about how the military establishment became stronger and more powerful after the end of World War II, and how close it got to big defence contractors and companies. Even then, the military-industrial complex had a lot of power over national security policies and foreign affairs decisions. This military-industrial complex routinely put its own needs ahead of democratic principles and the public good. In the same spirit, big businesses gained a lot of influence over economic policies and regulations. Not only do corporate leaders have most of the power within their own companies, but they also have a power over national economic plans, which often hurts smaller businesses and the public in the long term.

All of this would be impossible if the political institutions were not undergoing the same centralisation. The powerful few, once they attain positions of power, manipulate the political system to keep themselves in control. Additionally, many political leaders come from wealthy families and work for the military and business sectors. Through campaign donations and lobbying, their generational wealth has most of the power in politics. In other words, economic resources easily translate into political authority and public opinion. This convertibility ensures policy decisions are made to benefit the members of the power elite.

Concentrating power in the hands of the few , even if it is the outcome of institutional development, will inevitably undermine democratic processes and principles. Modern institutions, alongside the power elite, have slowly shut the public out of political decision-making , which has led to widespread feelings of helplessness on the ground, along with additional discouragement. Mills says that this slow loss of democracy is an existential threat to the very foundations of a free and fair society. It is not something that can be easily regained once it is lost. Because of their concentrated power, the elites are rarely held responsible for what they do, no matter how severe and serious their crimes. This leads to a vicious circle of apathy and hopelessness. People who don't feel like they can change things become less interested in politics and less involved, strengthening the elites' power even more.

Critics might say that Mills puts too much emphasis on the role of the elites and not enough on the power of the people and democratic processes. The other authors and examples discussed in this book should show that this concern with the influence of elites is completely warranted on Mill's side. His analysis is not too pessimistic as it presents possible challenges to the power elite; social movements and democratic reforms could bring about positive change and at the very least, weaken the elite. Widespread economic inequality, corporate influence in politics, and the power of the military-industrial complex are still pressing issues today. Mills gives us a framework for understanding how power is organised and maintained as well as a critical lens through which to look at how power and democracy work. Most importantly, the rise of 21st century totalitarianism is also understandable through this framework, as it shows us how institutions from different spheres collude and merge to form overarching systems of power.

The obvious idea that a small, linked group controls major parts of the social, economic, and political systems holds truer than ever. It will only become worse in the future if we do nothing about it. The power elite has changed over the years, alongside the social institutions themselves, but many of the features Mills described are obviously present. We can say that the current power elite is made up of politicians, government workers, and policymakers who hold power over national and international decisions, CEOs and other top executives of multinational companies;, especially those in the financial, energy, healthcare, and technology sectors, military leaders and defence contractors who hold the power over national security and defence policies. There are also other candidates for the power elite, for instance, the managers and executive board members of mass media companies and social media sites who orchestrate the flow of news and public conversation.

Tech billionaires are the newest member of the power elite. The rise of tech billionaires has changed the institutional balance of power in many new ways. Wealth and power has been attained by these people through their control of major technology companies. This success happened relatively quickly, and they have a massive impact on the world today. Because they have such a strong effect on many parts of society, especially the online world and social media, they can be thought of as a fourth pillar of the power elite. The development of digital infrastructure has also created new institutions that have, in turn, created new elites at the top.

Tech billionaires like Jeff Bezos, Bill Gates, Elon Musk, and Mark Zuckerberg have built companies that are pioneers in many important areas of the economy, from online shopping and social networks to space travel and AI. They are usually close to political leaders and can change policies through lobbying, donations to campaigns, and creating strategic partnerships. Tech giants run platforms that millions of people use every day. Sites like Google, Amazon and Facebook are inescapable in everyday life for most people in the West; we rely on them for information, commerce, socialisation and leisure. This gives them power to change public opinion, affect elections, and control the spread of information, whether true or false.

Big tech companies also collect vast amounts of data that give them new insights into people's habits, movements, and behaviours, giving them more power to control and even to predict social trends. This data is valuable to the political, economic and military elites. With these new technologies and methods of social control, the tech elites reinforce and uphold the whole of the power elite. A fourth pillar strengthens the whole system.

Jeff Bezos has an immense amount of power and influence, as shown by Amazon's dominance in e-commerce, cloud computing (through AWS), and its forays into media and healthcare. Amazon's effect on labour laws the way stores work, and increasing public concerns about data privacy contributes greatly to this power. Elon Musk's businesses have paved the way for electric cars (Telsa) and internet connections (Starlink); and they have also turned him into a key figure in futuristic technological progress. His ownership of X (formerly Twitter) puts him on collision course with those who wish to regulate free speech. The fact that Facebook has changed the way people interact with each other, talk about politics, and understand privacy shows how influential Mark Zuckerberg is. The platform's role in election meddling, spreading false information, and data breaches show the social reach of this influence. Facebook is not just a neutral medium for communication, it manipulates the allowed and desired content of public and private expressions.

Tech billionaires and their companies often push for rules and regulations that are good for them (or at least neutral) and bad for their competition. Usually, this means changing privacy, antitrust, and innovation laws. Their political power is shown by their ability to shape policy agendas and regulatory frameworks, their economic power is evident from the profits, and they even wield a degree of military power – since modern warfare has increasingly shaped by advanced technologies and digitalisation. Military power is not inherently violent, as subterfuge and sabotage show. X, Facebook, and YouTube are all very important in shaping public discourse and perception. This makes them potential tools of warfare as well.

Democratic processes, norms and social solidarity are not just affected by choices made through content moderation, algorithmic biases, and platform policies. They can also be affected by foreign governments through forms of digital warfare and by various agencies of the domestic government. Because these companies control such large digital markets and services, they can do more than set standards for the industry, change how customers act, and maybe even stop competition. Since they have become a vital part of the digital infrastructure we rely on every day, their potential military value has also shown itself. Not only can these platforms be used to wage covert operations by the US government itself, but also by foreign actors. This is clear from the widespread talk about Russian bots. Although sometimes overestimated, this practice is not benign, nor is it exclusive to Russia. It is not at all surprising that China, America's only real competitor (especially in technology), has a firewall that blocks out all Western platforms and provides its immense population with domestic alternatives. The Chinese technocracy is much more aware of the dangers of digital warfare than we are in the West.

The rise of tech billionaires as a new type of power elite shows how power relationships are changing in the 21st century. It is important to understand these dynamics in order to understand current political, economic, and social problems and to find solutions to the problems caused by the rise of a new totalitarianism. The writings of critical sociologists like Charles Wright Mills, especially his book *The Power Elite*, give us an academic framework with which we can more seriously think about the totalitarian threat. In our age, totalitarian governments need to be able to control information more than anything else. The powerful can control the mainstream narratives and stifle opposition by manipulating the information flows, setting the limits of public debate, and shutting down voices that disagree. In totalitarian systems, propaganda and censorship are used to keep the regime in power, and technological information control is a feature of those systems.

These days, technology plays a key role in keeping an eye on people and keeping society in check. Adding modern tech billionaires to Mills' analysis shows how control over digital platforms and data can be used to monitor and affect large groups of people. Totalitarian governments use surveillance technologies to silence dissent and make sure people do what they're told. Government use of advanced technologies can make it easier for a surveillance state to form. The way the Chinese government uses technology to keep an eye on and manage its people is an example of how the powerful can implement totalitarian practices. The social credit system is a complete way to keep people in line by rewarding and punishing people based on how they behave. Of course, in the West, we do not promote and accept surveillance because we like the idea of total control. We see it as a necessity if we are to maintain *security* and *safety* – or at least a sense of them.

In the West, governments and private companies are increasingly using surveillance technologies, and in new cunning ways. Yet, people do not worry enough about their privacy and civil liberties. It seems we have accepted these as the price for the perception of security and safety. These technologies are already being used for authoritarian goals, like keeping an eye on political dissent and managing how people act in public. When big businesses and tech companies lobby for policies, they usually favour decisions that hurt democracy and utilise their newest surveillance technologies.

Totalitarian regimes easily form when power is highly centralised, people are not held accountable, information is controlled, and technology is used to spy on people. This crucial work by Mills looks at these dynamics and shows how they can lead to the breakdown of democratic values and the rise of totalitarian rule. Most importantly, his critical analysis points to the importance of institutions. Logically, an elite is impossible without some form of social organisation. The political, economic and military (we may also add technological) institutions that Mills looks at are the most important social organisations of American society. The same goes for other societies and states. It is inevitable that with the rise of complex and interconnected institutions, an equally complex and interconnected elite would also come to be. The global village is overseen by a global aristocracy.

3

NEO-FEUDALISM AND TECHNOCRACY

Before going into further detail about totalitarianism, it is useful to consider two other possible labels for the concentration of power present in our age: neo-feudalism and technocracy. These two terms, alongside totalitarianism, are not unrelated; they are different descriptions of an increasingly obvious political reality. The best way to show this is to describe in what way our world is becoming re-feudalised and technocratic.

Neo-feudalism is a socioeconomic system in which the unequal and hierarchical systems of mediaeval feudalism are mirrored in modern society. This implies both the near absence of social mobility and extreme economic inequality. Medieval feudalism relied on severe economic disparity and a concentration of power within a limited elite, called the aristocracy. Neo-feudalism is seen in powerful contemporary agents (individuals, organisations or corporations) that function freely without oversight and above the law, much like medieval lords. Although modern Western societies generally accept and believe in some kind of egalitarianism, this asymmetry in power is often excused or ignored. We are all too aware that our egalitarian values are inept at bringing the powerful to justice. Some people are apparently just too powerful to be subject to jurisprudence. We do not have to go to medieval Europe to find examples of this injustice. The 2008 financial crisis and its aftermath is a contemporary example from America. Widespread economic unrest resulted from the 2008 financial crisis, yet very few Wall Street high-level executives received serious legal ramifications or were sent to prison. The majority of the prominent people engaged in the crisis escaped jail time. Charges and sanctions were levelled against several lower-level employees of different financial organisations, but they usually did not entail lengthy jail terms for prominent executives from large corporations. Among them were the executives of large financial firms, including JP Morgan, Goldman Sachs, and Lehman Brothers. Several companies paid fines and civil penalties to the government, but these were insignificant in the grand picture. For their part in the crisis, banks and other financial institutions paid billions in penalties and settlements, but individual CEOs did not go to jail as a result. Establishing obvious criminal intent or wrongdoing was challenging by the intricacy and complexity of the financial practices involved. Prosecuting top executives for their part in the crisis was difficult at the time because of the legal and regulatory environment. Many of the acts that fuelled the crisis were not obviously against the law as it stood. More than pursuing individual criminal cases, regulators and prosecutors concentrated on obtaining hefty fines and settlements from the financial companies involved.

Significant public and political criticism followed the absence of high-profile convictions; many felt that the financial sector leaders ought to have been held more responsible for the acts that precipitated the crisis. Egyptian-born Kareem Serageldin, who mismarked bond values to hide losses while he was an employee of Credit Suisse, is one of the very few globally who served jail time in relation to the 2008 financial crisis and the only US banker to do so. The criminal prosecutions in most of the legal actions were against institutions rather than individuals, resulting in only fines and settlements. These big banks and financial institutions could afford to pay the price, so they continued with the practices. The organisations responsible for the crisis were seen as too essential to the elites to be dismantled; after all, their crimes were against the many, not the few. Like all successful systems of exploitation, these banks robbed the poor, not the rich. That is why they got away with it. But what happens when someone does try to rob the rich?

One noteworthy exception when talking about people who were convicted of financial crimes during the 2008 financial crisis is Bernie Madoff. But his situation was unique, because the subprime mortgage market and the larger problems with the financial system that preceded the crisis had nothing to do with his offences. Madoff was the chairperson of Bernard L. Madoff Investment Securities LLC and defrauded investors of $65 billion by directing the biggest Ponzi scheme in history. When Madoff confessed to his sons in December 2008 they denounced him to the police. Quickly after, he was arrested. Among the many allegations against Madoff were securities fraud, investment adviser fraud, mail fraud, wire fraud, money laundering, lying, perjury, and theft from an employee benefit plan. Madoff entered pleas to eleven federal charges in March 2009. Judge Denny Chin handed Madoff the maximum term of 150 years in jail in June 2009. It was believed that this sentence would both dissuade others and reflect the seriousness of his acts.

Madoff's fraud cost thousands of ordinary people their investments, retirement accounts, and savings. However, additionally impacted were a large number of institutions and NGOs. Irving Picard was named trustee to liquidate Madoff's business and provide claimants with their recovered assets as part of continuous efforts to recover money for the victims. Based on most recent reports, many billion dollars have been recovered and given back to investors who were duped. On April 14, 2021, Bernie Madoff, then 82 years old, passed away in prison.

Although Madoff's arrest and the discovery of his scheme happened at the same time as the financial crisis, it is clear that his fraud was unrelated to the financial products and mortgage-backed securities that sparked the larger economic slump. Using the funds from newer investors rather than from actual investment earnings, Madoff's operation was a classic Ponzi scheme. Madoff was not a team player with his fellow financial elites. Instead of defrauding regular middle-class people, he set his sights on his wealthy investors and that was his big mistake. He ended up in jail not because of the severity of his crimes but because of the power of his victims. Likewise, the powerful financial elites escaped serious punishment not because their acts were benign (their greed caused global economic chaos), but because their victims were powerless. This double standard is a hallmark of feudalism. And it's reappearance in the financial world is a clear sign that society is being feudalised anew.

The process by which contemporary societies start to resemble feudal systems of the past—characterised by a return to hierarchical structures, economic inequalities, and decreased social mobility—is known as re-feudalisation in socioeconomic theory. It is not surprising that such a tendency takes place. A limited number of people or companies control a large amount of wealth and resources, widening the gap between the wealthy few and the rest of the population. Few people end up with economic power which translates into political power. This power entails a certain level of judicial immunity and sway. Like with the inflexible class systems of feudal countries, chances for social and economic progress disappear, and people find it harder and harder to raise their socioeconomic standing. As public services security, healthcare, and education are increasingly privatised, the position where money determines access to these services echoes the patronage systems of feudal times. Comparable to the absence of democratic government in mediaeval societies, democratic institutions and procedures deteriorate and decision-making gets increasingly concentrated and further away from the public.

Much like serfs depended on their lords, people and smaller entities become increasingly reliant on strong companies or individuals for work, services, and protection. With obvious gaps between the affluent elite and the general public, society becomes stratified, raising social tensions and instability. As their control over decision-making processes declines, the general public becomes disenfranchised, exacerbating feelings of helplessness and disappointment. This is not always so, as some part of the public adopts the servile mindset and gives into the culture of docility. After all, neo-feudalism does offer many new and exciting toys and consumer products to keep the people occupied.

Exacerbating social inequality, the quality and accessibility of public goods and services deteriorate as they come under more and more private ownership. As different parts of society grow more cut off from one another, social cohesiveness deteriorates and social and cultural fragmentation results. Society and culture become divided horizontally and vertically, the commoners are not only differentiated from the ruling elite – they also form new rivalries and antagonisms between themselves. The horizontal differences are strategically exploited, and often manufactured, in order to maintain the vertical power hierarchy.

The growth of the gig economy and precarious employment, which can offer minimal stability and perks, is reminiscent of the precarious life of serfs who had little influence over their working conditions. Feudal land ownership patterns are reflected in the growing difficulty of finding affordable housing, as big corporate landlords possess substantial shares of rental units. A lord is nothing without his land, and the land is nothing without serfs to toil on it.

Bill Gates, Co-founder of Microsoft and a well-known philanthropist, is a good example of a neo-feudal lord. Gates is now among the most prominent private owners of farmland in the USA. Significant discussion and controversy about the political, economic, and social ramifications of his purchase of agricultural land has been generated. According to the most recent estimates at the time of writing this book, Bill Gates owns about 242,000 acres of farmland in the US, thereby holding the most private acreage in the nation. His landholdings include portions of Louisiana, Arkansas, Arizona, Nebraska, and Washington. Though Gates hasn't revealed the precise rationale behind these purchases, it is thought that his public interest in food security, environmental preservation, and sustainable agriculture, may have been major influences.

The Bill and Melinda Gates Foundation, which contributes about 20% of the WHO budget, has made grants to agricultural research and projects to raise crop yields and encourage environmentally friendly farming methods. Gates has a great deal of influence over the regional agricultural markets because of his large landholdings. He has severely impacted local economies and rental rates by his concentration of land ownership. Gates's engagement in agriculture may result in more lobbying and influence over agricultural laws and regulations. His views on pesticide use, genetically modified organisms (GMOs), and sustainable farming methods may influence laws at the federal and state levels, which will then have an impact on people's health and wellbeing. The concentration of land ownership among a small number of wealthy people begs concerns about the laws and rules governing property ownership. Due to this new feudalisation, policy to deal with land concentration and guarantee fair access to land for small and medium-sized farmers may require more attention.

Re-feudalisation is, in short, a return towards socioeconomic systems more like those of mediaeval times, characterised by inequality, concentration of power, and lower social mobility. This process questions the foundations of contemporary democratic and egalitarian societies. It emphasises the necessity of laws to deal with these new inequalities and safeguard the interests of the larger public. This change is cultural as much as it is economic and political. A new culture of docility is normalising these severe inequalities and leading to a servile mindset.

People are far too friendly and forgiving to our new overlords. Conversely, a new aristocratic mindset is developing among the elites. This aristocratic mindset aims to extol the inherent virtues, merit and competence of the ruling class. It presents elite rule as rule by the best, the literal meaning of aristocracy. They are in these positions of power, so the logic goes, because they are the most deserving – the best! The servile mindset that permeates the culture of docility confirms this all too eagerly. As in medieval times, the best that we commoners can hope to achieve is to serve the nobility effectively and be rewarded for our servitude.

ECONOMIST YANIS VAROUFAKIS previously served as the Greek Minister of Finance and has addressed the idea of techno-feudalism as a criticism of the existing socioeconomic structure. Varoufakis contends that contemporary capitalism has developed into a new system which he refers to as "techno-feudalism", typified by the hegemony of technology corporations and their unique hold over social and economic life. In his book, *Technofeudalism: What Killed Capitalism,* Varoufakis claims that we are witnessing a transformation of capitalism into something different, rather than merely an advanced stage of capitalism (usually called late-stage capitalism or neoliberalism). According to Varoufakis, tech behemoths are replacing conventional capitalism, propelled by markets and competitive dynamics. Examples of this include the big- tech firms, such as Apple, Google, Facebook, and Amazon, who have amassed enormous sums of authority, loyalty, money, and power. These corporations have an unprecedented degree of market control, political power, cultural capital and social engineering technologies that –far exceeds the authority of any mediaeval feudal lord. Data is the commodity under techno-feudalism much as land was in feudal times. As feudal lords ruled over territory and took rent from serfs, digital corporations own data and extract its value from their consumers. Data produced by users is monetised frequently without giving users any acknowledgement or a portion of the value they produce. This technological aspect is worth exploring in further detail. Although companies like Apple, Google, Facebook, and Amazon are all worth hundreds of billions, their source of income is not immediately clear. After all, we are encouraged to make profiles on these sites and use them without paying an entry fee or monthly subscription.

Social media platforms offer free accounts to anyone over a certain age, yet they bring in vast revenues. Social networks monetise their user-generated data through advertising, the offering of premium services, but rarely through subscriptions. Where they gain their revenue is much less obvious and much more nefarious. With their collection, aggregation, and sale of user data such as user interests, behaviours, demographics, and interactions to various platforms and marketers, data brokers are where the money is. Extensive user profiles generated from data taken from 'innocent users' enable advertisers to target particular audiences with tailored advertising. Businesses target people on Facebook, for instance, depending on their hobbies, location, age, and other criteria. Advertisers bid in real-time on platforms like Google and Facebook to display their ads to specific types of people. Maximising the revenue for the platform, the highest bidder has their advertisement seen. Paid by influencers and companies, sponsored content appears in users' feeds just as a regular posting but is identified as an advertisement.

Social media sites offer researchers, data brokers, and advertising agencies anonymised user data. A better understanding of consumer behaviour and preferences is made possible by deep analysis and psychological profiling using this data . Platforms provide companies and marketers with some analytical tools and insights based on user data, which help them enhance targeting and hone their marketing plans. There was some uproar both in the USA and Europe over the discovery of data acquisition by China, through platforms such as TikTok. The Chinese government regularly uses TikTok to mine data about it's own citizens. Western citizens, for whatever purpose, imagine that they are more protected than that, therefore and that such apps must be banned. China, like any other foreign government or domestic agent, can buy this data thanks to Western laws, therefore it is the law that needs to change.

Through subscription structures, several platforms provide ad-free experiences or more enhanced content and services. LinkedIn charges for premium features including improved networking chances, more sophisticated job search tools, and in-depth statistics. YouTube Premium offers access to unique material and ad-free streaming. Shopping functions have been embedded into social media sites like Facebook and Instagram, enabling users to make direct purchases, with the platform taking commission on each sale. To increase revenue, platforms like Snapchat and TikTok offer virtual items such as stickers, filters, and digital presents.

Data of interest to a data brokers includes social media activity, internet tracking, purchase histories, and public records. With this information they put together thorough profiles of each person. By combining data on the same individual across several platforms, data brokers can create comprehensive psychological profiles, giving advertisers and marketers more accurate targeting opportunities.

Data brokers frequently link their data with the back end of the social media advertising platforms to further improve these platforms' targeting capabilities. Facebook collaborates with data brokers, for instance, to provide marketers with further targeting choices. Including cross-platform targeting, enabling advertisers to reach consumers across several platforms and devices, guaranteeing a consistent and focused advertising experience.

The massive gathering and commercialisation of user-generated data creates some very concerning privacy issues. Consumers have little say over how their data is taken, shared and used. The majority of users do not have any awareness of what is going on, even though they sign a usage agreement. If we want access to these sites and platforms we must sign away a part of our privacy. This is rarely a free choice, as the modern economy and normal socialisation require us to use such services. Tech companies know this and freely abuse their monopoly positions and social significance.

The data industry is massive, valued above $300 billion in 2023, and restricting it through regulation means undermining hefty profits. Strict standards on data management and openness, together with more control over personal data, have been the goals of regulations like the General Data Protection Regulation (GDPR) in Europe and the California Consumer Privacy Act (CCPA) in the United States. Social media sites and data brokers ought to comply with these rules by enforcing more stringent data privacy practices, getting user permission, and offering ways for users to view and remove their data. It is not clear that this legislation does enough to undermine the techno-feudal tendencies present within the industry.

Varoufakis draws our attention to the way that tech behemoths extract financial rent from companies that depend on their platforms as well as from consumers. Like tenants under feudal lords, enterprises employing Google's advertising services or Amazon's marketplace are subject to fees and conditions set by these corporate behemoths. The feudal lords in this situation also work like gatekeepers, managing access to enormous consumer populations. This gives them immense economic power over the businesses that do the actual producing and selling. The feudal system rewards the parasitic, not the productive. Through their interactions, purchases, and data, users of these platforms support the revenue streams of these digital giants in addition to enjoying ease and access to a large variety of services and products.

Cloud rent, as viewed by Varoufakis, is the money these platforms make from fees and restrictions placed on the companies and users of their platforms. Companies who want to ensure their items appear on YouTube or search results pay premium prices to Google for ad spots, yet Google's algorithms still get to decide where and how visible they are. If sellers utilise Amazon's logistical services, as well as advertising, they pay listing, referral, and fulfilment fees. Amazon also sets conditions on which vendors have to abide, such as inventory and price guidelines.

Varoufakis points out that these services are not capitalistic in nature. Amazon and its equivalents, such as eBay or Alibaba, seem like giant digital shopping malls. Varoufakis discusses how, in the case of Amazon, artificial intelligence is used to sell us things that we didn't know we wanted or needed. Through its home assistant Alexa, Amazon can learn about its consumers directly and offer any products it deems desirable or necessary. This is not targeted advertising; it is highly advanced and ever-adapting consumerism with some surveillance thrown in. You no longer need to go out and look for different products you might need or desire. Your AI assistant, be it Alexa, Siri or Google, already knows what you like and suggests products that it knows you will want. In order for a product to be eligible for this algorithm, its producer must pay cloud rent to Amazon, or whatever cloud network that keeps track of its consumers.

Widespread surveillance is one of the ways techno-feudalism maintains its power. So they can forecast and affect future activities, tech businesses track and analyse user behaviour down to the smallest detail, therefore enhancing their influence and control over society. User data is not only an economic resource, however, it is also a political one. User choices and behaviour can be used to suggest which politicians and policies said user would be influenced by. Your data can be used to control and influence you, directly.

Modern technologies can determine where you are, and where you were; they also know your political beliefs, consumer choices, medical records and even your social credit. Varoufakis cautions that the political power big tech companies can distort democratic procedures and opinions on popular policies, making governments more receptive to corporate interests than to the concerns of the people.

Because a tiny fraction of the elite controls the wealth produced by data and digital platforms, techno-feudalism worsens economic inequality and threatens to solidify itself through our institutions. Varoufakis compares the industrial revolution with the contemporary digital era, naming it, 'The Age of Cloud Capital". Varoufakis contends that the enclosures —the privatisation and expropriation of common lands— preceded the industrial revolution and the steam engine. The British state aided this brutal process by uprooting peasants and combining land into private ownership. A labour force freed from land by the enclosures became accessible for industrial work in cities. The conditions were created by this social and economic upheaval for significant technological breakthroughs like the steam engine, invented by James Watt. The industrial revolution was not, as many have claimed, kicked off by this single piece of technology.

For any technology to be meaningful, drastic social changes have to occur. Varoufakis references the Great Transformation theory by Karl Polanyi, which explains how market society emerged in the 19th and early 20th centuries. Driven by the theft of common resources and imposed by official authority, this shift involved the commercialisation of land, labour, and money. It created economic categories and patterns we live by today. This Great Transformation was political and cultural as much as it was technological and economical. There was much resistance to these *abnormal* developments.

Varoufakis notes, in a similar spirit, that the Internet Commons had to be appropriated so that digital technologies and the contemporary tech industry would flourish. He speaks of how the internet changed from a public, free resource to a commercialised, privatised sphere, controlled by tech giants. Politicians have helped to bring about this shift; choices made about regulations and policies made it possible to plunder the

Internet Commons legally. Much of the digital infrastructure that still underlies the contemporary internet was created without the profit motive and made available to everyone. Varoufakis highlights significant technological developments that enclosed the digital commons, including the creation of Google by Sergey Brin and the growth of AI applications . Interestingly, both the Industrial Revolution and the Age of Cloud Capital were preceded by a series of events in which political collusion and the exploitation of common resources occurred before major technical breakthroughs. By concentrating once public resources in the hands of a few, both revolutions fundamentally altered the economic and social environment.

The story of the Internet is characterised by technological innovation, changing policy, and market dynamics. The Internet went from a government-funded initiative and digital commons to a commercialised and privatised domain, in just a manner of decades. First supported by the Advanced Research Projects Agency (ARPA) of the U.S. Department of Defence, the Internet was known as ARPANET in the late 1960s. With the use of this network, military and academic institutions were able to communicate safely and efficiently. The Internet was mainly a tool for academics and researchers during the 1970s and 1980s, guided by openness and cooperation, values that promoted the unrestricted flow of ideas and information.

Important technical developments of this time, such as the creation of TCP/IP protocols, established the groundwork for the contemporary internet. Through programmes like NSFNET, supported by the National Science Foundation (NSF), these technologies—which were the outcome of cooperative efforts between scientists and engineers—made it possible to expand the network to include more academic institutions. But everything changed in the early 1990s when the US government chose to give commercial companies control over NSFNET. This action was a part of a larger plan to promote investment and innovation while opening up the Internet for commercial use.

By offering an easy-to-use means of network navigation, Tim Berners-Lee's invention of the World Wide Web at CERN in the early 1990s transformed the Internet. The public's increased accessibility to the Internet, thanks to the creation of web browsers like Netscape Navigator and Mosaic, sparked an increase in Internet use and the start of online commercialisation. The NSF removed its prohibitions on commercial internet usage in 1991, enabling private businesses to use the network for business gain. This choice cleared the path for the emergence of online services like AOL and Yahoo! and e-commerce sites like Amazon and eBay, which pioneered the internet's marketing, sales, and consumer interaction possibilities.

Dot-com, or speculative investment in internet-based businesses, peaked in the late 1990s. The Telecommunications Act of 1996, deregulated the American telecommunications sector; this era saw enormous investments in infrastructure, including data centres and broadband networks. Major tech companies like Google, Facebook, Amazon, and Microsoft emerged during the boom using network effects and enormous volumes of user data to solidify their supremacy. By creating vast platform ecosystems which became essential to the online experience, these businesses created advanced advertising models based on user data. Their commercial models are based on the gathering, analysing, and monetising of user data, which brings with it serious privacy and data security issues.

Today, a small number of very powerful companies with considerable political sway, control most of the internet. Through lobbying, these corporations have influenced internet governance, intellectual property legislation, and data protection rules, reshaping the regulatory landscape. The tale of the internet's privatisation and commercialisation demonstrates how government policy, market forces, and technical innovation interact intricately to turn what was once a government-funded research project into a worldwide commercial infrastructure. This revolution has changed commerce, communication, and information exchange dramatically. It has also brought up important concerns about control, privacy, and the digital commons.

Varoufakis makes a strong comparison between the appropriation of the Internet Commons that allowed the emergence of contemporary tech giants, and the enclosures that made the Industrial Revolution possible. There was a great deal of state meddling and public resource theft in both periods, along with revolutionary, technical developments. This comparison helps us understand the power relations and economic changes in the "Age of Cloud Capital". Varoufakis considers digital infrastructure and data a digital common, or a public good. We naturally have a right to what is common and public; no corporation or government has the right to take it away from us. Neither do they have a right to place these commons and public spheres behind a paywall or a data-extraction scheme. Therefore, this would mean the creation of legal structures guaranteeing that we own the data they produce, and that it is used for the good of society.

Varoufakis advocates for worker cooperatives, decentralised technology, and ownership models centred in communities that democratise economic decision-making. This would undermine the concentrated power of tech giants and return the ownership of data to individuals. Strengthening antitrust laws would dismantle monopolistic IT corporations and stop them from abusing their market dominance, helping to reestablish competitive dynamics. In an economy marked by insecure employment, Varoufakis also believes in the concept of a Universal Basic Income (UBI) to reduce economic inequality and offer financial security.

Varoufakis' idea of techno-feudalism draws comparisons to the feudal systems of the past to criticise the enormous power and influence of tech firms. He urges significant changes to restore democratic governance, redistribute power, and guarantee that society shares the advantages of technical breakthroughs more fairly. Varoufakis, as a committed Marxist and socialist, naturally espouses the values of egalitarianism, internationalism and cooperation. Equally, he detests the concentration of power and resources in the hands of a shrinking elite that seems to overshadow democratic politics. However, Varoufakis does not sufficiently explain the political dangers of techno-feudalism, nor does he recognise its totalitarian nature.

Luckily, we do not have to stick to any single account of modern political and economic developments. Varoufakis helps us understand how the leading technological innovations of our age reinvented mediaeval feudal social relations. This techno-feudalism is only one interpretation of 21st century totalitarianism. It is seemingly paradoxical, as the prefix *techno-* describes something modern and advanced, whereas *feudalism* is an outdated and medieval, seemingly overturned, social system.

There is an important lesson here, one that concerns the relationship between technological and social progress. There is a widespread modern myth that technological progress somehow facilitates or supports social progress. Technology, it is believed, will make us better people and society more just. This myth is frankly dangerous, as well as being incorrect. The myth is debunked by the existence of totalitarianism, especially if we consider techno-feudalism or technocracy, which relies heavily on the use of modern technology and exploits social decay. We do not have to agree with Varoufakis to see this; old forms of social hierarchy eagerly utilise new technologies to regain and maintain their grip on power.

This seemingly strange coexistence of advanced technology and medieval social hierarchy is explored in the popular science fiction series of books *Dune*, now in film format. In the world of *Dune*, we find a form of techno-feudalism quite different from the one that Varoufakis describes. Frank Herbert's *Dune* series depicts a sophisticated and intricately detailed techno-feudal society in a far-off future in which advanced technology and interstellar travel coexist with a well-ingrained feudal political structure. A tight hierarchy distributing authority among aristocratic houses, each of which controls particular planets and their resources rules the political and social framework of this cosmos.

Within the *Dune* universe, religion and power are deeply entwined. The main character, Paul Atreides, manages to overthrow the current Emperor by associating with religious fundamentalists who fight on his behalf. Herbert uses these components to investigate issues of power, religion, ecology, and human potential, constructing a multi-layered story that looks at the intricacies of a far-future techno-feudal civilisation. Politically, the series has a clear message: do not trust messianic and heroic figures, they will do more harm than good.

Dune depicts a feudal system in which aristocratic houses fight for dominance under the Emperor and rule over enormous lands, (which happen to be whole planets). This hierarchical organisation, evocative of mediaeval Europe, implies that social organisation has stagnated or regressed in spite of the amazing technologies at hand. Rigid class divisions, fidelity to aristocratic houses, and the calculated marriage connections and grudges that uphold the status quo define the feudal system in Dune, as much as they did in medieval Europe. The feudal system of governance works so well in this story that it implies an affinity, or at least neutrality, between feudal hierarchy and technical advancement. It offers a good example to us as to what may happen if the current situation goes unchecked. The emperor plays a key role, the concentration of power within a few aristocratic families (in our case, the behemoth tech companies), points to a lack of social change, even if technology has the capacity to democratise power and improve socioeconomic conditions for most people. This resistance is strengthened by the way technology is used to uphold rather than to challenge authority. Although *Dune* is about the lives of the nobles and their political battles, we do frequently peer into the lives of the commoners. We see that the fundamentalists lead difficult lives and distrust foreigners who usually exploit or exterminate them. The aristocracy seems to lack any basic human rights that protect all its population; the powerful do as they wish. Despite the technology, there is no universal standard for all of humanity.

In *Dune*, it is completely up to the whims and values of the aristocratic house that rules the planet that you live on.

The series' depiction of the continuous fight for power and control in a beautifully imagined universe connects profoundly with its suggestion that real development involves not only technological innovation but also fundamental changes in social and political arrangements. Technological advancement is not enough for historical progress; in fact, it can be counterproductive.

TECHNOCRACY, in general terms, is an administrative structure in which decision-makers are chosen according to their level of competence in technical and scientific domains. The administration must be logical and effective. Technocrats and specialists in this system, are in control, instead of elected officials, and decisions are based on efficiency, facts, and analysis rather than on political factors. When technological control methods, such as data monitoring and surveillance, are employed to impose complete control over society, technocracy naturally leads to totalitarianism. In a neo-feudal setting, technocratic institutions maintain inequality by putting the elite's interests and efficiency as their top priority, frequently at the price of greater social wellbeing and basic freedoms.

We have seen totalitarianism ingeniously uses technology to stay in power. The concentration of economic power is also a hallmark of neo-feudalism and can reinforce totalitarian control over all social spheres. In totalitarianism and neo-feudalism, technocratic structures offer knowledge and instruments that can improve control systems. Technocracy is an instrument of control utilised under totalitarianism, rather than a separate system. There is a strong synergy between these three concepts. All three can coexist in a society where technology and knowledge are used to concentrate and preserve power in the hands of a few, whether in the political, economic, or administrative domains. Totalitarianism concentrates on political control, neo-feudalism on economic inequality, and technocracy on supposed expertise in governance and science. Technocracy can unintentionally foster neo-feudal and totalitarian systems by encouraging efficiency and competence, if these efficiencies maintain the current power dynamics, often at the expense of humanity.

Totalitarian governments can use technocratic knowledge to put in place expansive and pervasive systems of monitoring and control. One such system has already been suggested – a Digital ID which will combine vaccine passports and centralised digital currency. If implemented, it has the potential to enable governments to monitor your spending, keep track of your medical history, and keep score of your personal carbon footprint. This is a clear and present danger to all of our personal choices and freedoms, standing in open sight. As you can imagine, both in theory and in practice, technocracy raises a number of important issues that have drawn a great deal of criticism and anxiety. Often neglecting conventional democratic structures and procedures, technocracy concentrates power in the hands of a small number of specialists or technocrats. This concentration of power is inherently authoritarian, even if it is presented as beneficial. Indeed, technocrats like to present their rule as a both efficient and humane, even though these two values clash regularly.

Most people, the *commonfolk*, may find it challenging to comprehend the intricate technical factors that go into the decision-making processes in technocratic regimes. This lack of openness undercuts public confidence in government and democratic accountability. But this is not an issue for technocracy, as transparency is not one of its values. Technocracy categorically values control, predictability and efficiency at the price of individual freedoms and personal preferences. It is a creep, as citizens realise that bureaucratic orders and algorithms begin to control their life more and more, limiting their freedom and determining their behaviour. Varoufakis points out how our AI assistants train us to train them, so that they can better sell us personalised products and gather even more data about us. Putting technocratic ideas into practice frequently entails collecting great deal of seemingly arbitrary data, presenting us with serious privacy issues. People's choices and activities are tracked and examined all the time, not just for commercial purposes.

Technocrats put economic and technical efficiency first at the expense of cultural vibrancy and national sovereignty. Essential human traits like empathy, fairness, and humour go unaccounted for in decisions made with data by computers. Technocracy has the ability to dehumanise people by viewing social and economic problems as technical problems to be resolved. Everything can be solved at a price. There are no tragic human flaws and existential limitations. This reduces people to numbers or resources which can be controlled, instead of appreciating their intrinsic finitude and dignity. Because people with access to technology and technical know-how acquire greater power and influence, technocracy worsens social inequality in many ways. Access to elite education and advanced technology is already limited to the wealthy. Most of us, and especially groups on the margins of society, are shut out of the decision-making processes – as we lack the expertise and know-how to act rationally in service of the technocracy.

Job losses brought on by automation and artificial intelligence (AI) are one example of how technocratic policies can cause major economic displacement. This tends to aggravate current economic disparities and spark social upheaval. Of course, AI and automation are not natural enemies of humanity, it is up to us how we use these technologies. Automation can lead to an increase in leisure time and an easier workload, but also to unemployment and the complete replacement of whole sectors of the workforce. It is clear which one technocracy favours. Long-term sustainability may not be as important to technocratic systems as immediate efficiency increases. Ultimately, judgements made in the rush for quick outcomes may be unsustainable both socially and environmentally. Over reliance on technology can lead to vulnerabilities since it makes civilisations reliant on intricate systems that could malfunction or be taken advantage of. This reliance on technology also inhibits human inventiveness and adaptability.

China's application of technocratic ideas illustrates these problems. The degradation of privacy and individual freedoms is best shown by the Chinese social credit system, using a digital ID to monitor their behaviour. Each person is given a ratings according to their levels of behaviour and compliance to the system. Significant ethical and human rights issues arise from this enforcement of conformity and punishment of dissension, even while its goal is presented as building a harmonious community through behavioural incentives.

Even if technocracy seeks to enhance government via scientific and technical knowledge, it raises serious issues with democratic loss, individual autonomy, ethical issues, social justice, and sustainability. These difficulties emphasise the need to strike a balance between technical effectiveness and democratic principles while maintaining the importance of human rights and moral issues in order to guarantee that technological developments benefit society as a whole.

4

THE WAR FOR TECHNOCRACY BY PROFESSOR DAVID A. HUGHES

Professor of International Relations at the University of Lincoln, David Hughes was interviewed on *Counterpoint*[1]. He has authored a series of books about our current political environment, its history and potential future. In *Covid-19, Psychological Operations, and the War for Technocracy*, Hughes gives us a concise history and explanation of technocracy. His follow-up, *Wall Street, the NAZIS and the Crimes of the Deep State* was released after our first interview in 2024, and completes a valuable contribution to the advancement of our knowledge of what is happening, why, by whom and for what objective.

He contends that the Covid-19 pandemic was not a random event but a premeditated and meticulously orchestrated psychological operation designed to facilitate a global shift toward technocracy, the fulcrum of 21st century totalitarianism. This psychological operation created so much shock and fear it demoralised, disoriented, and debilitated the global

1. https://podcasts.apple.com/gb/podcast/10-professor-david-hughes-covid-19-media-and-control/id1710094803 And https://youtu.be/5X6P8or-duI

populations so it could weaken any resistance to a planned transition from liberal democracies to a global technocracy. This shift is often characterised by advanced technologies and psychological manipulation. According to Professor Hughes, bio-digital totalitarianism happens where control is maintained through constant surveillance and social engineering.

Hughes supports this contention by referencing government documents that indicate a premeditated strategy. He highlights an early report in 2020 from the UK's Department of Health and Social Care, the Office for National Statistics, and the Home Office, which admitted that the health impacts from lockdowns and the lockdown-induced recession were greater in terms of quality-adjusted life years than the direct Covid-19 deaths. This, Hughes argues, shows that governments were well aware that their policies would cause significant harm, yet they proceeded nonetheless. He suggests these policies were framed necessary for saving lives, but in reality, were designed to cause maximum disruption and fear.

A significant portion of Hughes' analysis focuses on the psychological operations employed during the pandemic. He compares these to known techniques of psychological torture, drawing parallels between the methods used in the MKUltra mind control experiments of the mid-20th century, and the measures implemented during the Covid-19 pandemic. These techniques include inducing chronic stress, sensory deprivation, and self-inflicted pain. Hughes argues that these methods were used to create a state of chronic anxiety and compliance among the global population.

He also discusses the role of masks, lockdowns, and constant media bombardment in spreading fear and maintaining a state of high alert. Hughes suggests that these measures were not just public health responses but were deliberately designed to control and manipulate the population psychologically. The use of fear and trauma, he explains, makes the mind more susceptible to propaganda and programming, a concept rooted in psychological warfare techniques.

Professor Hughes further explains how these psychological tactics have historical precedents and are part of a broader strategy to implement a technocratic regime. By breaking down individual resistance and fostering a sense of helplessness, these techniques pave the way for the acceptance of more intrusive forms of control, such as biometric surveillance and digital currencies. The psychological impact of these measures has been profound, leading to widespread demoralisation and disorientation.

To provide a broader context, Hughes traces the roots of technocracy back to the early 20th century, with figures like Howard Scott and M. King Hubbert envisioning a society managed by technical experts rather than elected representatives. This vision involves eradicating private property, centralising resources, and conditioning individuals to fit predetermined roles within the technate. Hughes argues that the implementation of technocracy requires a scientific dictatorship, where control is maintained through advanced technologies and psychological manipulation.

In his book, Hughes examines China's role as a model for global technocracy, highlighting how Western investment and technology transfers facilitated China's development into a highly centralised, technologically advanced society. He points to the integration of biometric technologies and constant surveillance in everyday life as key components of this technocratic control. If such a system is fully implemented globally, Hughes warns, it could lead to irreversible enslavement.

The concept of the "Internet of Bodies," central to technocratic control, involves integrating biometric technologies and constant surveillance into everyday life. Hughes cautions that if such a system is fully implemented it could lead to irreversible enslavement. He cites examples of how biometric surveillance, central bank digital currencies, and social credit systems are already being tested and implemented, particularly in China, and are likely to be expanded globally.

Professor Hughes's analysis of the Covid-19 pandemic and its aftermath paints a stark picture of a world transitioning towards technocratic totalitarianism. However, he also emphasises the importance of awareness and resistance. By understanding the psychological and social mechanisms at play, individuals and communities can better resist the encroachment of technocratic control. He calls for a renewed commitment to democratic principles and social justice, arguing that only through collective action and solidarity can the global population thwart the ambitions of the transnational ruling class.

The Counterpoint interview I held with Professor Hughes brings to light the significant parallels between the current global shift and historical totalitarian regimes. Hughes argues that the current trajectory mirrors the political economy of 1930s Germany, where a gradual erosion of democratic principles paved the way for totalitarian control. This is the main topic of his second book, *Wall Street, the Nazis and the*

Crimes of the Deep State. He emphasises that the process of transitioning to technocracy is incremental and involves multiple stages of social division and control, as outlined in Stanton's ten stages of genocide. According to Hughes, the first four stages—classification, symbolisation, discrimination, and dehumanisation—were already evident during the Covid-19 pandemic. In forensically comparing the slide of Germany after *The Enabling Act* period in 1933, to the global political economy since 2020, Professor Hughes reveals some startling juxtapositions.

The Enabling Act of March 23rd 1933, followed the Reichstag Fire Decree, emergency legislation that President Hindenburg, on the advice of Chancellor Hitler, passed on February 28th 1933 and which set aside rights protected by the Weimar Constitution. This was after the arson attack the day before on the Reichstag which was blamed on communist operatives by Hitler. It followed exactly four weeks after Hitler was sworn in as Chancellor of Germany. *The Enabling Act*, officially called the *Law to Remedy the Distress of People and Reich,* gave the cabinet, led by Hitler, the power to make laws without involving either the Reichstag or President Hidenburg. It set aside the checks and balances of the German system of Governance and was passed 444 votes with 94 against. In comparing then and now, Hughes makes the following observation;

> *'In both cases, power was seized in a climate of fear triggered by a false flag operation, in which people willingly surrendered their rights, and legislatures and judiciaries capitulated to executive power. A multi-year process of legislating tyranny was set in motion, its apparent lawfulness fooling most people into believing in the endurance of liberal constitutionalism. What is taking*

> *place, now as then, is a revolution from the above, a top-down remaking of society to serve ruling class interests, conspicuous by its attacks on the working and middle classes. Gleichschaltung -the production of ideological conformity -is a striking feature of both ages, with the citizenry, the professions, the churches, the Left, and the trade unions all immediately falling into line with official ideology and offering no resistance for fear of being 'switched off' (fired, censored, shut down etc). Centralised control of the media in both eras has resulted in the people being barraged with propaganda; the media space has become a war zone"*

During Covid, the Irish Supreme Court ruled that Irish Government's emergency powers were constitutional, mimicking Canada which ruled that its powers were *'justified as reasonable limits in a free and democratic society'*. The Canadian Government in Ottowa, led by Trudeau, would later raid and close the bank accounts of truckers for protesting peacefully outside the nation's parliament in the freezing Canadian winter. In a bitter irony, the *Malicious Practices Act,* which passed March 31, 1933, and which criminalised making negative comments about the Nazi regime, 89 years later was bookended when the Nuremberg Public Prosecutor opened a case against Holocaust survivor Vera Sharov for campaigning peacefully outside the Nuremberg Palace of Justice against Covid vaccines.

In 2024, Ursula Von Der Leyen made tackling *misinformation* and *disinformation* the centrepiece of her policy platform as President of the EU. She was also Trustee of the World Economic Forum. In 1934 Hitler declared that *'The German revolution will be concluded only when the entire German Volk has been totally created anew, reorganised and reconstructed'* Within months of Covid, WEF chief Klaus Schwab, son of Nazi industrialist Eugen Schwab, announced the *'Great Reset'*. The Mises Institute, Hughes reminds us, observed that the WEF wants to *'lead the world into a new era without property or privacy'* noting that totalitarianism requires the subordination of individual rights to the common good, which the Nazis called *Volksgemeinschaft* (national community).

Hughes relies on the 19th century term Robber Baron when identifying some of America's wealthiest families -Bush, Rockerfeller, DuPont and Dulles - as players in the deep state. American oligarchs, he reminds us, played both sides in World War Two, including Henry Ford, who built vehicles for both the Wehrmacht and the US Army, including deploying slave labour at his Cologne plant. Prescott Bush, a board director of W.A. Harriman & Co, sold stock in Nazi companies, including to Joseph Kennedy, ambassador to the UK from 1938-1940. Bush was a partner in Brown Brothers Harriman, an investment bank established in 1931, which by 1938 had sent millions of dollars in gold, fuel, steel, coal and US treasury bonds to build out the Nazi vision for Germany.

General Motors was owned by the du Pont family led by Irenee du Pont, who was obsessed with Hitler's principles, including eugenics, racial purity and antisemitism and who had conspired in the Business Plot to bring fascism to the USA in 1933. GM invested heavily in I.G. Farben plants in Germany right up to 1939, where 0.5% of the salary roll went into the coffers of the Nazis. GM executive James Mooney like Henry Ford, was awarded the Grand Cross of the German Eagle, and by 1939 GM controlled 70% of the German automobile market as it retooled to feed Nazi war production.

Both GM and Ford would go on to handle repairs and modifications to German army vehicles from neutral

Switzerland. These are just a few examples from Hughes's book, which names Rockefeller's Standard Oil and Chase National Bank, ITT, IBM and several others trading with and financing the Nazis. The IBM president Thomas Watson who was directly paid 5% of IBM transactions with the Nazis, was awarded the Merit Cross of the German Eagle with Star by the regime, the highest medal of honour for a foreigner. Big corporations, no matter what is said on the front door, crave monopolies and giant contracts associated with fascism; it is a licence to print money. But it doesn't end at money; it ends at power, ideally totalitarian power, the lure of dynasties.

A key architect in the Bank for International Settlements, founded in 1930 by world central banks, was the Reichesbank president Hjalmar Horace Greely Schacht. The German banker had been trained on Wall Street. BIS was central to funnelling Anglo-American finance to the Nazis and throughout World War Two, its board was dominated by Nazi industrialists. In 1944 US Congressman John Coffee stated, *'The Nazi government has 85 million Swiss gold francs on deposit in the BIS. The majority of the board is made up of Nazi officials. Yet American money is being deposited in the bank'*. Today, BIS is the architect and promotor of Central Bank Digital Currencies, which its chief, Augustus Carstens, has stated publicly will be fully programmable and subject to complete surveillance by central banks.

Professor Hughes traces the US security state to the 1947 National Security Act which he identifies as a Wall Street promotion that led to covert operations eventually coming under the CIA. This established the modern Deep State, whose primary purpose, he states, was to *'facilitate political violence to expand capital accumulation'*. The chief lobbyist for the CIA creation was Wall Street lawyer Allen Dulles who would later lead the CIA, where he oversaw the 1953 Iranian coup, Project MKUltra mind control and the covert 1961 Bay of Pigs Invasion for which he was fired by President John F Kennedy. Dulles became a member of the Warren Commission that investigated Kennedy's assassination in Dallas on November 22nd 1963. Dulles disliked Kennedy, a man whom he described to journalist Willie Morris as *'that little Kennedy, he thought he was a god'*. When tackling the Deep State in his book, Hughes doesn't beat around the bush;

> *'The Deep State amounts to a high-level conspiracy between key elements of Wall Street, intelligence and other government agencies, the military-industrial complex, the police, multinational corporations, think tanks, foundations, the media and academia. Regardless of which government is nominally in charge, the deep state subverts democracy and the rule of law to make sure that ruling class agendas are continuously advanced. Although there are tensions and power struggles between different classes, factions tend to coalesce and unite around certain fundamental control paradigms and policies for their mutual benefit. The deep state makes its most significant interventions in the form of 'deep events' i.e. events which profoundly transform the trajectory of politics and society yet whose provenance is ambiguous e.g. the JFK assassination, 9/11 and Covid 19."*

In April 1939, Goebbels announced a new order for Europe under the intellectual leadership of Nazi Germany and Fascist Italy. Hughes follows the money, *'the same month senior figures in the US, Britain and Germany agreed a massive US gold loan that would underpin the New Order, the loan being made through the lawless Bank for International Settlements'*. Planning for a new world order can be traced back to the post-war era in the 1950s and 1970s, when both climate and pandemics were identified as triggers by organisations like The Club of Rome to lay the ground for one world government. In 1990, George Bush Snr made a specific speech about a new world order, echoed two years later in the Wall Street Journal by Senator Joe Biden titled, *How I learned to love the New World Order.* In a 2009 interview for the FT, George Soros, the billionaire financier of NGOs and the centrepiece of WEF *Stakeholder Capitalism,* claimed that China needed to be brought into the creation of a new world order.

Throughout Covid, the New World Order (NWO) appears in the open, *Forbes* evidently briefed in May 2020 headlined, *'Are we ready to embrace a New World Order?'* Chicago mayor Lori Lightfoot even called for US agency heads to pledge *'allegiance to the New World Order and good governance'.* In Australia, which witnessed some of the most aggressive Covid crackdowns, the New South Wales chief health officer, Kerry Chant claimed in 2021, *'We will be looking at what contact tracing looks like in the New World Order'.* Reprising his Wall Street Journal article in March 2022, President Biden, sensing a generational pivot pronounced, *'Now is the time when things are shifting, there's going to be a New World Order out there'.* In an insight into the origins of the NWO, Henry Kissinger concluded the WEF June 2023 conference when interviewed by Klaus Schwab, his protégé, by saying *'What a wonderful opportunity to conclude our week here with such concrete proposals and ideas of how we can really create, I would say, a New World Order'.* Schwab's other mentor was former Fine Gael Attorney General and Goldman Sachs Chairman Peter Sutherland, who, as UN Ambassador for Refugees, advocated widely in Europe for open borders to arrest population ageing.

The Nazis targeted the most vulnerable in society, beggars, drug addicts, prostitutes, homosexuals and pacifists for taking money from the public purse in defiance of Nazi law and order and undermining the image of their Aryan race. Many from 1937 ended up tagged and imprisoned in concentration camps and used for slave labour. Today, Israeli academic and WEF advocate Yuval Harari speaks about a useless class, the economically redundant who are excluded from contributing as technology drives us forward towards transhumanism. The unspoken question is, what follows? The culling of the so-called useless class? Harrari hints at the answer; '*You want to know how super-intelligent cyborgs might treat ordinary flesh-and-blood humans? Better start by investigating how humans treat their less intelligent animal cousins.'*

In his first book, *The War for Technocracy,* Hughes explores the concept of the "Big Lie," a propaganda technique fully described by Adolf Hitler in *Mein Kampf.* He argues that the pandemic narrative has employed this technique by presenting an exaggerated, cognitively overwhelming threat for the average person to comprehend. This, he explains, creates a state of cognitive dissonance where people cannot reconcile the propaganda with their everyday experiences, leading to widespread compliance and suppression of dissent.

One of the most striking aspects of Hughes' analysis is the comparison of pandemic measures to psychological torture techniques. He discusses how the constant state of fear and uncertainty induced by media bombardment and government policies mirrors the tactics used in psychological torture to break down individuals' will and resistance. Hughes points to the use of masks, lockdowns, and social distancing as tools to create social isolation and sensory deprivation, weakening social bonds and increasing dependence on authority.

He also highlights the role of dehumanisation in fostering compliance and how the narrative around "*anti-vaxxers and conspiracy theorists*" has been used to stigmatise and marginalise those who question the official narrative. This process, he argues, is designed to create social division and prevent unified resistance against the technocratic agenda.

The implications of these psychological operations are far-reaching. Hughes warns that the erosion of individual freedoms and democratic principles during the pandemic sets a dangerous precedent for future crises. The normalisation of emergency measures and surveillance technologies during the pandemic has paved the way for more intrusive forms of control, such as biometric surveillance and digital currencies. Huges would argue that the groundwork is laid.

Hughes' vision of 21st century totalitarianism is one where scientific management and control supersede democratic governance. This shift, he warns, is driven by a transnational elite that operates above national boundaries and democratic institutions. He claims they have been planning the transition to technocracy for decades, using crises as opportunities to implement their agenda.

He emphasizes that implementing technocracy requires not just technological advancements but also psychological manipulation to gain public compliance. He argues that the Covid-19 pandemic was used as a pretext to introduce and normalise these control mechanisms. Fear, trauma, and social division, he explains, are key elements in maintaining control over populations and preventing resistance.

Despite the grim analysis, Professor Hughes remains hopeful that awareness and resistance can thwart the technocratic agenda. He calls for a renewed commitment to democratic principles and social justice, arguing that only through collective action and solidarity can the global population resist the encroachment of technocratic control. Hughes highlights the importance of documenting and understanding the psychological operations at play, as this knowledge is crucial for resisting future attempts at social engineering.

5

PROFESSOR FRANCIS BOYLE: COVID 19 IS A BIOWEAPON

The Covid-19 pandemic has ignited intense debates about the virus's origins. One of the most compelling voices in the Counterpoint interview series[1], which also resonates with the work by Professor David Hughes, is that of Professor Francis Boyle, who authored the Biological Weapons Anti-Terrorism Act of 1989. This act, passed unanimously by both houses of Congress and signed into law by President George Bush Sr., was designed to implement the Biological Weapons Convention in the United States. Boyle's early assertion in January 2020 that Covid-19 is a bioweapon deserves attention, given his extensive background in bioweapons monitoring.

Boyle's journey into the world of biological warfare began in 1983 when he was asked to handle legal aspects related to the field by the Council for Responsible Genetics. With three degrees from Harvard, he was well-equipped for this task. In the Autumn of 2019, while finishing his book *World Politics,*

1. https://podcasts.apple.com/gb/podcast/19-professor-francis-a-boyle-harvard-bioweapons/id1710094803

Human Rights, and International Law, Boyle began monitoring reports of a new pneumonia-like illness emerging in China. By mid-December the first public cases were reported, and by January 2020, Boyle came to the conclusion that Covid was an offensive biological weapon of war. He cited his extensive experience in monitoring disease outbreaks and his involvement in biological warfare programs since 1983 as the basis for his judgment. Boyle believed the virus had been genetically engineered to be more lethal and infectious, leaking from the Wuhan Institute of Virology's Biosafety Level 4 (BSL-4) facility.

Boyle's alarm went out on January 24, 2020, through several hundred media outlets. In his alert he insisted that all BSL-3 and BSL-4 labs worldwide must be shut down immediately to prevent further catastrophes. His assessment of the Wuhan lab's role was informed by a documentary he consulted on, *Anthrax Wars* (2009), which discussed the existential dangers of BSL-3 and BSL-4 labs. He reiterated this position in his book *Resisting Medical Tyranny*, covering the first two years of the Covid-19 pandemic.

Around the same time Boyle made his assertion in late January 2020, a counter-narrative emerged, spearheaded by figures like Anthony Fauci and Jeremy Ferrar, suggesting a zoonotic origin for the virus. This narrative claimed that Covid-19 organically transferred from bats to humans, a story Boyle found implausible given the virus's rapid and highly infectious spread. Boyle's long-standing expertise in bioweapons and the political machinations surrounding them made him certain of a man-made origin. Professor Boyle faced immediate backlash. The Associated Press labelled him a conspiracy theorist and a purveyor of fake news, a narrative that disseminated globally. Despite the assault across global media on his credibility, Boyle stood firm, convinced that his interpretation was correct and grounded in decades of experience.

He pointed out that key U.S. agencies, including the CDC, NIH, and the Pentagon, were possibly involved in the development of Covid-19. He argued that figures like Fauci (NIAID) and Collins (FDA) were fully aware of what was happening in Wuhan due to their financial and operational ties to the lab. This assertion suggested a broader, more coordinated effort in managing the virus's narrative and the global response.

Boyle highlighted the Food and Drug Administration's (FDA) dual role in developing and approving treatments and vaccines. He found this particularly troubling, noting a conflict of interest in the FDA's involvement in creating the virus and then sanctioning the specific vaccines designed to combat it. This dual role raised ethical and safety concerns, especially given the experimental nature of the mRNA technology used in the Covid vaccines. Boyle drew parallels between the Covid-19 vaccines and earlier instances of experimental vaccines used by the U.S. Military, notably during the Gulf War. He referenced the anthrax and botulinum vaccines administered to troops which led to widespread illness known as Gulf War Syndrome. This historical precedent underscored his scepticism about the safety and efficacy of the Covid-19 vaccines, predicting a similar or worse outcome given the scale of distribution.

Boyle's expertise in international law and human rights also informed his critique of the global health governance during the pandemic. He criticised the World Health Organization (WHO) for its role in the crisis, alleging that it acted in concert with major powers and pharmaceutical interests to mislead the public and implement draconian measures. The WHO's sponsorship of the Wuhan lab was particularly damning, in

Boyle's view. The organisation, along with the CDC and NIH, had a vested interest in covering up the lab's role in the pandemic's origins.

Boyle has also addressed the implications of the World Health Assembly's 2024 attempts to establish a global technocracy through a pandemic treaty and amendments to health regulations. He argues that these efforts were based on the false premise that Covid-19 occurred naturally, rather than was a man-made bioweapon from a laboratory. This lie, he asserted, was being used as the backbone to justify the creation of what he terms a "*Global Totalitarian Medical Police State*". Despite these challenges, Boyle remains hopeful that continued public scrutiny and resistance could prevent such an outcome.

6

TOTALITARIANISM IN THE 20TH CENTURY

A PERSON MIGHT SUPPORT totalitarian policies because they feel anxious and unsafe, and over time, they may fall for the totalitarian ideology believing it wholeheartedly. Eventually, they may become disillusioned with the ideology but continue to support the totalitarian regime because it benefits them materially, particularly if they have a cozy and secure government job or be a high-ranking official. This example is hypothetical, but it helps us conceptualise the three main motivations for totalitarian support: emotionality, ideology and interest. If we understand these motivations, we can better understand how societies end up supporting totalitarian regimes.

Societies, by definition, are complex and stratified, and include both vertical and horizontal diversity. If any ideology or system is to appeal to a whole society, it must be multifaceted. Most people who support political projects do so because they feel it is the right thing to do. Anxiety, fear, shame and insecurity creates desperation, opening up the possibility for authoritarian solutions. Pride, on the other hand, makes people blind to the negative effects of totalitarian collectivism. Emotions are public; feeling something as a society makes individuals more conformist. Even without a basic understanding of the issues at hand or the solution proposed by totalitarian leaders, large portions of society accept totalitarianism to go along with the crowd, because it seems like the right thing to do.

There are those who passionately believe in totalitarian ideology and see it as a force for good. People motivated by genuine belief tend to be the most ardent and vocal supporters of the totalitarian regime. They become its active foot-soldiers and willing informants, these are the ones who will kill and die for the regime. Their dedication is matched only by their blindness.

Finally, a section of the population, usually a small elite, accepts totalitarianism as a means to an end. Interest transcends emotions and belief. Historically this group has been comprised of industrialists and party officials whose dedication to the ideology and cult of personality is usually shallow and formal. They see totalitarianism as a business opportunity, a way to ensure profits and privileges. Totalitarianism of the elite motivated by interest alone, is a solution to an ancient problem: democracy. Any system that takes power from the hands of the many, and consolidates it in the hands of the few, is seen as worthwhile to the elites.

These three approximate groupings are not definite and exhaustive but merely help us grasp the situation in greater detail. Motivations change, as well as the way in which people pursue their motivations, so in the case of totalitarianism, we must always avoid reductionist methodologies that hyperfocus on a single explanation.

Totalitarianism is a form of government characterised by centralisation of authority under a single political party or leader, and the suppression of opposition through authoritarian measures. This can be our working definition. It is important to immediately note something about this definition: totalitarianism is not simply a harsher form of authoritarianism or autocracy. There is more nuance to totalitarianism; it is not exclusive to the sphere of politics. As the name suggests, totalitarianism is *total* – it seeks complete control over society. It cannot accomplish this task without the passive or active support of many parts of society. This is why this book is divided into different topics: culture, politics, economy, science, social media, climate, etc...

Totalitarian regimes desire absolute control over all aspects of society including economy, culture, education and media. The state uses many forms of soft power to maintain power and suppress dissent including propaganda, censorship and mass surveillance. However, it never shies away from using hard power if needed. The history of 20th century totalitarianism is the history of mass and unprecedented violence. There is no reason to expect anything else from its 21st century counterpart. It may seem more subtle and soft now, but that is only because we are still at its early stages.

Totalitarian regimes are often based on an all-encompassing ideology that seeks to mobilise the masses and create a unified society. Examples include National Socialism in Germany, Communism in the Soviet Union, and Maoism in China. Not all authoritarian regimes are totalitarian; some may lack a total ideology or mass mobilisation efforts. This ideology is usually incoherent and disingenuous. Totalitarianism has no real values but uses temporary values packaged into ideology in order to gain mass appeal and avoid commitments to any lasting principles. Totalitarian ideology is amazingly flexible, as it is unwilling to commit to anything that might hinder its own power and expansion.

Totalitarianism abolishes the distinction between public and private life, as control over all aspects of social life means control over the individual. It merges state with society, culture and economy. In turn, the individual is subsumed under political power and has no available sphere of independence and self-expression. This includes monitoring citizens' behaviour, thoughts, and beliefs and enforcing conformity through coercion and indoctrination. You may not care about totalitarianism, but totalitarianism cares about you! It is precisely this attempt to completely subdue and pacify the individual that distinguishes totalitarianism from authoritarianism.

Just as it is important not to completely equate totalitarianism with authoritarianism, we also must not associate totalitarianism with "right-wing" politics and ideology. Totalitarianism surpasses the right/left dichotomy because totalitarianism is not committed to any particular values, ideals or ideology. Although the extreme right wing has traditionally been linked to notable instances of totalitarianism, such as Nazism and fascism, totalitarianism can take on diverse ideological forms. For instance, totalitarian governments based on leftist ideologies included Maoist communism in China and Stalinist communism in the Soviet

Union. Totalitarianism has no standards; it uses whatever is available at the time: class tensions, ethnic hatred, economic chaos, cultural anomie, etc...

When we remember the totalitarianism of the previous century we tend to think about its final and most atrocious acts, such as the Holocaust, Russian Gulags and China's "Great Leap Forward". These mass killings should not deceive us, totalitarianism is not identified by atrocities; it has a subtler history. While developed totalitarian regimes do tend to exhibit overt displays of state power and repression, less developed ones operate more indirectly, using techniques such as propaganda manipulation, and co-option to establish and maintain control. Totalitarianism evolves gradually, with authoritarian leaders steadily consolidating power over time. Totalitarianism centralises as much power as it can – as much as society allows it.

In her groundbreaking book, *The Origins of Totalitarianism*, Hannah Arendt offers a thorough political analysis of totalitarianism and its importance for the contemporary world. This book is the first systematic analysis of totalitarianism written immediately after the Second World War. In it, Arendt demonstrates the establishment of the totalitarian worldview and its methods of implementation, its operation at the level of political movement and, finally, of political order. In doing so, she strictly limits totalitarianism in time and space, taking into account Hitler's and Stalin's regimes.

Arendt explored the characteristics of totalitarian governments, their ascent, and the means by which they impose social control. Arendt's critique draws attention to a number of important features of totalitarianism that are relevant to modern concerns, including originality, ideology, terror tactics and use of technology.

According to Arendt, 20th century totalitarianism is a unique and unprecedented type of government in which the state completely dominates every facet of society. Alongside authoritarian political control, this also involves mass mobilisation, cultural propaganda and ideological manipulation. Arendt saw totalitarianism as more than just authoritarianism. It was a new political beast that could only arise from within modern society, its culture and technology. Totalitarianism was an indirect product of the Enlightenment, it corrupted the rational tendency to gather, amass and systematise knowledge into a political principle.

Arendt highlighted how important ideology is to totalitarian governments. Totalitarian ideologies, like Stalinism and Nazism, offered widely understandable worldviews that legitimised the state and provided an explanation for its overreaching actions. Since these states were prone to strange, erratic and destructive decisions, the ideology needed to be flexible while remaining absolute. Ideology was explicitly acknowledged as crucial for the state, and special ministries, offices; commissariats were created to spread state ideology.

Ideology was only one instrument of control; Arendt also highlights the use of terror as a tool of totalitarianism. Totalitarian regimes employed systematic violence and intimidation to suppress dissent, instil fear and maintain an atmosphere of uncertainty. Constant fear and violence were necessary for totalitarian regimes to succeed. The employment of terror was intended to induce fear and obedience in ordinary citizens as well as in real or perceived opponents of the regime. Totalitarian governments aimed to eradicate all forms of dissent and foster an atmosphere of dread and uncertainty using arbitrary arrests, incarceration, torture, and executions. The ultimate goal of terror is complete dominance over every facet of human existence.

Fear is a useful tool for social engineering that easily manipulates people's attitudes, convictions and actions. Totalitarian regimes aim to shape people into obedient subjects who follow the rules of the state by continuously monitoring, intimidating, and coercing the populace. The goal is to make individuals internalise political terror. Arendt studied how terror affects people psychologically—both victims and offenders. Terror causes sufferers to feel helpless, alone, and alienated, which breeds hopelessness and resignation. Participating in violent and repressive behaviours can degrade a person's moral character and cause them to lose their conscience and empathy as they grow insensitive to the pain of others.

20th century totalitarianism would have been impossible without 20th century technology. Arendt explores the role of technology in facilitating totalitarian control, particularly in the realms of propaganda, surveillance, and mass communication. This aspect is highly relevant in our digital age, where advancements in technology have enabled new forms of state surveillance, censorship, ignorance-manufacture and manipulation of information. Technological advancements such as administrative systems and surveillance tools have made it easier for authoritarian societies to monitor and manipulate their citizens. Totalitarian governments used highly developed monitoring systems, including informant networks and covert police units, to keep an eye on the whereabouts and actions of its populace.

Modern technologies including data collection and wiretapping, allowed authoritarian governments to continue widespread social control and repression. Technological developments in the armed forces and industrial sectors made it easier for authoritarian governments to mechanise and bureaucratise violence. Totalitarian nations used their industrial infrastructure to carry out mass murder and support military campaigns. With the employment of tanks, aircraft, and chemical weapons, they were able to inflict previously unheard-of amounts of devastation and violence on a worldwide scale. The Holocaust was would have been unimaginable without the proper technological tools to carry out mass killing on an industrial scale.

Arendt examines how technological advancement affected the state of humanity, emphasising how the emergence of mass society and industrialisation led to a sense of alienation and rootlessness among people which was then identified and exploited by totalitarian governments in order to control and enlist the support of the populace. Human autonomy and dignity were further undermined by the dehumanising ideology of authoritarianism and the depersonalising consequences of contemporary technology. Arendt observed how totalitarian regimes only further atomised and isolated individuals, eroding social bonds and collective solidarity. This fragmentation of society made it easier for the regime to exert control and suppress dissent. In our modern world, concerns about social polarisation, alienation, and the erosion of democratic norms echo Arendt's warnings. Totalitarianism arises out of social problems, the chief among them being the erosion of social bonds.

It is for this reason that there is serious cause for concern in relation to the misgendering of our children, as advocated in UN papers on education. This undermines the family unit, which is the basic structure of society . Homogenous countries with strong familial bonds represent a threat to totalitarianism, because the first loyalty of any person is to family and community. On March 13th 2024, the Irish People overwhelmingly rejected changes to the Irish Constitution that sought to undermine the definition of marriage by allowing for 'enduring relationships' and the removal of the woman in the family home, despite overwhelming political and media support for the change. It was a moment of hope for the people and a setback for the Irish Government, who's campaign was led by NGOs. The people had smelled a rat, and both of the proposed constitutional amendments were defeated by an average of 70%. In the totalitarian mindset, the veneration of and total control by the centre cannot take root unless social bonds can be destroyed or rendered impotent. Taken to the extreme, this elevates the State to a level of higher importance than the bonds of family, which explains why citizens under totalitarian regimes behind the Iron Curtain routinely reported on neighbours and family members as a civic duty.

The adjective totalitarian and the noun totalitarianism, still so prevalent in contemporary political jargon, derive from the Latin word *totus*, meaning whole, complete, comprehensive. This completeness refers to the degree of dominance or control and/or authority established over society in this particular type of political regime. It is, therefore, about comprehensive domination or absolute power over society. Totalitarianism is not only all-encompassing but it is also intensely encompassing, its control is never shallow.

As Arendt states, totalitarianism is a novelty in human history and political theory, introducing new methods of control and forms of reality that cannot be ignored. The first part of the 20th century gave us the rise and fall of fascism as a form of totalitarianism , while the last decade of the 20th century showed the limits of communism, which is another form of totalitarianism. Totalitarianism fundamentally differs from the other forms of political repression we know - such as despotism, tyranny, and dictatorship - by the specific connection between totalitarian ideology, isolation and terror. It abolishes any autonomous activity of individuals and communities. Totalitarian regimes are not satisfied with simply isolating people; they actively produce isolation by creating a rupture between the individual and the world which destroys private lives, hence the attempt to destroy the family. Isolation is the essence of totalitarian rule.

Wherever it came to power, totalitarianism established completely new political institutions and destroyed all existing social, legal, and political frameworks of the land. Regardless of the specific national tradition or the particular spiritual source of its ideology, totalitarian rule always transforms the public space into a mass society, replaces the multi-party system with a one-party dictatorship, shifts the centre of power from the civilian government to the military and the police, and pursues a foreign policy aimed at conquest. Mass society is a precondition for totalitarianism, as strong social bonds prevent mass mobilisation, indoctrination and widespread fear.

Totalitarianism is an unprecedented form of organisation which dedicates all of its activities to controlling the masses. The image of totalitarianism is a mass of people huddled around a leader who embodies the movement and inspires it with a driving force. Sympathisers, party members, and members of elite formations form successive layers whose task is to distil reality and fill the gap that separates the central ideological fiction from the outside world. The totalitarian leader is an ambiguous character, more of a mascot or performer – a personification of the regime . The leader is there to give totalitarianism a *human* face - a repellent one to be sure, but a human one none the less. The totalitarian apparatus is comprised from institutions (the party, bureaucracy, police, military, commissions, ministries, etc), so that it is able to function, even without the leader. This is what distinguishes totalitarianism from dictatorships and tyrannies.

As we have seen, Totalitarianism is not necessarily monolithic, not reliant on a single idea, leader – *or enemy.* It is flexible, the leader is disposable, important enemies are interchangeable. Totalitarianism is characterised by the multiplication of rivals. We can see this in both fascism and communism. For example, the sham trials in the Soviet Union during Stalin's rule show that anyone can be the enemy. Once totalitarianism defeats an eternal and malevolent enemy, it immediately finds another.

In order to survive, totalitarianism needs both outer and inner enemies, yet it is the inside enemy (the traitors, intruders and dissidents) that are its weakness. This is why the police are usually more important than the military. Once the original opponents are removed, totalitarian ideology conjures up new ones. The war must go on, the masses are never truly saved from the beastly enemy. The war against the external threat takes the form of conquest, while the war against the internal becomes terror.

Terror and conquest are used blatantly in the name of an ideology that legitimises the totalitarian regime. This extreme and constant violence requires an ideology based on Manichaean perception where, "Manichean" refers to a dualistic worldview in which the world is divided into two opposing forces, typically good and evil, light and dark, or other similar dichotomies. Most famously, Augustine of Hippo was a Manichean before converting to Christianity and becoming Saint Augustine.

Our current culture of docility and spectacular science works as a helper to this simplistic, black-and-white ideology, leaving little opportunity for subtlety or complexity, competing forces or ideas. The Nazis had their "race science", and the Soviet Union had Marxism-Leninism. These served as pseudoscientific frameworks that grounded totalitarian ideology in "natural" and "historic facts". Violence becomes total precisely when the will of the state is thought to be in submission to the laws of history and nature. The Manichean divide deeply divides people (the higher races vs the lower races, exploiters vs the exploited), and makes antagonism a part of everyday life. Terror isolates the members of mass society, whilst conquest isolates the society itself. The false remedy for this isolation is precisely totalitarian ideology. Totalitarianism, through violence and ideology, destroys and recreates society and man in its own image.

The original account of totalitarianism developed by Arendt has a few interesting details that we ought to contemplate. The first point is Arendt's dating of totalitarianism, as something uniquely modern. Arendt claims that this is also true for antisemitism and imperialism. Although there were authoritarian regimes, racial discrimination and colonial conquests before the modern age, modernity offers a new set of challenges. Karl Popper claims that totalitarianism goes back to Plato and his utopia, however I have no intent of addressing these historical claims, as such, but what is important to note is that if Arendt is correct, the danger of totalitarianism will only grow as we become more technically advanced. There is a connection – maybe even a coevolution – between modernity and totalitarianism about which we must be aware. Our contemporary age is more vulnerable to totalitarianism than the early 20th century. This is especially clear from two general trends: the decay of social bonds and the advancement of technology.

The second point is that totalitarianism seems to be restrictive and precise, it focuses on some things and ignores others. It might be said that it is an irrelevant term now that the Soviet Union regime is no more, and China has opened up. But similar objections aren't made about other political terms like dictatorship. The aspects of totalitarianism we explore show that it is not as straightforward as other systems. Social bonds, relationships and culture are of much more interest here because totalitarianism is much more interested in them. Totalitarianism is a concept that helps us understand certain kinds of social organisation, even if they change over time. It is not a purely political concept. We should refine our understanding of totalitarianism, rather than abandon it completely, to better understand how these regimes work and in order to combat them before it is too late.

Finally, totalitarianism exhibits incredible mutability, the capacity to change. This has menace because 21st century totalitarianism is still in its infancy and hasn't solidified as yet. We can see the governments of the world are still trying out different tactics and methods. We must also be aware of *totalitarian ingenuity*, so we can identify and combat it wherever it appears. Our current focus is on culture and social bonds because these are the breeding ground of totalitarian tendencies. The culture of docility and weakened social bonds allow elites to realise their power fantasies which is why this book aims to show the importance of critical thinking in combating it.

7

CRITICAL THINKING IN THE FIGHT AGAINST NASCENT TOTALITARIANISM

Critical thinking is the answer to totalitarian ingenuity. Both are dynamic in nature but have completely different goals. Critical thinking emancipates us through our own efforts, it is the most basic form of resistance. It enables authentic communication, as opposed to idle chatter. Critical thinking enables us to ask the right questions, so we can have impactful conversations.

This type of thinking is a cornerstone of informed decision-making and a vital skill in today's information-rich society. It involves the objective analysis and evaluation of an issue to form a judgment. It is crucial to be able to see through manipulative propaganda, psyops and mass psychosis. This is a cognitive process characterised by the ability to think clearly and rationally, to understand the logical connection between ideas and most importantly the ability to see the interconnections between seemingly unrelated events. It encompasses several key skills including observation, analysis, interpretation, reflection, evaluation, inference, explanation, problem-solving, and decision-making.

In essence, critical thinking means that we rigorously question ideas and assumptions rather than accepting them at face value from Government, media, academia and NGOs, always asking *cui bono*? Who benefits? It is about being active rather than passive, deducing consequences from what we know and seeking out new and relevant sources of information to better inform ourselves. Anyone can learn this skill by practice; it has little to do with IQ, some of the worst inversions of it can be found in academia. Critical thinking is not just limited to the ability to argue or present information in a debate, but is the routine systematic process of questioning, analysing, and synthesising information to reach well-founded conclusions. It allows for more effective and creative problem-solving, ensuring that all decisions are well thought out and not based on incomplete or biased information.

Imagine you're scrolling through social media and you see a shocking headline. A critical thinker wouldn't just hit the share button right away. Instead, they'd dig a little deeper – check other sources, see if the information adds up, and decide if it's worth sharing. It's about being curious and a bit sceptical, always wanting to get the complete picture. For those engaged in manipulation, propaganda and mass psychosis operations, the critical thinker is about as welcome as a sniffer dog on a smuggler's yacht; it is why critical thinkers are undermined, de-platformed or attacked with tropes and personal abuse. Critical thinkers, especially those in centres of influence, invoke fear because of their capacity to break through the utopian illusion; this is why they are singled out for rough treatment.

Utopianism is the search for a perfect society where the political, economic, and social processes all work together perfectly to make sure everyone is happy and healthy, forever. Utopian ideas have led to the rise of many totalitarian governments. Historically, the goal of utopian thinkers has been to imagine ideal societies. This usually means eliminating poverty, crime, and unfairness, creating a peaceful and wealthy community . Utopian leaders such as Plato and Marx claimed they would make society perfect by making big necessary changes and putting a certain philosophy into practice. For instance, the goal of the Bolshevik Revolution was to create a society without classes, and the goal of Nazi Germany was to make a state where everyone was of the *"perfect Aryan race"*. To achieve these demanding goals, totalitarian governments need to concentrate power, as these radical changes can only be made by a strong, united leadership. Force and violence, propaganda, censorship, and suppression of criticism have their role, but also their limits. The final utopian goal justifies all the extreme acts required to reach it.

Utopian ideals put the needs of the collective ahead of the needs of individuals, which means that personal freedoms and individualism are outlawed in totalitarian regimes. They must ensure that people's beliefs, culture, and even their schooling are in-line with the state. The wants and goals of the state come before those of individuals. Since there is only one ideal of the good and perfect, there is no need for diversity among societies and individuals. Groupthink and conformism become the norm when a central authority can establish a single standard, absolutely. Even though utopianism strives towards a perfect society, totalitarian measures have always caused unintended catastrophes, from famines and wars to cultural stagnation and pseudo-science.

MANY DYSTOPIAN BOOKS, such as *1984* by George Orwell and *Brave New World* by Aldous Huxley, examine the connection between idealistic goals and totalitarian governments. These works show how the search for the perfect society can lead to systems that are cruel and dehumanising. The literature and historical examples show how dangerous it is to use totalitarian methods to make utopian dreams come true. There must be a balance between idealism and respect for human rights and individual freedom.

On this note, it is necessary to consider anti-dystopianism as a political platform and value that can guide us through the rise of 21st century totalitarianism. Anti-dystopianism means fighting the rise of totalitarian dystopias. This approach does not try to unite people around a vision of a perfect society, instead, it aims to unite people through a shared concern about a potential dystopia. Unfortunately, it is much more realistic to politically unite people around a threat, than a positive image of the future. As a whole, we may disagree about concrete values, laws and policies, but if we are faced with the rise of 21st century totalitarianism, common ground can be formed to create a united front against a terrifying dystopia. Preventing a technocratic and biomedical dystopia should be a shared sentiment and we cannot afford to be divided against this common enemy of humanity. Let us further define its formation in this century.

8

TOTALITARIANISM IN THE 21ST CENTURY

Totalitarianism in the 21st century is becoming more subtle than it has ever been before. The fast growth of technology, especially in areas like monitoring and information control, has the potential to weaponise totalitarianism in the 21st century across diverse channels that the monsters of the last century could only dream about.

Companies and governments now have access to personal information like never before, allowing them to monitor and control a huge number of people. This problem is exacerbated by the fact that many people use social media and other online platforms carelessly. As we have already seen, these platforms enable governments and their working groups to spread propaganda, silence dissent, and manage public conversation.

Another reason for subtlety is due to the rise of banal technocratic and authoritarian leaders, who, unlike Hitler and Stalin, want to keep their power concealed while they weaken democratic institutions. These leaders use fear and social differences to get what they want, by censoring the media, attacking independent institutions, denigrating anyone who speaks out against them and deploying ranks of fake fact checkers who, funded by corporations and institutions, support their paymaster's agendas and vigorously attack counter narratives. These new leaders, parties and groups transcend the traditional left/right political split. As far as we can see, they have no real values or ideology.

Totalitarianism is not necessarily inevitable in the 21st century. There are many points of resistance to its impulse. Some individuals and groups work to protect democratic values and culture, utilising independent media and critical thinking. People are becoming more aware of authoritarianism and are fighting it. Covid lockdowns, in particular, have woken people up to the dangers of uncontrolled state power and the loss of personal freedoms. Bear in mind, however, the majority of populations facing nascent totalitarianism in the 20th century were aware of it rising but severely underestimated its potency and capacity. We do not have to repeat their errors. Totalitarianism is no longer a new phenomenon; we have seen its effects. There are plenty of reasons to be afraid, but not to despair. Hope is apparent in the many thought leaders who have already diagnosed this current trend towards totalitarianism and the social movements opposing it. One of these is the Professor of Clinical Psychology at the University of Ghent in Belgium, Mattias Desmet.

In the summer of 2022, a lone middle-aged man on his bicycle led a large parade of cars and lorries out a narrow road from Skibbereen in West Cork. What stood out for me, was not the frustration of the drivers stuck in traffic behind him, or his cycling in the middle of the road, but the fact that he was breathing through a covid mask. Around the same time, I met an old friend at his request, to discuss a financial puzzle. A multi-qualified and successful businessman, he was always an exemplar of quiet, reserved, and critical discussion about complex economic, financial and business interplay. As the business bit came to an end, the subject turned to the epidemic. He informed me that he had stopped following me on Twitter due to the contrary opinions I was expressing. When I tried to explain , he pulled his hands up to his ears and began rocking and humming, as if he couldn't bear to hear it!

Both men, the cyclist and the businessman, display behaviour which shows they had become part of what Desmet calls a mass formation, both of them were traumatised by the propaganda and fear mongering from the government in different ways. *The Psychology of Totalitarianism*, published by Desmet in 2022, is a game changer for those seeking an explanation for the frustrating impenetrability of the indoctrinated mind when confronted with counter-facts and data relating to the worldwide pandemic narrative. Mattias Desmet arrived just in time with a model to explain how the public is susceptible to this mass formation (much like starlings in a murmuration) and how and why propaganda can profoundly alter human society and invite totalitarianism under certain conditions. Unsurprisingly, Professor Desmet's work is greatly influenced by his research into the works of historian and philosopher Hannah Arendt.

Mass Formation and Professor Mattias Desmet

Desmet regards totalitarianism as a *mechanistic* ideology that plans for a world headed by mundane technocrats, who use their technical abilities to run society. This mechanistic ideology treats humans as purely biological organisms while ignoring the moral, symbolic and complex psychological aspects of humanity. It leads to the creation of disassociated individuals who are easily controlled and prone to mass formation.

He sees large-scale and long-lasting mass formations that lead to authoritarianism as the manifestation of a mechanical worldview. Rulers can come and go, but the ideology endures until it is confronted, or it self-destructs and implodes. At its most extreme, Stalinism stigmatised, ostracised, and slaughtered segments of the population that did not conform to its chosen image of the ideal man and rejected the totalitarian system. Under Tzarist Russia, less than 20 death sentences were carried out each year, but in the first few months after the 1917 Russian Revolution, there were 540 executions rising to 12,000 per year until 1937, and 600,000 per year thereafter.

Although totalitarianism as it existed in the 20th century is unlikely to reemerge in the same form, it has not disappeared, and continues to play a central role in the strategy and policy of institutions such as the World Economic Forum (WEF). 21st century totalitarianism is built on two pillars. The first is to present a positive picture of a paradise where everything will be delivered without a struggle (utopianism). In the words of the World Economic Forum, *"you will own nothing and be happy"*. There is no conspiracy here; the objectives and ideology of the World Economic Forum, which meets annually in Davos, Switzerland, are published and promoted openly. The second pillar, which has received less attention, is that it cannot be realised without a massive increase in public fear and terror until a pivot point is reached, when personal liberty is sacrificed for a sense of safety.

Since the beginning of the 21st century, there has been a noticeable acceleration in the development of surveillance technologies and a reduction in personal liberties under legislation that arose from fears about terrorism and, in recent years, fears about a virus, the solution to which was to jab ourselves with experimental mRNA drugs, imprison ourselves at home, wear masks, and enforce the rules among ourselves. Within three months of the lockdowns, in June 2020, the World Economic Forum, led by Prince Charles, unveiled its vision for a sustainable future, which included using the transhuman technology envisioned in the fourth industrial revolution. The *Great Reset* was swiftly incorporated into speeches by US President Joe Biden, Canadian Prime Minister Justin Trudeau, and New Zealand Prime Minister Jacinda Ardern.

Professor Desmet observes that the psychological processes that led to 20th century totalitarianism are already obvious in our century. This includes infiltration, e-mail monitoring and eavesdropping on mobile devices, and overt surveillance in the form of public space camera networks that can geolocate you based on face recognition and cell phone data. While the populations in the democratic West are not subject to the hegemony of the Chinese public, which uses a combination of camera surveillance and a social credit system to alienate, isolate, and fine Chinese citizens who are deemed noncompliant with society rules as determined by the Chinese Communist Party, the West is well on its way to a similar dystopia. Despite abundant evidence, including WHO policies that urged against locking down populations during a respiratory virus outbreak, the West replicated the Chinese lockdown measures. Both Australia and New Zealand, models of what we once thought as strong democracies, applied the harshest lockdown regimes using the false belief that a respiratory virus could be controlled by subjecting their population to brutal restrictions.

The path is clear. There is a push to speed up the implementation of digital IDs in the EU, which can serve as a wallet for vaccine passports, personal carbon restrictions, and central bank digital currency. This is no longer a conspiracy hypothesis but is in the works. All they need is an event that will lead to the next great moment of opportunity, when fear and worry create a need for increased protection by the state. By August 2024 the WHO had declared Monkeypox as the next Public Health Emergency of International Concern (PHEIC). It may be followed by a UN attempt to proclaim a planetary emergency based on contentious temperature data modelling by the UNIPCC and the vilification of atmospheric CO2 despite its greening effect.

To quote Desmet: "*The moment Arendt had anticipated in 1951 seems to be rapidly approaching; the emergence of a new totalitarian system led not by 'ringleaders' like Stalin and Hitler but by dull bureaucrats and technocrats*"[1] This potential rise of a totalitarian state can also be seen on a cultural level, as evidenced by the proliferation of rules, particularly those governing what words are "acceptable" or "unacceptable" in public speech. At the time of writing this book, the Irish government has proposed legislation that, for the first time in Irish legal history, will criminalise ideas rather than action. It is meeting resistance and may be forced to dilute. The "Hate Speech Bill" will allow police, armed with a court warrant, to

1. The Psychology of Totalitarianism, page 91

enter a home and seize all mobile devices and laptops, seeking evidence for any content that could be deemed offensive against an identified minority, whether it had been published or not. Critics argue that the goal is to stifle free expression. Hate is not defined in the Bill.

The growth of 'woke' culture, as seen in the *#MeToo* movement, has resulted in an explosion of new social offences, crimes, microaggressions and laws governing practically every aspect of human interaction. This includes the new norm requiring society to acknowledge various, often fluid, gender identities.

Desmet claims that human attempts to eliminate risk, fear, and uncertainty through laws and rationality must eventually fail. His theory argues that social movements like *#MeToo*, climate fanaticism, gender activism and the pandemic are symptoms of a larger problem. Gender identity activists would have us believe that the pronouns we use in everyday speech are hugely offensive to certain segments of the population, whilst climate activists would have us believe that limiting human travel, freedoms, and food will save the planet from burning up. These phenomena arise as a result of a population's desire for authority to remove the burden of hazards and insecurity, in return for a loss of freedom. It is why policymakers, bureaucrats and technocrats easily step in to fill the hole with additional rules, regulations, norms and legislation.

We should not be astonished by the human inclination to form mobs, to give up their individual identity for the perceived safety of a group and, in doing so, erase all capacity for critical thought; this is as old as time and the seed corn of revolutions. Desmet contends that mass formation, i.e. groupthink, is a complicated and dynamic phenomenon analogous to how convection patterns emerge in water when heated, first unnoticeable until churning into steam. He remarks witheringly that the coronavirus crisis is the first time in history that the worldwide population has been subjected to such a mass formation for an extended length of time. It inspired him to write his book to explain the phenomenon.

Professor Desmet has developed a model that describes the four interconnected conditions that he claims must exist before mass formation can take root in society. The first is general loneliness and social isolation, which weakens social relationships within a population. Ironically, the age of mobile phones, Wi-Fi, and the Internet appears to have weakened, rather than strengthened, social bonds. No one answers their phone; communication is mostly streamed and not spontaneous or mutual; actual real discussions are mostly by appointment, and in business, most websites no longer include phone numbers; instead, talk to the bot or send an email. The art of letter writing is fading, as is corporations' ability to create personalised responses from a blank sheet. Bots and other AI are increasingly performing human tasks, reducing one-to-one engagement between humans.

On February 9th, 2022, the British Medical Journal released the findings of a meta-study on loneliness across 113 territories or countries, which included 57 studies.[2] It determined that a significant proportion of the population in many countries

2. The prevalence of loneliness across 113 countries: systematic review and meta-analysis, Surkalim, Luo, Eres, Gebel, van Buskirk, Bauman and Ding Ding. BMJ 2022;376:e067068

experiences serious levels of loneliness, small wonder that former US Surgeon General Vivek Murthy described loneliness as an epidemic. According to another study published in The Lancet 2018 by JT Cacioppo, one-third of the population in industrialised countries experiences loneliness, with one in every twelve people experiencing it at a problematic level. According to Desmet, approximately 30% of people living in industrialised countries report chronic feelings of loneliness and isolation, and this figure is rising, recalling Arendt's observation that "*the chief characteristic of the mass man is not brutality and backwardness, but his isolation and lack of normal social relationships*."

The second condition for a mass formation logically follows from the first, which is a general sense of meaninglessness, of being hollowed out, disengaged and uninterested in work, as if sleepwalking through existence. In sociology this condition is called *anomie,* the lack of clear and meaningful values in a society. In philosophy, it is called nihilism – the inability or refusal to believe in anything. This state, whatever we choose to call it, points towards leading an existence that is unable to make sense of its surroundings. A disassociation from body, mind and spirit. This does not mean that there is a lack of available science, interpretations, wisdom or common sense, of what the philosopher Miranda Fricker calls hermeneutic resources. There might be an abundance of these, but they are ineffective and shallow. People are in an emotional state where they are unable to make sense of their reality.

The third condition is free-floating anxiety, which was common during the early phases of the Covid pandemic. This feeling was largely caused by overwhelming fear-based media attention and high levels of public interaction. Those of us who experienced it will not be surprised. Untreated free-floating anxiety, is a broad feeling of concern that is not consciously related to any specific object, and as it increases in intensity it can lead to panic, paranoia and other such pathologies. Those who are isolated, disassociated, or feel a sense of meaninglessness are presumably more subject to free-floating anxiety. According to Definitive Healthcare LLC in February 2024, anxiety is the most common mental health disorder in the United States, affecting 20% of the population and expected to affect 300 million individuals worldwide[3].

The fourth condition is a sense of frustration and aggressiveness, which follows on from the previous three. These emotions prompt a search for an object or cause to blame for feeling this way. Isolation, meaninglessness and anxiety make people increasingly irritable. Their aggressiveness is not a response to a concrete threat or hostility; it is a consequence of the psychological state they are living in. Because of this, they are able to change the object of their ire according to the needs of the mass formation or the totalitarian state.

Desmet thinks that for mass formation to take hold in a population, almost a quarter of it must experience feelings of isolation, loneliness, a general sense of meaninglessness and anxiety, as well as impatience and anger. This group is susceptible to propaganda through the mass media that associates an object with these emotions – the proverbial enemy. For the Soviet Union, these became the vestiges of imperial Russia, the middle classes, and eventually the Kulaks; for Nazi Germany, they became the Jewish race; and for the rest of the world, the Covid-19 virus and the unvaccinated.

---

3. https://www.definitivehc.com/resources/healthcare-insights/most-prescribed-anti-anxiety-drugs

The identification of the source of concern for this cohort ignites a common bond, an adversary on whom to focus collective attention and unleash unrestrained wrath, results in a massive release, even a sense of intoxication to sustain the mass formation. There becomes a perceived purpose for living where there wasn't one before, leading to the group thinking and acting in tandem. The most radical followers of the mass formation lead the group, such as in Germany with the SS and in Covid with the *Zero Covidistas*. You'll recognise them: those measuring the two-meter social distance in the shops, wearing masks even when driving alone (or cycling), and cheering the Government broadcasts. They were the ones condemning the small minority who refused or couldn't take the miracle 'vaccine' jabs to stop the virus spreading and protect Granny and Grandad.

The unvaccinated were the bad guys, the holdouts, enemies of the state without social solidarity; misfits who were refused access to public venues, and conspiracy theorists. The mass formation covid ritual was formed by adhering to the regulations, the mask serves as a sign of compliance, dancing and singing *Jerusalema* became the anthem swirling on social media. Mass formation becomes impervious to sound counter-science. The facts that vaccines do not stop transmission or prevent you from contracting the virus, that masks provide little or no protection, and that lockdowns are a horrible public health policy that would cause more harm than good, none of it mattered. The mass formation clung tightly to the absolute claims of a government sponsored spectacular science, until the centre of power announced that covid lockdowns could end.

The propaganda was based around the virus. It becomes the lead news item day after day, particularly in the highly concentrated media of small homogeneous countries such as Ireland, where vaccine compliance reached 85% of the population and healthy children were routinely jabbed despite the fact that they were more vulnerable to the stated side effects of emergency use drugs than to Covid itself. The fear-based propaganda created widespread conformity to the rules, regardless of whether the regulations were founded in error or were contrived disinformation; it was about *being seen* to comply. The culture of obedience was quickly instituted, virtue signalling was rewarded, reinforcing the fear and false claims.

In totalitarian systems, the middle cohort of the population, estimated to be 40% to 60%, goes along with the propaganda but does not support the extremes. They keep their heads down, fearing the penalties of being isolated or fired for speaking up or expressing doubts about the science and rationality of the mass formation. This is the quiet majority about whom Paul Simon sings in *The Sound of Silence* before their *Neon God*. Inevitably, the mass formation's impact eventually wears off on some, and those on the periphery begin to awaken one by one.

One out of every five or ten people see right through the lies and propaganda, recognising the reality from the outset. They see the illusion as clearly as looking through a pane of glass. In 20th century totalitarianism, this group of people would have been suppressed or eradicated through executions, incarcerations or expulsion; in the 21st century, they are cancelled, blacklisted, silenced and banned. Cancellation can result in a loss of office; disciplinary action was taken against doctors for failing to obey orders to inject patients with medications for which they did not get informed consent, along with a media backlash and social media uproar.

Totalitarianism is primarily sustained by indoctrination and propaganda pushed into the public realm regularly through the mass media. This necessitates the silencing of opposing voices, not just in the public but also in the domestic sphere. This distinguishes totalitarianism from dictatorships, having far-reaching effects on social isolation and disintegration. The totalitarian aims to prohibit individuals from assembling in large like-minded groups and seeks to undermine social and family bonds, replacing them with the most important bond: the bond to the totalitarian system itself. Totalitarianism is distinguished by its use of social engineering. It does not settle for ruling over society as it is, instead, it tries to create an atomized mass society in its image.

Some of the hallmarks of mass formation were readily apparent in coronavirus society. As the crisis progressed, propaganda became more aggressive, and repression of opposition rose in lockstep. It has remained in place. In March 2024, when I was preparing an open public meeting in Cork City to discuss the WHO pandemic treaty, a local radio producer cautioned that he could not publicise the event or conduct an interview about the WHO for fear of putting its radio station licence at risk. He apologised, acknowledging that this was not journalism, but that in truth, it was totalitarianism in character. It was one of four experiences I had in 2024 when engaging with mainstream media, no one wanted to touch a story about the WHO despite Ireland's membership, and its disastrous performance.

Desmet argues that dissenting voices inevitably grow and have an impact on the middle cohort because these individuals are silent, but still not hypnotised. The noticeable turning point occurs when the comedians begin to delve into public conversation with sharp observations and laughter.

Totalitarians are strict, but fragile. They cannot handle laughter. When the public laughs at their leaders, the illusion is fully broken. We're not quite there yet, but we're getting close.

PROFESSOR DESMET HAS OUTLINED a theory of mass formation; we can appreciate and use it without wholly accepting it. His work has drawn some critical analysis by other academics, notably David Hughes, Valerie Kyrie and Daniel Broudy, in their article, *Covid-19 – Mass Formation or Mass Atrocity?* published on the website *Unlimited Hangout.*[4] The trio first outline how the Covid-19 pandemic changed the character of scientific endeavours. The government and other powerful actors used pressure, defamation, and censorship to create a new science, which the authors call *The Science™*, which is a compilation of pseudo-medical justifications for overreaching government involvement and violations of individual rights. These developments were clearly dangerous since science had fallen under the jurisdiction of new pandemic laws and political authorities. The fast-moving health science of this period was an unfolding spectacle, shaped by the commercial interests of the pharmaceutical industry. They give an example of distinguished Stanford University epidemiologist Professor John Ioannidis, who on St Patricks Day, March 17th 2020, was so concerned that the scientific research surrounding Covid was a fiasco in the making that he went public, causing a furore. The US government ignored his warning, and many

4. https://unlimitedhangout.com/2022/11/investigative-reports/covid-19-mass-formation-or-mass-atrocity/

others like it, and went forward with their implementation of the public health emergency regardless.

As Hughes has written about extensively, the application of psychological operations and propaganda techniques makes it easier to weaponize science and medicine in near-military ways. Part of the Covid public health emergency involved deliberately withholding life-saving drugs, such as hydroxychloroquine, which has been given to hundreds of millions of people for more than 50 years. The impact of this action will never be known. Our knowledge of the virus and possible preventive measures was purposefully kept to a minimum by governments through censorship and sidelining. From June 2020, there was a growth to the public understanding of Covid-19, after which public understanding was hampered as individuals have been threatened, fired, censored, de-platformed, and professionally assaulted for daring to question the public health orthodoxy. The directives are still on Government statutes, enabling medical boards to revoke the licences of medical practitioners who undermine their vaccination campaign.

As stated before, a small minority, Desmet claims, opposes the propaganda and hypnotic influence from the outset, up to 60% of the populace voluntarily complies without being hypnotised and up to 30% of the population completely surrender to the process of mass formation.

The main flaw, however, that Hughes, Kyrie and Broudy identify in Desmet's book, is his "*exoneration*" of political leaders. According to Desmet the mass hypnosis is partially self-inflicted; the totalitarian measures being welcomed by the majority of the people. He sees the political leaders as also being subject to the hypnosis, not necessarily having any particular ulterior motives; they are also victims of the same psychological tactics used on the masses, rather than being purposeful, evil actors. This is where the criticism is grounded, as Desmet's psychological findings of mass formation does not extend to seeing it as a purposeful creation, a mass psyops event, which is the conclusion reached, in particular in both Professor Hughes books, and which is why he draws upon the juxtaposition to the Enabling Act period in Germany. It is true that Desmet discuses conspiracies in his book, but he is much more nuanced. In broad terms, he identifies conspiracy theorising as a counterproductive tendency that tends to connect too many unrelated patterns. Conspiracy theorising stems from the same source as a complete submission to mass formation: ignorance.

In his study of the psychological phenomena behind totalitarian rule, Desmet presents leaders who reduce individual autonomy to fulfil the needs of the general public. Governments were not *forcing* people to give up their means of subsistence, socially isolate, and abandon education – they were giving the hypnotised masses what they wanted. Desmet's theory calls for a major reassessment of the Covid-19 history, which lessens all the resistance to government aggression and suppression. Desmet underplays the active and constant refusal to accept totalitarian measures engendered by the elites. This is why the authors of the article flip Desmet's study of mass formation and discuss *mass atrocities*: acts of extreme violence committed by state or non-state actors against civilians and noncombatants, often resulting in crimes against humanity.

News sources and historical texts both regularly record these cases of severe violence. Policies such as lockdowns, treatment-suppression and vaccination mandates that followed from the

Covid-19 response have led to foreseeable and preventable deaths. Further acts that cause serious pain and/or suffering include injuries from vaccinations, widespread unemployment, poverty, and hunger. Desmet has identified the psychological elements that contribute to mass atrocity. Free-floating anxiety, isolation and meaninglessness leading to psychopathy, is also a mass atrocity. It seems that Desmet is coy in accepting the possibility of motivated and intentional mass atrocity. As stated before, totalitarianism for him is self-inflicted by the hypnotised masses and compliant leaders. He does not focus on the possibility that totalitarianism is favourable to the elites and that it is deliberately implemented through measures to create a mass formation. Desmet's account of totalitarianism does not suggest confrontation with political elites as a means to change the circumstances; rather, it demands critical self-reflection from the hypnotised and deceived.

We can use Desmet's theory as a basis for understanding the situation, regardless of his oversight. The normal roles and connections in society become warped in conditions that lead to atrocities. In every circumstance, humans play the roles of victims, offenders, active observers, *and* passive spectators. The mass formation theory holds that the underlying ideology of totalitarian governments is the real source of power, not the leaders of those governments enforcing the ideology. This is why Desmet's view does not see the political elites, or any other actors, as instigators of totalitarianism. Ideology rules, rather than the elite.

Finding the people behind the atrocities committed under the cover of Covid-19 would demand a study of political science, social research, and investigative journalism. Both the pandemic and its response are parts of the same atrocity, requiring the critical attention of both academics and laypeople. Although it is important to engage with the psychological elements that help to create circumstances that result in mass atrocities, I believe we should not accept the psychologism that reduces totalitarianism to individual, or collective, neuroses. Totalitarianism is just as much a product of clear and cunning reason as it is permeated by anxiety and loneliness. Mass formation, as a dynamic, does not remove the possibility of pre-planned totalitarian measures.

Hughes, Kyrie and Broudy try re-politicise Desmet' theory and amend it with further psychological conditions, such as system justification. System justification describes cognitive prejudices that cause people to minimise or ignore the structural weaknesses of their society, driven by the desire to see one's social structures as legitimate, just, fair, and moral. Methods for system-justification include ignoring the facts, endorsing the status quo, blaming victims, and embracing views that uphold the system without question. System-justifying encourages assigning responsibility to victims, ignoring corruption and increasing a tolerance for civilian casualties during wartime.

Desmet, the paper argues, engages in a form of victim-blaming by holding people who are under the influence of mass formation responsible for their own weakness and deception. They may be the victims, but they are also the perpetrators. It seems that Desmet engages in system justification, to a degree, in his *The Psychology of Totalitarianism.* System justification, however, serves as an enticing and intellectually satisfying cloak, and it is argued that it enables the perpetrators of mass atrocities to remain unnamed and anonymous, as is also the case in Desmet's book.

By treating mass formation as a normal phenomenon that arises when intricate social systems arrange themselves, Desmet himself engages in moral disengagement. Using the "*agentless passive voice*" creates the morally disengaging idea that mass atrocities are being committed by unknown forces. They merely happen. Huges, Kyrie and Broudy argue that Desmet ignores the impact of propaganda and the mass media when discussing how mass formation develops, both historically and in our own time. They suggest his book also fails to cover the disastrous results of the pandemic countermeasures and the authoritarian way they were implemented.

Moral erasure is a psychological term that means when the pain of others is hidden from view, doing harm to them becomes easier. The world has currently become a petri dish for medical research, with over 5.5 billion people receiving experimental injections without any long-term safety information available. The public health policymakers knew in advance that worldwide lockdowns would have negative effects, including more emotional pain inflicted by governments to encourage behavioural changes. Critics have pointed out there is a higher prevalence of anxiety, depression, drug abuse, and complex grieving as a result of the lockdowns.

As well as the experimental vaccine trials during the Covid-19 pandemic, the population also underwent non-pharmaceutical interventions including social separation and universal masking, but Desmet's book avoids mentioning this. As Desmet himself notes, stress can lead to higher death rates, nevertheless, he ignores the possible repercussions of exposing the human population to artificially produced stress through lockdowns which could be characterised as a period of intense stress.

Desmet's focus ignores any analysis of the criminal mindset which is present in totalitarian regimes. His mass formation theory overturns any possibility of mass atrocity as a direct violation of the Nuremberg Code and a planned crime against humanity. The concept of mass formation introduced by Desmet implies a certain inevitability and innocence in the purposeful annihilation of a civilised society. As his critics point out, the slow takeover of civil society has been a key element in the US ever since the national security state was established in 1947. Complex grieving, substance abuse, despair, and anxiety all rose in frequency , yet Desmet's theory fails to tackle this troubling political history.

For Desmet, the transition from democracy to a totalitarian technocracy, with the coronavirus crisis acting as a major catalyst, happens without elite collusion or malicious motivation. This is surprising given that he also mentions the stress needed to convince people to accept transhumanism and intrusive bio-surveillance. There is a risk that applying the theory of mass formation to the reality of Covid-19 can encourage apathy among bystanders who do not hold their leaders accountable for the mass atrocities committed – in their name, supposedly. Desmet's attempt to reduce socio-political events to natural psychological patterns is, paradoxically, a hallmark of the mechanistic ideology he criticises.

Hughes has written extensively about a covert war on a civil society. Working behind the scenes with psychological warfare and the media, different US administrations have repeatedly broken international law and perpetrated war crimes. According to Huges and his co-authors, the United States is no longer a constitutional republic under the rule of law since Wall Street and large financial firms are free to engage in illegal activities without being held accountable by the law. Similarly, as long as it is done in the framework of covert intelligence collecting, the UK Coronavirus Act and the Covert Human Intelligence Sources (Criminal Conduct) Act allow the state to carry out illegal acts without being prosecuted in Britain.

The Covid-19 epidemic is a prime example of the disregard for legal norms. Under the rule of law, large pharmaceutical companies would be accused of domestic terrorism and of trying to coerce communities into getting the vaccine. That our own legal institutions are unable to address open and cruel violations of our basic rights is a clear indicator of a hostile takeover by totalitarianism.

By stressing the popular involvement in mass formation, Desmet's theory on the psychology of totalitarianism ignores the analysis of the criminal mindset of totalitarian administrations. This does not mean that the theory of mass formation encourages the acceptance of anarchy and the institution of totalitarian rule. The psychological approach advanced by Desmet still has a vital role to play in grasping the human propensity to disassemble into mass formation under certain conditions. Given what has happened, the obvious question it raises is, if mass formation as a phenomenon was understood long before Professor Desmet's excellent work, could they have created this human murmuration effect quite deliberately as a weapon to be deployed in parallel with Covid?

9

TOTALITARIANISM IN THE DIGITAL AGE

Totalitarian regimes have historically used technology to control and manipulate their populations, and the digital age presents new and unique challenges in safeguarding against such abuses of power. The rapid advancement of technology needs to be counterbalanced by constant vigilance to protect democratic values and individual freedoms. We can do this by prioritising transparency, accountability, and defining the ethical use of technology. By staying informed and actively participating in discussions about the impact of technology on our lives, we can work towards creating a future where technological advancements can serve the greater good.

It is self-evident that, unchecked, the rise of social media and surveillance technologies will exacerbate the reach and control of the totalitarian mindset. It seems that they have done this already. For example, the Bank for International Settlements (BIS), is planning for the absolute surveillance and spending control of programmable central bank currencies. By understanding the potential dangers of technology in the wrong hands, we need to take steps to protect our freedoms and privacy and to support civil society so we can collectively advocate for ethical and responsible use of technology. Abuses that include the creation of echo chambers, the censorship of the information we are fed, and their combined effects on our capacity for critical thinking need to be tackled.

The Colosseum, an architectural wonder, has symbolised the majesty and power of the Roman Empire since its original construction. It is a tribute to a society's interests, values, and entertainment preferences, as well as to ancient architectural genius. However, closer examination reveals a startling parallel between ancient Rome's sociocultural environment and today's digital age.

In AD 72, Emperor Vespasian authorised the construction of the Colosseum, initially known as the Flavian Amphitheatre. This massive structure, completed by his son Titus in AD 80 and later remodelled by Domitian, could accommodate more than 50,000 spectators. It grew into the focus of Roman public life, attracting individuals from all social classes to witness and participate in games that would be considered unnecessarily violent and brutal by today's standards. Gladiatorial bouts simulated naval battles, animal hunts, and public executions were commonplace, providing a visceral depiction of life, death, and the unpredictable nature of fate.

The Colosseum had a greater social purpose than just the immediate appeal of these events, however. It reinforced a sense of social cohesion and, more subtly, acted as a control mechanism. Juvenal, the Roman poet, famously stated the ruling class used "bread and circuses" (*panem et circenses*) to appease and divert the people's attention away from political unrest and the Empire's broader problems. The Patricians maintained control and avoided potential civic uprising by occasionally providing free grain and funding lavish theatrical spectacles. The dramas, discourses, and spectacles that internet platforms use to enthral modern society, are similar to those of the amphitheatre and, interestingly, both use thumbs up and down to decide the fate of its protagonists.

Furthermore, the Colosseum's activities were not solely for entertainment purposes, they were heavily reliant on embedded symbolism. Gladiatorial bouts, for example, represented military victories showcasing the strength of the Roman legions. These events also helped to establish a social order. While women, slaves, and the general people were sent to the upper decks, literally and metaphorically far away from the centre of power, the privileged snagged the best seats near the stage. The digital age has also divided society into categories. As in the Colosseum's central arena, influencers and prominent personalities frequently control the debate, while the greater userbase—the audience in this case—participates mainly as observers or as passive consumers. Likes, shares, and retweets are the modern equivalents of the Roman audience's acclaim, jeers, and cries; they create stories, and influence outcomes.

Digital platforms, like the Colosseum, perform two functions: they test and support societal acceptance. They can reinforce popular beliefs, but they can also provide a platform for dissident voices that was previously unavailable. Power relations on the Internet remain complex. The nobility of antiquity, or the present tech behemoths, wield disproportionate power over the narrative. The Colosseum represented a microcosm of Roman political, social, and cultural life, as well as a social standard and in the digital environment today, the similarities are evident. The platforms we utilise have a greater influence on our interactions, values, and impressions than we may realise. We, like the Romans, are caught up in the complicated dance of power, spectacle, and story, both as participants and as viewers.

Roman arenas and theatres were some of the primary gathering locations for large populations from various classes and backgrounds. The senatorial aristocracy, middle-class equestrians, and even slaves cheered together, uniting society through shared joys and sorrows. Not only were the recreated naval battles, lion fights, and gladiatorial competitions enjoyable, they were stunning, visceral demonstrations of the Empire's might. The capacity to summon men and beasts from across the realm to battle to the death in the heart of Rome was a strong symbol of imperial sovereignty. It demonstrated Rome's reach and riches.

These shows also had a crucial impact on the economy. Thousands of people worked there, including builders, custodians, merchants, gladiators, animal handlers, and charioteers. However, this economy had a dark component: the slave trade prospered thanks to the Colosseum. A vast number of gladiators were slaves, trained solely for combat, their blood spilling for the entertainment and profit of others. Today these roles are performed by bots.

Some of the staged events had deeper meaning. Triumphant general processions, war loot displays, and public executions of rivals all contained significant cultural and political messages. These rites established myths that favoured the ruling elite, defined heroes and villains, and imposed social behaviours. It was not enough to declare a senator as a traitor, he had to be publicly denounced, tarred and feathered. Arenas like the Colosseum caused much moral debate. Philosophers such as Seneca opposed the bloody contests, viewing them as a sign of Rome's moral decay. But these were moral games for the Roman masses, gladiators were believed to represent Roman honour, valour, and tenacity. Their willingness to face death served as both a lesson and a spectacle. The brutality was an essential part of life in Rome.

Emperors such as Augustus and Trajan created legacies by displaying their conquests in the arena. Later in the Roman Empire, particularly under Nero, arenas were used as sites of Christian persecution. Christians were either executed in mass or thrown to the beasts. Ironically, these actions, which were designed to display Roman control over a "threatening" religion, contributed to the popularisation and dissemination of Christian martyrdom.

Arenas fostered community despite their associated brutality. Locals established a common cultural and social identity as they cheered on their favourite gladiator, witnessed the excitement of a chariot race, or watched stories dramatized in the arena. These arenas were more than just brick and mortar structures, they were thriving cultural, political, and societal hubs, reminiscent of the complexity of the civilization that gave origin to them.

Though actual battle is absent in the digital sphere, ideological clashes happen regularly. On social media there are numerous debates that devolve into confrontations, abuse, and animosity, discourses that frequently take on symbolic importance. A popular hashtag or viral meme begins to represent broader social issues, and people engage in these online battles with the same zeal as ancient Romans would do for their beloved gladiators.

However, unlike their historical counterparts, contemporary platforms have the potential to democratise, as surely, after all, their origin is democratic and egalitarian? In theory, everyone has a voice on modern platforms, and the ancient arenas were essentially spectacles designed by the elite for popular consumption. Because of the adaptable power dynamics on the Internet, grassroots campaigns and organic movements that challenge the traditional ought to emerge, but the possibility for democratisation has many sides.

Where there are too many voices information overload occurs, and the value of individual speech is lost in an endless flood of tweets, updates, and postings. On top of this, the algorithms of modern platforms prioritise information that encourages user involvement, frequently bypassing complicated and nuanced debate in favour of dramatic or contentious content. Elites can buy their way into the conversation. Roman emperors routinely financed entertainment and sports to gain popular support and maintain social order. Similarly, if you pay the platforms enough, your sponsored posts go to the top of the feed. Voyeurism and the desire to enjoy public spectacle are centuries-old human characteristics. Sensational content, whether scandal, controversy, or public humiliation, is absorbed by modern users with the same elation that an ancient Roman could have had when viewing a gladiator's life-or-death struggle. Add in the overwhelming prevalence of facelessness and a toxic cocktail emerges. Platforms allow faceless participants to publish their thoughts, feelings, likes and dislikes of publicly identifiable people, without restriction, and they do so, frequently dripping in balefulness and hate. It is ubiquitous.

As you can see, even as circumstances and technology change, basic human instincts remain constant. Social media, video streaming services, online forums, and other modern digital platforms function as massive virtual arenas. They host a variety of spectacles, from meme culture's virality to heated debates in the comment sections. These are dynamic spaces where stories are told, identities are formed, and society's ideas are reflected and reinterpreted; they are not passive content repositories. Like the featured events in historic venues, the "trending" sections on platforms like X or YouTube illustrate what is now capturing people's attention. Where in ancient arenas, physical space limited the numbers in the audience, digital platforms transcend physical space and, even national boundaries. Because performances (whether tweets, films, or postings) may be watched, judged, and remarked on by a global audience, their universality enhances the spectacle. With this greater reach, the stakes rise since content creators are the new performers, fully aware of the vast, invisible audience they serve. The fast feedback loop enabled by likes, shares, comments, and reactions is the modern version of the cheers and jeers that once filled historic amphitheatres.

The design of computer systems, which are built around data analytics and algorithms, has a significant impact on the type and content of spectacle. By selecting material based on what the viewer wants, algorithms generate personalised newsfeeds that appeal to individual interests and preconceptions. Though it boosts user engagement, customisation traps users in echo chambers where the content they encounter reinforces their beliefs. Algorithmic determinism reduces the variety and unpredictability of traditional public displays. Instead of giving you a little bit of everything, sites like Facebook and X are designed to show you what you want – or rather, what you respond best to.

Another essential aspect of digital platforms as public spectacles is the democratisation of performance. In the past, only a few people could perform in arenas, but now, anyone with an internet connection can create content. Being a content-creator is much safer than being a gladiator, and in this crowded digital age, the pursuit of virality can lead to sensationalism, incorrect information, and a blurring of moral boundaries. Furthermore, the ephemeral nature of digital content—a viral success today may become a forgotten meme tomorrow—creates a persistent performance environment in which creators are constantly looking for the next big thing to capture people's attention. There is no time to linger on the importance of current event, there is always a need for something greater. If not greater, then at least novel, or more shocking.

Public figures—celebrities, politicians, influencers, and even viral sensations—have become the modern gladiators. They compete against each other for public opinion, global scrutiny, and celebrity status. The ever-changing rules and dynamics of digital platforms promote the artificial creation of petty rivalries and feuds.

Throughout history, gladiators were either volunteers, slaves, or prisoners of war who risked their lives in the pursuit of riches, freedom, or notoriety. Even though they are not as physically vulnerable as those of Ancient Rome, public figures now fight an ongoing battle in the digital arena for relevance, adulation, and, on rare occasions, redemption. These fights take place on social media, news websites, and other digital channels. Every tweet, photo, speech, and scandal is analysed, debated, and shared by a worldwide audience. Likes, shares, comments, and trends are the modern-day equivalents of ancient crowd replies in the rapid feedback loop. A mistake can cause someone to go viral for all the wrong reasons, yet a great message can elevate a well-known figure even further. As in Rome, a thumbs up or down can determine the remainder of one's life. A game-changing blog post, a viral video, or even a tweet can immediately make someone famous. This transformation also has benefits; it encourages diversity and gives voice to those who were previously silenced. However, this increases the turmoil in public opinion. The internet public's judgement is swayed by fads, algorithms, and fleeting emotions, so today's hero could be tomorrow's monster. Fame becomes a fleeting currency. Individuals dedicate their whole lives and careers to attain it, only to lose it in a day. The show must go on; the gladiatorial meatgrinder does not stop.

Digital platforms as public spectacles demonstrate the cyclical nature of human history, in which old structures and behaviours reemerge in new, technologically improved versions. With the internet's pervasive reach and instantaneity, today's digital Colosseums serve as spaces for performance, assessment, validation, and critique, evoking the spirit of the ancient public spectacle. Consumption is never without consequence. Our blind involvement in, and acceptance of, the digital Colosseum, foments the rise of totalitarianism precisely because it fosters a culture of docility and increases our susceptibility to manipulation into a mass formation.

The digital age has also presented us with the issue of permanence because previous statements, actions, or arguments can resurface at any time, necessitating accountability, reassessment, or, on rare occasions, forgiveness. This is paradoxical, since the digital age relies on rapidity and constant creation of novelties by content mills. Things are buried under new products and posts but never lost. The algorithmically driven digital Colosseum's design compels new digital gladiators to play to the gallery, select the optimal photo, and optimise for algorithmic prominence. Authenticity is a carefully designed and managed product.

All digital platforms—social media, video streaming, and e-commerce—use algorithms based on user engagement data to maximise user engagement and content consumption. A burst of likes, shares, and comments signals a post's popularity to an algorithm, driving it to more feeds, ensuring greater visibility, and multiplying its impact. On the other hand, content that receives less or more negative interactions may be degraded. Depending on the user, this algorithmic loop can either silence or amplify voices, transforming digital judgement mechanics into a powerful weapon. Winners tend to win while losers keep losing.

This automated assessment has a more sophisticated side. Even though algorithms are important, the significance of user psychology cannot be overstated. Liking anything extends beyond mere adoration. It can be a social connection tool (liking a friend's post to show support), an identity marker ("*This aligns with my beliefs, so I like it*"), or even a method of organising material for later use. Similarly, disagreement, apathy, and digital tiredness may be signified by a *dislike*. This method has issues, even though it is democratising. Content homogeneity can develop from the pursuit of likes when content creators cater to what they consider to be popular sentiment rather than genuine expression. This issue has only worsened with the widespread use of AI. Many pages, especially on Facebook, are automated to produce completely inauthentic and homogenous posts in large quantities, some pages are silos of mass produced and identical content that has no real value besides being real estate for advertisements.

There is a dangerous propensity among many users—particularly younger ones—to equate digital approval with self-worth. Seeking constant digital approbation has negative consequences for one's mental health. It leads to a disconnect between the offline and online worlds, especially when confronted with our seeming irrelevance in the real world despite having hundreds of friends and likes on social media.

Overall, digital appraising mechanisms are a double-edged sword. They carry risk of mental weariness, inauthenticity, and algorithmic silos, even though they provide previously unheard-of opportunities for exposure and involvement. Knowing these dynamics allows us to participate more intentionally as digital citizens; differentiating real from algorithmic rubbish and ensuring that our digital acts encourage, validate, and motivate others in the vast online arena. There is a stunning lack of responsibility and authenticity in these public arenas. This is partially because they are digital, but also because you can be faceless. People tend to become harsh, negative and overly critical when they believe there are no consequences for their actions. Once upon a time, communities gathered around campfires to share stories, sing songs, and look to each other for approval, laughter, or applause. Our stories are now online, our songs are on TikTok, and instead of campfires, we gather around bright screens. One thing remains timeless: our fundamental desire for approval. All of us seek approval, a sense of belonging, and recognition. In the present era, likes, shares, and comments are king. We must ask, what are the political implications of this need?

We are social beings, our ability to connect and integrate into social networks has traditionally been critical to our survival. Having the group accept and value you ensures your access to resources and safety. Our psychological constitution evolved over time in response to the need for social acceptability. Sociality is not a luxury or secondary characteristic; it is a means of surviving.

These basic social dynamics are mirrored on the internet and in the digital world, but on a scale that was previously inconceivable. Digital media has evolved into a tool for expressing one's identity, beliefs, achievements, and ambitions. Every tweet, video, or post reflects our desire for recognition. Every like provides a small confirmation that we are valuable, that our opinions are respected, and that we are included in society. The internet is so large and fast that it adds layers of complexity to these interactions. In contrast to in-real-life contacts, where validation is sometimes delicate and qualitative, online platforms provide unambiguous, hard measurements. When using the number of likes, retweets, or followers to measure acceptability or popularity, comparisons and rivalries are unavoidable. After all, it is a numbers game. Plain and simple.

Dopamine is a neurotransmitter, or a chemical messenger in the brain, that performs various vital roles in the body. Dopamine plays an important role in the reward system; it is released during pleasurable events and enhances feelings of delight and reinforcement, prompting a person to actively engage in specific activities that produce dopamine. It is essential for motivation and helps to explain human behaviour. Social media platforms are designed to induce dopamine release through multiple processes, producing a reward and reinforcement cycle that becomes addictive, especially for younger people. Each like, comment, or share results in a dopamine boost. This positive reinforcement drives users to share more content and seek additional social recognition. The unexpected nature of social media (not knowing which postings will be liked or shared) generates a gambling-like scenario in which users repeatedly check their accounts in expectation of a reward, a process known as variable-ratio reinforcement. Successful posts are emulated, whereas unpopular ones are avoided in the future. This is how our brains learn what to do online.

Social media frequently encourages comparison with other users, which can elicit both positive (when we believe we are doing well) and negative (when we believe we are failing) emotional responses. Both scenarios increase engagement as users aim for the dopamine hits associated with each perceived social achievement. Features such as the continuous scroll and video autoplay are intended to keep users engaged for extended periods of time. The limitless feed of new information keeps the dopamine flowing. Quick, regular incentives might impair the capacity to focus on things that do not bring instant fulfilment. Attention deficits are quickly becoming a new standard among the newer generations that are emersed in these applications. The social comparison enabled by digital media can cause emotions of inadequacy, anxiety, and depression. As time passes, we tend to prioritise social media engagement above personal interactions and obligations, hurting both our relationships and our own mental wellbeing.

The urge to present the best version of oneself online can lead to selective sharing, which involves exhibiting just the highs rather than the lows. Personal and business profiles are heavily curated to show the best version of someone. We call this our *best self,* but it is nothing more than a comical exaggeration of our good attributes with the suppression of everything else. This false presentation only further fuels the feelings of inadequacy. Comparisons with this well-constructed reality also fuel an inauthenticity cycle, where people further diverge from their true personality and strive to compare themselves to other inauthentic influencers.

Relying too heavily on validation received online leads to many problems. Fluctuations in online measurements cause anxiety, low self-esteem, and mood swings. Internal self-worth indicators become supplanted by external validation. The demand for approval leads people into echo chambers, where they only network with others who share their beliefs. This has important political consequences, as it can lead to increased social division and narrower worldviews. In essences, I believe social media tends to destroy our sense of self-worth and makes us reliant on external validation. When we are made to feel worthless, we are more prone to accepting leaders who give us a sense of value and direction.

Metrics such as likes, shares, and follows provide a clear, even addicting impression of our resonance in a vast digital environment filled with noise. These metrics signify a person's digital relevance. Gather enough, and you can rise above the din, become well-known, and possibly achieve digital immortality. One could argue they strengthen one's voice, provide approval, and boost one's sense of worth. They transform someone from a mere player on the virtual stage into a hero beloved and admired by a passionate audience. On the flipside, however, there is a depressing fact. Dependence on these metrics can lead to a vicious cycle of anxiety, self-doubt, and a distorted sense of oneself. When people's self-worth becomes dangerously linked to these fluctuating metrics, they begin to constantly seek digital approval, sometimes going beyond the realms of their personality to gain momentum. This can result in an online persona that is often very different from who the person truly is. Living with such a paradox may result in acute existential anguish and cognitive bewilderment. The true self and its digital representation are constantly vying for supremacy and the relentless pursuit of quantifiable popularity subtly damages the quality of human bonds. Quantity of likes, not quality of interaction is what matters in the digital age. Real human relationships risk being replaced by transactional ones when exchanges are quantified by metrics and reciprocity is based on mutual digital elevation rather than genuine emotional resonance.

For millennia, people have sought approval, fame, and admiration. However, the dynamics of social recognition are heightened and magnified in today's digital arena, with alluring benefits and frightening consequences. The stakes have gone up. This internet adoration becomes like a lighthouse, temporarily lifting the person above the never-ending clamour of online voices. As with all ascendible hierarchies and social stratification, the higher you go, the greater the fall. The same media outlets that promote approval may also emphasise criticism, exaggerate resistance, and broadcast condemnation. A single error, an ill-timed remark, or an unpopular position can rapidly change adulation into scorn. Online reactions are immediate and ubiquitous, so one can go from hero to pariah in a matter of seconds.

This oscillation has significant psychological consequences. Many people regard the digital world as an extension of themselves, a reflection of their individuality, rather than a foreign environment. As a result, the highs of digital approval can induce euphoria—the sensation that a large, anonymous number of people adore you. On the other hand, at its lowest, digital disparagement can plunge a person into a downward spiral of loneliness, stress, and self-doubt. On the Internet, all things are possible. We are made to live in a constant state of uncertainty and risk. Crucially, this fosters a cautious and conformist society which feeds into the suppression of dissenters who are perceived as a threat to tribal ideals, until there is full silence and unity of belief. It explains the successful enforcement of lockdowns, the glib acceptance of the so-called vaccines and the belief in the infallibility of leaders in public health science, bolstered by ubiquitous mainstream media punting and policed by online algorithms to shut down dissent.

Political Correctness or Language Policing?

For self-preservation, people self-suppress opposing views, manicure their online accounts, or parrot popular opinion even when it contradicts their genuine convictions. After all, hitting the like button is so easy. The echo chamber effect that emerges from such behaviour stifles diversity of thought and limits the depth of debate. A culture of docility is created through fear of exclusion and desire for recognition.

Political correctness represents a cultural effort to avoid language and acts that could potentially offend or marginalise specific groups of people. However, a closer look reveals that the word *political correctness* is itself a politically correct term, it conceals what is more appropriately described as language policing. The concept of political correctness arose in the late twentieth century as part of a larger push for greater social fairness and inclusion. Its supporters urge for the use of polite and inclusive language to promote equality and avoid any form of harm. For example, employing gender-neutral terminology such as "chairperson" rather than "chairman" avoids excluding women from recognition.

Despite its supposed noble intentions, political correctness is a euphemism that softens the image of what is ultimately a regulatory framework for language and behaviour. By framing the issue as one of correctness, it implies a binary division between right and wrong, acceptable and unacceptable. This dichotomy obfuscates the complexity and nuances of personal expression and culture. The word also implies we have a choice to conform with progressive values rather than admitting there are coercive methods behind these social "norms". Satirising powerful groups is certainly not politically correct, but morally, there are times where it can be the right thing to do .

The term *language policing* better describes the regulatory component of enforcing precise language and behavioural standards. Language policing entails monitoring, criticising, and restricting speech that deviates from what is deemed acceptable. It represents a concerted effort to control not only what is said, but how it is said, and to whom. Regulation of language goes beyond social disapproval to encompass institutional frameworks , workplace guidelines, and has legal repercussions. Language policing affects the whole of culture and public expression. Like most of the elitist progressive politics, it is aimed at creating an aura of benevolence without actually helping anyone. In more authoritarian settings, language policing is used as a mechanism of control that prevents public criticism of power. This is the implied threat we are facing from the so-called hate speech laws, which has the intention to send a cold chill through anyone that dissents.

Language policing employs a variety of tactics including social ostracism, complex institutional punishment, and digital surveillance. Social ostracism emerges as public shaming, cancel culture, and social media backlash, where those who defy the accepted standards face rapid and frequently brutal consequences. Institutional rules in businesses and educational institutions enforce codes of conduct that require politically correct language and behaviour, which may result in disciplinary punishment for noncompliance. In the digital realm, algorithms and content moderators on sites such as , YouTube and Facebook actively monitor and filter speech that is judged unsuitable or damaging.

While the ideal of creating a more respectful society is admirable, accomplishing it through strict control discourages open dialogue and the interchange of opposing viewpoints. Respect, inclusivity and fairness are nice values, but we must be suspicious of authorities that demand we sacrifice our most basic freedoms in exchange. Fear of retaliation or social marginalisation leads to self-censorship, people avoid discussing sensitive or complex matters entirely. This climate stifles intellectual development through lack of the vigorous debate required for a thriving democracy. Of course, this benefits the promoters of political correctness. The reasoning behind what is deemed acceptable language is rarely explained, it is a dogmatic codex that requires blind obedience and it comes with no surprise that it appeals to authoritarian personalities.

In his legendary work *1984*, George Orwell depicts the language police, or Newspeak authorities, as a powerful arm of the totalitarian state entrusted with regulating and manipulating language to serve The Party's interests. Newspeak is the official language of Oceania, the novel's fictional superstate, and its primary goal is to limit freedom of expression by eliminating words and notions that could potentially undermine The Party's power. Orwell saw language policing, particularly repressive government control of language, as a dangerous tool for stifling free thought and expression. The language police in *1984* are portrayed as highly organised and omnipresent, with the ability to punish people who transgress from the mandated, politically correct, rules of language . They continually monitor and regulate all types of communication including written text, speech, and even ideas. Language crimes are a heavy offence and are severely punished.

Newspeak is distinguished by its limited vocabulary and the removal of terms that could be utilised for subversive or rebellious reasons. for example, The Party replaces phrases like "freedom," "rebellion," and "revolution" with terminology like "thoughtcrime," "doublethink," and signs saying "Big Brother is watching you," to promote its ideology and control over the populace. Orwell's portrayal of language police in *1984* warns about the risks of nefarious linguistic manipulation and censorship in totalitarian countries. Power over language and thought shows a high level of established control that indicates something more than authoritarianism. Authoritarian regimes impose restrictions on what can be publicly expressed, but they are inept to stop thinking and private conversations. *1984* shows what happens to language under totalitarian rule: it becomes a way to access our private thoughts and control us from the inside. With Newspeak, the citizens of Oceania are not just afraid to speak their thoughts, they become unable to have thoughts at all. Orwell shows language manipulation as a form of mind control, demonstrating how The Party employs it to shape people's perceptions and suppress opposition.

Orwell's critique of language extended beyond *1984*. He identified and criticised already present political distortions of language in the British Empire, particularly the deterioration of language in political speech. He emphasised the fact that confusing and euphemistic language is routinely used by politicians to conceal the truth and manipulate public opinion. Beyond highlighting the destructive power of rhetoric, Orwell highlights the importance of verbal clarity and precision as well as resisting the desire to conceal meaning with jargon. As he illustrated with his book, language policing is not just a type of authoritarian control that harms democracy and individual liberty, it can become totalitarian and destroy the history, culture, creativity and freedom of a whole society. Language should be used to communicate and express ideas, not to coerce or manipulate others, but this ethical ideal is routinely ignored in contemporary politics and public spaces.

Language policing in practice is a risky business and not foolproof. People can resist or evade censorship by using coded language, euphemisms, or alternative modes of communication. Despite what Orwell said, unclear and deceptive language is sometimes the only way to express oneself authentically. Furthermore, attempts to control language may elicit opposition or backlash, particularly if regarded as too restrictive or overbearing. People are generally ready to alter their speech to some extent out of respect or politeness, but there are clear boundaries. Language policing also has unforeseen repercussions, such as driving dissent underground, fuelling animosity, or resulting in a loss of linguistic variety and complexity. These last two, variety and complexity, are not welcome by the totalitarian who seeks to foster a culture of fear and self-censorship by actively suffocating open discussion and creativity to create a culture of docility. Docility implies a substantial simplicity and uniformity. But totalitarianism requires a language full of spectacle, not substance.

The potential success of language policing is determined by a variety of elements, including the context in which it is performed, the scope of enforcement, and the objectives of those carrying it out. In the short term, language policing can be effective controlling public speech and shaping political views, particularly in online environments and certain organisational settings.

Algorithms can be effective mechanisms of language policing by restricting certain words or ideas and encouraging specific linguistics, thereby creating the illusion of conformity and agreement. This short-term approach doesn't fundamentally alter our cognitive and social capabilities, however, language policing can have a long-term impact on individual and social norms and behaviour. When specific terminologies are constantly reinforced, and transgressions are punished or discouraged, people internalise them and govern their own language accordingly, even in the absence of direct enforcement. This is the dream of totalitarianism, the complete internalisation of Orwell's Big Brother style surveillance.

Language is so much more than an exterior expression; it is a gateway to our inner self, our thoughts and our creativity as human beings. Hence the need for totalitarian governments to control it. Arendt investigated the function of language in totalitarianism, emphasising its relevance as a tool for manipulation and control in totalitarian institutions. She did not talk directly about language policing but believed that totalitarian regimes use a distorted form of language to impose a unified and seemingly inevitable viewpoint on society, resulting in a false reality in which opposition is stifled and individual autonomy destroyed.

Language Distortion

In her book, Arendt describes the propaganda tactic of totalitarian dictators, particularly Hitler and Stalin, who used the guise of infallibility and prediction to justify their political plans of action. By presenting their plans as prophetic announcements they manipulated the public perception and created a sense of inevitability. Hitler's speech from 1939, where he prophesied the annihilation of the Jewish race in Europe, actually was a declaration of his intention to wage war and commit genocide. Similarly, Stalin, in a 1930 speech, described his political opponents as representatives of "dying classes," foreshadowing their coming physical liquidation. In both cases, the tactic serves two purposes: first, it gives the impression that the dictators' actions are predetermined by historical or natural forces absolving them of responsibility; second, it serves as a retrospective justification once the actions are carried out. Their prophecy later becomes an alibi, allowing them to claim that the events were inevitable and, thus, not their fault. Such totalitarian propaganda strategies are only feasible and effective once totalitarian movements with authoritarian leaders have taken control. The method of infallible prediction shows the ultimate goal of world conquest, as all lies and predictions can only be realised in a world completely controlled by the dictator. This shows us something crucial about totalitarianism: it has to be *total.* Total control is not just its goal, but also its method. It needs control over everything so that nothing can contradict it. By guaranteeing triumph and success regardless of momentary failures, these regimes provide individuals willing to be integrated into larger, all-powerful forces with a sense of security and certainty. Whether the Nazis shaped legislation based on heredity or the Bolsheviks exploited economic forces as historical judgements, both regimes promised victory and success in any cause or business, appealing to the abstract desire for triumph .

Prophetic language distortion is not limited to fully developed totalitarianism. It is all around us. Vladimir Putin, Russia's enduring President, has frequently used rhetoric that portrays him as a strong and resolute leader, critical to Russia's stability, rebirth and historical importance. Putin's language about the Ukraine war frequently portrays Russia's activities as defensive responses to foreign threats and measures to defend ethnic Russians and Russian-speaking minorities in Ukraine. But this is not all; he also sees his invasion of Ukraine, the so-called "special military operation", as an act of historical rectification. According to this logic, Putin is not waging war against a smaller neighbouring country; he is simply correcting historical accidents. The fact that he has to use force is due only to Ukrainian unreasonableness. Putin, however, has an arguable position when he mines under the breach of historic agreements that limited NATO expansion eastwards after the collapse of the Iron Curtain. He is correct from a strategic defence perspective to resist NATO on his southern flank. Putin has used prophetic language in a number of ways. For instance, he justified his continued central position through language that presents him as the only saviour of Russia from the chaos of the 90s. Why is Putin the only person who can lead and save Russia? Well, it might have something to do with the fact that all the alternatives are jailed, dead, bribed or intimidated. Putin may be lying when he says that he is Russia's only saviour, but he is slowly turning this lie into reality. What he prophesied in the 90s is slowly being realised through his open use of censorship, political suppression and assassination.

Language policing is routinely used in Russia to regulate public speech and crush opposition. Russia has strict rules that criminalise extremist speech, a wide term that is frequently used to target political opponents and government critics. Because of their ambiguity, these laws can be used flexibly and randomly in order to stifle opposing viewpoints, limit freedom of expression and create a paranoid political atmosphere. The Russian government has also passed rules to monitor internet information, such as social networking sites and messaging apps. These regulations require platforms to store user data within Russian borders and to comply with government demands to remove content that is illegal or damaging to national interests. Again, since "national interests" is a loose term, no one is safe, and everyone is subject to potential persecution.

The Russian government controls much of the mainstream media and often bans anything that criticises it or supports the opposition. This has escalated with the war in Ukraine. Independent journalists and media outlets endure threats, intimidation, and even imprisonment for covering difficult topics. Covering the war unfavourably has become a risk that no one, aside from several independent bloggers, is willing to take. Part of Putin's plan to reinvigorate the Russian identity and empire has been the erasure of differences and diversity within Russian borders. The Russian government has passed laws that limit LGBTQ+ advocacy and expression, including one that prohibits "propaganda of nontraditional sexual relations" among children. This regulation is used to restrict LGBTQ+ content and silence activists who support LGBTQ+

rights. Corrupt oligarchs are seen as beneficial partners, but minorities are dangerous traitors or infiltrators.

Contemporary examples of language policing can also be found in various other contexts and are by no means limited to Russia. Language policing happens right here at home; in government offices, corporate environments, educational facilities, social media platforms and political movements and is slowly becoming a widely accepted practice.

Governments continually pass laws or regulations prohibiting particular types of words that are judged rude, hateful, or politically incorrect. Hate speech laws in numerous nations seek to prohibit the use of rhetoric that supposedly incites violence or prejudice against specific groups based on traits such as race, religion, or sexual orientation. An increasing number of companies have codes of conduct or diversity and inclusion policies in place that restrict language use in the workplace. These policies may appear to restrict discriminatory language, harassment, or offensive humour while encouraging courteous communication among employees, yet the practices are difficult to judge because their idealistic goal, preventing harm to minorities and marginalised groups, seems justified. More often than not, these rules are often used for other means, and perverted into a mechanism of control.

Social media networks such as Facebook, X and YouTube have community guidelines and content moderation procedures in place to manage user-generated content. These guidelines frequently restrict what they think is hate speech, harassment, and other forms of harmful or abusive language. The rules may be enforced via automated filters or human moderators. Again, there seems to be nothing wrong with this in theory, but in practice, these guidelines are implemented selectively to adhere to the so-called common good. Paradoxically, hateful content drives engagement and captures attention. Let's be frank, social media platforms do not care about determining what is actually hateful and what is not, because they have no interest in stopping the cash cow that is hate-fuelled online activity.

Activist groups and social justice movements frequently engage in language policing to encourage inclusive and respectful discourse while challenging language that promotes stereotypes or marginalises specific groups. This includes the use of gender-neutral language, raising awareness about ableist or racist language, or pointing out examples of cultural appropriation. Most of this "activism" happens online and is usually political in a superficial sense, it boils down to using certain language and signifiers in order to craft a favourable online identity.

Some of these organisations have adopted policies requiring the use of gender-neutral pronouns like "they/them" rather than traditional binary pronouns like "he/him" or "she/her." In certain situations, gender-neutral language campaigns have resulted in the modification of classic literature or historical writings to replace gendered pronouns with gender-neutral equivalents. Some radical proponents of gender-neutral language demand the complete eradication of gendered terminology from language, even when the term has been traditionally accepted and has no negative implications. Terms like mother and father should be replaced, it is said, with gender-neutral alternatives like parent or caregiver.

WHITEWASHING, another form of language policing, refers to the practice of altering or suppressing information, events, or historical narratives to portray a sanitised version of reality. It entails the intentional omission or manipulation of facts to present a false or incomplete image of previous events or societal issues. Typically, the deeds of the powerful require the most whitewashing, especially if those powerful persons appear on our banknotes or hold other prestigious positions. History is frequently whitewashed to minimise or eliminate controversial or uncomfortable aspects of the past. Governments censor and rewrite textbooks to downplay their role in previous crimes, or to promote a more positive national story. Whitewashing is also common in the media, as news organisations or government agencies distort information to shape public opinion or pursue a specific agenda. This can include censoring news reports, manipulating photographs or footage, or disseminating propaganda.

Whitewashing is a form of agnogenesis, or ignorance creation, and it happens before our eyes all too often. Two derivative forms of whitewashing present in the West are *greenwashing* and *pinkwashing*. Pinkwashing is the deceptive practice of corporations or organisations utilising support for LGBTQ+ causes or feminism as a means of marketing products or increasing support. These practices utilise progressive language while also engaging in actions that usually damage LGBTQ+ people and women. For example, a firm might sponsor a Pride parade or event to appear supportive of women's rights while neglecting issues like employment discrimination or the gender pay gap. Pinkwashing can also occur at the governmental level when politicians or governments utilise support for LGBTQ+ rights to divert attention away from other concerns or to boost their international image. Governments engage in pinkwashing by emphasising their support for LGBTQ+ rights while ignoring or prolonging human rights violations against LGBTQ+ people. Corporations have accepted pinkwashing as a marketing strategy. Far from preaching progressive values, companies utilise support for LGBTQ+ people for their own profit. This is quite easy to see: go to any social media platform during Pride Month (June) and look up the regional accounts of any major company. A clear and distinct trend emerges. The regional accounts corresponding to markets where LGBTQ+ rights are already accepted all have a rainbow flag in their logos. Pinkwashing is a way of abusing genuine commitment to causes in order to push political agendas and promote products.

Greenwashing is a similar trick, it refers to the practice of using misleading or false claims about their environmental practices or products to appeal to environmentally conscious consumers. Companies advertise a product as eco-friendly without providing any evidence to support these claims. Some companies in the oil and gas industry have been accused of greenwashing by promoting themselves as environmentally responsible while continuing to engage in environmentally harmful practices such as fracking or offshore drilling. More recently, major carbon emitters, energy companies, have rebranded themselves as environmental champions. They engage in greenwashing by renaming, rebranding, or repackaging products to convey a false impression of being natural, harmless or chemical-free.

Even ExxonMobil, the company responsible for spilling 11 million gallons of crude oil in 1989, has a page on their website where they express their approach to sustainability. Coca-Cola, the number one plastic polluter in the world, has also expressed concerns about pollution – but has announced that it has no plans to discontinue the use of plastic bottles. Automobile, fashion and food companies are also at fault here. The term, "save the environment" originated in the 1960s when the hotel industry encouraged guests to reuse towels to "save the environment," however, it was to primarily to reduce their laundry costs.

Whitewashing, pinkwashing and greenwashing are just three examples of language distortion that organisations, both private and public, use to promote a better image of themselves. As much as language is policed and restricted, it is equally distorted and misused. Words are either forbidden or evacuated of all meaning. We associate authoritarianism with language policing, but language distortions are an equally important part of totalitarianism.

Individuals or collectives also use language distortion to create false meanings that benefit them. Hermeneutics is the philosophical discipline that deals with interpretation and understanding, and Hermeneutical injustice, a term coined by the philosopher Miranda Fricker, refers to situations in which people have been wrongfully stripped, or prevented, of the cultural and linguistic means of understanding their social position and environment, and the ability to communicate their experiences to others. Language policing and distortions perpetuate hermeneutic injustice because specific experiences or viewpoints are marginalised or removed from the mainstream narrative, preventing people from properly interpreting and communicating social reality, resulting in misunderstandings, misinterpretations, or dismissals. In extreme cases, such as in Orwell's *1984,* hermeneutical injustice comes from the complete abolition of certain words. Big Brother abhors words like "freedom" and "independence" because the regime does not want the residents of Oceania to interpret themselves as free and independent.

Miranda Fricker's book, *Epistemic Injustice,* identifies both testimonial injustice and hermeneutical injustice as two important forms of epistemic injustice, where epistemology is the philosophical theory of knowledge. Fricker coined the term testimonial injustice to describe the experiences that women and minorities face in many situations, but chiefly within the legal system. Fricker takes the example of the classic American novel *To Kill a Mockingbird* as a paradigm case of testimonial injustice. Specifically, the jury's prejudice against Tom Robinson interests Fricker as a social epistemologist. In the story, a fully white jury finds the maimed Robinson guilty of a crime he could not commit. The obvious truth of the situation did not fit the jurors' racist prejudice and stereotypes of Black people, and Tom Robinson`s testimony is deemed false, and rejected. Frickerclaims bias conditions a person`s ability to know things, or accept new knowledge. Testimonial injustice occurs because the hearer cannot accept the speaker's testimony as fact – not out of valid epistemic reasons, but because of the prejudicial bias of the hearer and the identity of the speaker.

Testimonial injustices happen all the time due to prejudices based on identity such as race and gender, occupation and class. Basing your distrust in someone on the basis of a past experience of their particular actions can be justified, it is not unreasonable to believe a person who has lied repeatedly before is lying to us now. However, basing distrust on the basis of identity alone is unacceptable, both ethically and epistemologically. The deficit of credibility that certain groups suffer requires them to exert themselves additionally (or over-prove), to attain a normal level of credibility. We do not hold the same standards to everyone.

You can see it with certain privileged groups or respected individuals, who's testimony is automatically elevated above others, giving them inherently more credibility for no reason other than their social status. The white woman who accuses Tom Robinson of a crime in *To Kill a Mockingbird* is precisely such a person. Her testimony, as a white person in America in those times, is accepted without question. Many respected people in society are given too much credibility, such as politicians, CEOs, influences, scientists, etc... Society encourages us to elevate these types of people above all doubt due to their success in one field. It seems we have an innate tendency to assume fairness and associate success with celebrity. So, if someone seems accomplished, they must know their stuff and we should believe them. Of course, celebrity does not mean competency, and success is in one arena of life is not a reliable way to determine a person's integrity.

To learn things means you must be actively and practically engaged in the world. It also implies you have the ability to be social and learn from, and can relate to others. Understanding this epistemic dimension of our lives and our tendency to bias based on cultural prejudices is crucial for any democratic or emancipatory project as it undermines us as epistemic agents and as whole human beings. To be a good listener and avoid testimonial injustice, we must accept others as fully capable – until they are proven otherwise. We must better develop critical thinking skills to help us determine who is deserving of credibility, and who is not. The last thing we need is for government officials, propagandists or commercials to tell us what and who to believe.

It is true that some people are cognitively limited, lacking the words, ideas, symbols and opportunities required to express themselves, both as individuals and as a collective. Fricker focuses mainly on racial and sexist injustices, but minorities and women are not the only victims of this hermeneutical injustice. A whole culture can suffer, for example a colonized nation which had it's language, religion and customs erased and undermined. They cannot understand themselves as they once did, and much of their culture becomes lost. Hermeneutical injustice illustrates the lack of "resources" that are required in order to form any kind of understanding. Cultural concepts, the richness of meanings, indigenous symbols, certain texts, songs and slogans. All of these are resources which help us interpret and understand our own experiences and the experiences of others. Of course, the significance of these resources change over time. Some are rejected or relegated, others accepted or reinvented. The important thing is that a culture, in the most general sense, offers people different ways to understand themselves, their environment and other people. Culture helps us to make sense of the world and our place in it.

Totalitarianism strives to limit understanding and to reduce us to one dimension, therefore it necessarily leads to, and relies upon various hermeneutical injustices. This can mean banning whole words and concepts, as in the book *1984*. It can also mean forbidding certain slogans and symbols, or burning richly cultural books, as they did in Nazi Germany.

Hermeneutical injustices have been happening in the background throughout history, infiltrating themselves into our psyche, and their importance should not be overlooked. The conception of the idea of race, and that one race is superior to another, for example. Race distinctions, particularly in the case of Black and Native Americans, have been forced upon entire continental populations at the expense of their own cultures and modes of self-interpretation. Through enslavement, destruction of socialisation processes and forms of education, to cultural genocide and human genocide (for millions of inhabitants of North America), countless cultures, languages, interpretations and knowledge have been lost. Those that survived this destruction have often been marginalised and shunned. Yet being in the majority does not guarantee immunity to hermeneutical injustice, with the rise of 21st century totalitarianism, there is a real possibility that this form of injustice will continue to spread .

The wonderful thing about culture is that it is never finished; we are always creating new stories, new art and new ways to interpret our world. It is exactly this that upsets totalitarianism; it seeks to establish total control, but the dynamism of human creativity and culture prevents it from solidifying. This is why Totalitarianism may have its own pseudo-culture of docility, but it is one-dimensional, sterile, static and most importantly: controllable. There is no room for self-understanding and genuine communication in the culture of docility and this is exactly what hermeneutical injustice describes.

10

THE RISE OF SPECTACULAR SCIENCE

TRUTH IS war's first casualty.

Technology platforms, fact-checkers and the mainstream media quite clearly can be captured, and science can be purchased with grants and supports. Once venerated repositories of peer-reviewed studies can be whitewashed. The World Health Organisation targets misinformation and disinformation as the primary enemy of its Pandemic Agreement, and deplatforms and attacks those offering counter science using its main tool of propaganda, the mainstream media and same said fact checkers, we are experiencing an information war.

In practice, as we have learned from the UNIPCC leaked emails; once believed to be infallible, we have proof that science *can* be corrupted if there is enough power and money at stake. Editors and contributors from leading medical journals are not immune from its effects.

Integrity within science means the rigor, reliability, credibility, and vastness of scientific methodology and research is designed to seek truth, and is not altered to favour specific, desired results. Our idea of science has always been that which upholds and exemplifies its own values. Scientific hypotheses and theories are supposed to be falsifiable, meaning they can be tested and potentially proven wrong, through empirical observations or experimentation. Falsifiability is essential to distinguish what is true. When we think of science, we assume that there is careful experimental design, proper controls, adherence to the sources, contextual interpretation, accurate data collection and statistical analysis. In order to be rigorous, science **must** have established and transparent methods. Researchers are also expected to provide detailed descriptions of their methods and make their data openly available for scrutiny and replication by other scientists. This is the true nature of true science! Where appropriate, scientific research undergoes a peer review, where other experts in the field critically evaluate the research, oftentimes anonymously, before it is deemed publishable in reputable scientific journals. Peer review ensures the quality and validity of research within a field. Through peer review, a scientific community maintains high standards through constant self-criticism and self-evaluation. Scientific discoveries should also be reproducible; meaning that other scientific researchers should be able to independently replicate similar results using the same methods and data provided by the original researchers. Reproducibility strengthens the confidence in the validity of the findings – however, this is not always feasible. For instance, large-scale social research that requires help from the state is rarely reproducible. Scientists conducting any kind of research must be transparent and disclose their methodology – even if their results are not feasibly reproducible.

Experts in a particular field often gather to form a consensus around particular scientific issues. While this does not guarantee certainty, it gives the scientific community an agreed benchmark upon which they can base further research. Scientific consensus can also rely on meta-studies which aim to show the overall results of research in a field; abstracting out details from many research papers in the same field, to reaching general conclusions. These traits all characterise and form what I would call "Sound Science", or science with integrity. Yet as we have seen, what passes for science now, has become a social endeavour which is prone to many shortcomings and forms of corruption. One of these corrupted forms is what I call "Spectacular Science". It is opposed to sound science, because it, covertly or openly, has a different goal: the maintenance of a culture of docility. Because of this, spectacular science is not simply bad science – it has its own agenda, and standards.

Those carrying out Spectacular Science are not inherently opposed to the scientific principles as I laid out, they follow them, but only to the extent they have to, in order to accomplish their real goal. Spectacular scientists offer popularity as a substitute for thought, and usually carry an excess of confidence as a way of covering up a lack of knowledge, using casual lying as a response to criticism.

Spectacular Science is the product of a certain kind of politics - knowledge is power, and so is ignorance! Spectacular Science is necessary for the political elites, so they can maintain the semblance of authority they have assumed for scientific reasons. They produce all kinds of spectacles, not just scientific, to create a cultural environment of ignorance within society, which as we have seen, is a hermeneutic injustice. Spectacular Science is an instrument of an outdated form of politics that most thought was extinct: totalitarianism. Totalitarianism in our century is only possible by creating a society of illusion and docility. Throughout the so-called pandemic, time and time again, public health authorities and political leaders quoted from a science that they knew, or ought to have known, was neither sound, nor truthful. It was never the truth that the covid vaccines would stop transmission. It was never the truth that the spike protein would not go beyond the injection point. It was never the truth that taking the covid vaccine would prevent infection. This Spectacular Science that was presented to us by those in power became dogma, and, ultimately, was deployed to vilify and demonise the unvaccinated, who were treated as lepers once were, precluded from social access and viewed as carriers of a live infection.

The political elites projecting and staging spectacular science are not suited to a modern democratic and liberal society. In order to attain and maintain power, they distort all aspects of society through their own kind of spectacular science to create a culture that aligns with their own vision. This is a culture where docility is established as the only legitimate way to address large and consequential societal problems: the elites decide, and we accept without question. When culture is made docile, it becomes passive and loses its creativity and spontaneity – it is unable to criticize, create and offer new possibilities. The everyday life in a culture of docility is shaped by politicians who would like to be intellectuals, and intellectuals who would like to be politicians.

Culture is our shared conceptual and symbolic framework through which we express ourselves, and how we understand the world. Without a flourishing and active culture, we cannot imagine or communicate alternative scenarios and new possibilities for living. Culture is our most precious terrain and the most intrinsic field of resistance.

A narrowing of culture through trained docility could eventually produce a society that is unable to resolve various social problems, meet its own material needs, maintain a stable natural environment and raise healthy individuals. Inevitably, such conditions lead to a potential collapse into authoritarianism and, potentially, totalitarianism. The culture of docility, because it diminishes imagination and the will to act, is a systematic producer of misfortune.

If cultural and social values, alongside competing perspectives about reality, are not considered in open discussion, there is neither a public nor a culture. The public that cannot grasp cultural, economic and scientific issues accepts its own insignificance and its inability to understand the basic issues of everyday life. To be sure, many issues are technical and require professional expertise, but the public is not some uneducated mass, and has the potential to be a body of well-informed and conscious citizens. We value science informers and popularisers; the public wants to know, and likes to seek the advice of experts. The important thing here, is that the public, ideally, asks for guidance but does not forfeit its right of judgment. The public has a right to question everything, yet this right is basically non-existent if the people it questions are already captured by the regime. Restricting the flow of information to the public deliberately putting a stamp of approval on the decisions of elites and experts, is a sure pathway to creating a non-democratic society. Debate in a docile public sphere are conducted for the sake of empty argumentation, verbal competition, petty drama and maximal viewership – in a single word: for the sake of spectacle. They become an expression of doctrinal fervour and proud thoughtlessness – a manifestation of speech without content. The whole purpose of the public in a culture of docility is to speak meaningfully as little as possible and to listen and obey as much as possible.

False openness, false solidarity, false cultural value, false multiculturalism, false authenticity, false publicity... These are all characteristics of the farcical nature of a culture of docility. Anyone who deviates from the track defined by those in control poses a danger of being marginalised from society. This is when the culture of docility spawns conflict in its original sense, the culture then creates their proverbial enemy deserving of public brutality. The public become primed to confront anything that represents a potential threat to the culture of docility and its servile values.

People who embrace an open culture for all of its beauty do not fear an internal struggle because they have faith in their own strength. They encounter and create new possibilities because they are not afraid, and can embrace change and the unexpected. The culture of docility, on the other hand is fundamentally controlled by a fear and uncertainty in its own strength. Deep down, the people in it know what it is, they know that it cannot survive in openness. Everything new, different and uncontrollable is seen as a threat.

Universities in cultures of docility use citations (references to other people's work) as a measure of the quality of their own scientific works. A Spectacular Scientist may have dozens of citations, while never referencing a single scientific paper or text outside of their own circle. Academic disciplines often operate this way, with researchers primarily interacting with colleagues within their own field. This leads to isolated groups within the larger scientific community. These academic silos produce a lack of exposure to alternative perspectives or interdisciplinary insights, reinforcing the perpetuation of accepted theories within specific disciplines. Spectacular Science is one such academic silo; a repository of claims which have not been challenged to any great extent. The scientific community is a social group like any other, subject to the same emotions, interests, miscommunication and mistakes. Our disenchantment with science, spectacular or not, begins with the realisation that scientific credibility is based on mutual citation among popular scientists who may be working to an approved agenda that serves some higher order. Where there is no healthy criticism, where scientists cannot be challenged, then there is no science.

All of this context is necessary in order to understand how bad science and self-serving agendas can persist within scientific communities and universities. Although my interest is in spectacular science and its influence on culture and the public, all of these points apply all forms of science. Since the scientific community has its own subculture of docility, it is affected by inertia. Once a particular idea or theory becomes established within a scientific community or academic discipline, it can be difficult to dislodge, even in the face of overwhelming contradictory evidence. People who have taken credit and kudos for accepted theories that form a backbone of scientific thinking are too comfortable in their hierarchy, and do not want to be challenged. They take advantage of the humans tendency for inertia, which happens in all other social spheres as well including culture, art, politics and technology . It is a sort of mood or approach that is too comfortable with itself, and lacks the will or desire to innovate, actively shutting down anyone that questions it. When science becomes docile, it paves the way for more a robust and active spectacular science.

Institutional incentive structures within universities and research institutions prioritises the publication of research that aligns with established paradigms or popular theories – or, indeed, with specific commercial interests, the UN IPCC is a prime example. This pressure to conform to the prevailing norms can discourage researchers from pursuing alternative hypotheses or challenging existing theories. Research funding is often directed toward projects that align with mainstream scientific paradigms or address popular research topics. As a result, innovative ideas or alternative theories that challenge the status quo struggle to secure funding, limiting the opportunities for their exploration and validation. Just like the dollar outweighs the vote in democracy, the dollar overrides the discoveries of sound science. Remember, from 2020 to 2022, despite rampant money printing directly into the veins of the economy, not a single Irish economic scientist, academic or journalist published a paper warning of the inevitability of excessive inflation. Not one. Think about what that says about a culture of docility.

Scientists, like all other human beings, exhibit confirmation bias, the tendency to favour the information and data that confirms our existing beliefs, at the expense of evidence that contradicts them. This bias can lead researchers to interpret new data in ways that support outdated theories or ignores evidence that challenges established ideas. Confirmation bias is present everywhere, and I will address how it influences other parts of society (and how it helps totalitarian tendencies) as well as how to counter it. Confirmation bias is a psychological mechanism and cannot be easily sidestepped, rather, it must be habitually exposed and taken into consideration. Since confirmation bias cannot be effectively eliminated, it must at least be made clear.

Besides inertia, funding and confirmation bias, we have to deal with academic conservatism. Scientists exhibit intellectual conservatism when they adhere to established theories rather than entertain new or unconventional ideas. This conservatism is reinforced by peer pressure within academic communities, where dissenting voices may be marginalised or ostracised. Academia is usually seen as a source of constant progress and innovation, but this is true only in a limited sense. As we have seen with science, academia has its own idea of progress, one might say a tradition of progress, that it adheres to. It tries to conserve this tradition of progress against alternative viewpoints and deflect criticism.

Academic teaching tends to emphasise the transmission of established knowledge and theories rather than teach critical inquiry or exploration of alternative perspectives. This traditional approach to education perpetuates outdated ideas and discourages students from questioning established beliefs. It is the mechanism of academic conservatism, where academic conservatism perpetuates its own bad ideas at the expense of better alternatives. Ideally our goal should be to conserve our best cultural accomplishments and abandon the harmful ones, and to do this we need clear standards. This is why transparency, critical thought and democracy are important. They should be the standards by which we judge what is worth conserving, not petty emotions, dogmatism and private interests.

A culture of docility combined with academic conservatism cannot be a good base for any kind of decent science. The academics want to show they're doing a good job, and the docile want to be fooled and amused in order to maintain their innocent servility. Spectacular science rises to meet this demand, for example using red heat maps to denote temperatures deemed excessive across regions, whereas the same maps used before the era of spectacular climate science, often reported higher numbers but were absent of the 'scary' deep red tints, presenting weather as normal.

Spectacle works because the culture allows it to work. Ideally, critical thinking, cultural creativity and sound science must crush dangerous illusions. It is not enough to criticise and expose the lunacy of spectacular science, we must nip it in the bud by combating docility, declaring it an unacceptable cultural value.

GROUPTHINK IS a psychological phenomenon that occurs within a group of people, when the need for conformity and docility in a group results in irrational or dysfunctional decision-making. It may be a misnomer as it has little to do with thinking, rather, it is collective irrationality. This irrationality can be dangerous for the group itself, and its dissenters. In the context of science, groupthink happens when scientists within a particular field stick too closely to a prevailing consensus or dominant paradigm, stifling dissenting viewpoints or alternative hypotheses.

Before the entire Irish banking system collapsed on foot of the property bubble burst, critical economic analysis was attacked by the Irish Taoiseach Bertie Ahern, Government parties, banks, developers and investors alike. Everyone was getting rich on rising property values, anyone from accountants to lawyers were in on the game. A quarter of the Irish economy depended upon the denial of a credit bubble even in the face of outlandish expansion in consumer credit, pitching Ireland into the top ranks of excessive credit globally. Academics, with a few exceptions, stayed quiet, including those within the Central Bank, as they knew which side their bread was buttered on. Scientists are no different and feel the pressure to conform to the prevailing beliefs or theories within their field in order to gain acceptance, funding and recognition. This pressure, whether active or passive, can discourage individuals from expressing dissenting opinions or pursuing alternative lines of research. Our old friend, confirmation bias, also reappears here. This confirmation bias can reinforce the existing group consensus and impede the consideration of alternative explanations.

Other group dynamics, such as the need for cohesion or avoidance of conflict, can influence decision-making within scientific communities. Scientists, like all human beings, are attached to group coherence through positive and negative emotions. The need for cohesion is exemplified through pride and ease. When our group is coherent, it is strong and resilient, and we are proud of the fact, and at ease. It is possible that scientists safeguard a consensus because it shows the coherence of their community and contributes to their feelings of pride and ease.

Novel ideas can be accepted or rejected by influential members of the scientific community, however the support of a specific idea might encourage groupthink by stifling other viewpoints. Furthermore, scientists may be persuaded to adopt the dominant consensus view despite conflicting data with pressure coming from institutional constraints such as financial incentives or chances for career development which can obstruct sincere scientific research and advancement. Here is a classic example from medical history: Hungarian physician Ignaz Semmelweis.

In the mid-19th century, Semmelweis observed that the cases of puerperal fever (a deadly illness affecting women after childbirth, more commonly called postpartum infection) were significantly higher in maternity wards staffed by doctors compared to those staffed by midwives. He hypothesised that the difference might be due to doctors performing autopsies and then delivering babies without proper handwashing, whereas midwives did not engage in autopsies and had cleaner hands. Semmelweis introduced a handwashing protocol using chlorinated lime solution for doctors before delivering babies, and the mortality rate from puerperal fever dramatically decreased. However, his ideas were met with scepticism and resistance from prominent figures in the medical community at the time. Many doctors were offended by the suggestion that they were transmitting disease and rejected Semmelweis's findings. One influential figure who opposed Semmelweis's ideas was Carl Braun, a prominent obstetrician in Vienna. Braun publicly criticised Semmelweis's findings and discouraged their adoption, contributing to the rejection of handwashing practices in many medical institutions.

Semmelweis's observations and recommendations were largely ignored during his lifetime, it was only years later that handwashing became widely accepted as a crucial practice in preventing the spread of infectious diseases in healthcare settings. This example illustrates how influential figures within the scientific community can impact the acceptance or rejection of certain ideas even when supported by empirical evidence, and how resistance to change can contribute to groupthink within the scientific community.

As we have seen, scientific consensus , may not always reflect the complete or final truth about a given topic. Scientific consensus can also be misrepresented or misunderstood by the public or policymakers, leading to misconceptions or inappropriate decision-making. Miscommunication of consensus findings can arise from oversimplification, sensationalism, or deliberate distortion by vested interests. And this is how "Spectacular Science" has been able to rise its ugly head.

I think the writer Michael Crichton sums it up beautifully in this quote from a paper he wrote entitled, "Aliens Cause Global Warming,"[1] which is an excellent treatise on how bad science can become part of popular culture.

> *"Let's be clear: the work of science has nothing whatever to do with consensus. Consensus is the business of politics. Science, on the contrary, requires only one investigator who happens to be right, which means that he or she has results that are verifiable by reference to the real world.*
>
> *In science consensus is irrelevant. What is relevant is reproducible results. The greatest scientists in history are great precisely because they broke with the consensus."*

1. https://stephenschneider.stanford.edu/Publications/PDF_Papers/Crichton2003.pdf

11

CANCEL CULTURE

Cancel culture is the practice of withdrawing support or recognition for persons, organisations, or public figures that have said or done anything deemed disrespectful, provocative, or undesirable. This includes voicing unpopular beliefs or engaging in controversial behaviour ranging from asking questions to harassment. The process comes with broad public condemnation, magnified by social media platforms, in which people or groups draw attention to alleged infractions and demand accountability. Punishment usually involves some kind of deplatforming, which can lead to boycotts, petitions, public shaming, and requests for resignation or removal from positions of power.

This phenomenon fosters a mob mentality encouraging online harassment and the stifling of opposing viewpoints with the most vociferous mob leaders typically holding faceless accounts. It also usually involves disproportionate consequences, a lack of due process, and leads to the deterioration of free expression and intellectual diversity. The effectiveness and moral implications of cancel culture have still not been thoroughly discussed. If there are enough willing participants, anyone can cancel anyone. Cancellation can be a spectacle in itself, or a political move.

Right-wing views typically present cancel culture as a form of censorship and ideological intolerance committed by liberal or progressive activists. Many right-wing critics say that cancel culture suppresses free speech by creating an environment in which people are afraid to express opposing views or engage in contentious debates. They frequently cite examples of persons facing career or social consequences for voicing politically incorrect or socially unacceptable viewpoints. Cancelation mobs do not believe in due process, the innocent, by their existence alone, are proven guilty.

The left sees cancel culture as a tool used by marginalised communities to hold powerful people and institutions accountable for their actions. It challenges oppressive structures while also boosting the voices of people who have previously been silenced or marginalised. Cancel culture is frequently portrayed as a vital component of accountability, at least online. It is viewed as a means of enforcing repercussions for harmful behaviour, especially when established channels of responsibility, such as legal or institutional action, have failed to address underlying concerns.

There is no reason to accept the claim that cancel culture is used by the marginalised to push back against the powerful. Usually, it is the other way around. The powerful oppress the powerless, and social media is just another dimension of this oppression. Justice requires a careful process of investigation, examination and judgment – all of which are not to be found in cancel culture. What is called social justice is more aptly called mob justice – an illusion of justice that is vengeance in disguise.

Liberals, progressives and leftwingers are by no means the only instigators of cancel culture. Right-wing influencers and groups have organised boycotts of corporations considered to support progressive causes or engage in "woke" behaviour. Companies such as Nike, Budweiser, Starbucks and Ben & Jerry's have been boycotted because they support social justice movements or progressive agendas. American conservative lawmakers and activists have also recently attempted to restrict the teaching of critical race theory (CRT) in schools and government entities. CRT is an academic legal concept that investigates how systemic racism interacts with the law and society. Right-wing critics believe that CRT encourages divisiveness and anti-American sentiment among young children, prompting attempts to enact legislation prohibiting its teaching in certain jurisdictions. Critics of cancel culture often characterise it as driven by a mob mentality, where individuals or groups seek to publicly shame and ostracizes others for violating perceived social norms. Mob mentality quickly forms groups of people united around a goal: to expose, shame and punish a perceived culprit. This behaviour is often performative, with people engaging in virtue signalling to demonstrate their own moral superiority without genuinely addressing any of the underlying issues. Where there is shame, there is also pride. The feeling of pride drives much of cancel culture and it focuses on signalling virtue, supremacy and purity.

Cancel culture undermines the norms of due process and justice by circumventing the traditional resolution processes such as legal proceedings and institutional investigations. The justice system takes time and is rarely spectacular, and often it is not even cathartic. Cancel culture needs a spectacle and a quick catharsis, this is why people are penalised based on accusations or allegations that may lack sufficient evidence or an opportunity for defence. It is not incorrect to view cancel culture as a threat to intellectual diversity, open discussion and free speech, especially on college campuses and in mainstream media. The pressure to conform to dominant ideological norms causes self-censorship and the suppression of opposing opinions, ultimately limiting the flow of ideas and impeding intellectual development.

Cancel culture is frequently characterised as a reaction to political correctness, language policing and rigid ideological orthodoxy. Additionally, cancel culture emphasises victimhood and hypersensitivity to perceived slights or offences. Both right and left political values can be turned against cancel culture, even though both engage in it. Overall, right-wing interpretations of cancel culture emphasise concerns about free speech, individual rights, and the erosion of traditional legal proceedings. Left-wing criticisms of cancel culture stem from concerns about its capacity to limit free expression, encourage intolerance, and further marginalise certain communities. Wherever you fall on the political spectrum, you have reasons to be concerned about cancel culture.

Cancel culture is a product of political, cultural and economic tendencies which are enabling the rise of 21st century totalitarianism. Rooted in the online culture of social media, this cancelation epidemic has spread far beyond our smart devices, infiltrating numerous aspects of our lives. To understand the scope and intricacies of cancel culture, it is useful to first examine and understand the context of its creation.

In the new digital landscape, every person, regardless of socioeconomic, ethnic, or geographic background, was given opportunities to speak, listen, watch and follow using a variety of social media platforms. Twitter (now X) and Facebook became arenas where conclusions appeared quickly and the users wielded power, often unrestrained and unbridled. We have already seen how the algorithm is influenced by likes and shares, and how followers, likes and shares have come to affirm a person's sense of self-worth. Online culture on social media was always fast, with rapidly changing hashtags, fads and fascinations. Sensationalism feeds the algorithm, and overall, this format cannot help but influence the attention span and desire of its users. Quickness and ease of consumption became the determining factors in the creation and dissemination of content.

As the digital sphere became increasingly integrated into the fabric of daily life, the effects of online activity began to resonate offline, spilling over into mainstream media. Today, online callouts, cancellations and even expressions of disagreement can have real-world consequences including job losses, social isolation, and mental health issues. Celebrities, once thought to be immune in their ivory towers, have seen their careers jeopardised as a result of previously unknown misdeeds. And it isn't just the celebrities who feel the heat. Everyday people, from academics to retail clerks, may have to confront the wrath of an outraged digital mob, having their mistakes, and opinions, magnified and judged in the court of public opinion. Because of the speed of online engagement, there is always a need for fresh blood.

In 2017, Kevin Myers, a forty-year veteran Irish journalist whose writing was widely regarded as both challenging to historical paradigms of Irish self-image and brilliantly argued, wrote some clumsy lines in the Sunday Times about a pay dispute in the BBC. He drew a link between the business and pay negotiation acumen of two of its leading presenters, both Jewish women and both of whom he praised. Mr Myers, who does not use social media, has long been an advocate for Jewish tradition in an historically Christian country and is recognised as such by Jewish institutions. It did not matter. He awoke on a Sunday morning to discover that his career had been destroyed, he'd been cancelled, the lines had been extracted, and the piece, which was buried behind a paywall, had gone viral globally, aided in particular by JK Rowling's Twitter reach. The mainstream media joined the mob, with the Irish State broadcaster RTE in particular branding Mr Myers a *Holocaust Denier*, and the Sunday Times, which had published the essay, dismissed him to protect itself. Despite his 25 years of authoring *The Irishman's Diary at the Irish Times*, his erstwhile colleagues turned on him, joining in the outcry and condemnation.

Once the mob died down, hopelessly outgunned, Kevin Myers took a single defamation case and sued RTE for a clear case of premeditated defamation in labelling him a Holocaust Denier. He won a significant settlement before a High Court action because RTE didn't have any evidence to prove otherwise. As part of the settlement in 2019, RTE reported the fact that a settlement had been reached in an agreed script on its main news, then deleted it from its archive while across in the Irish Times, the editors remained entirely silent on Myers's success. The Irish Times, whose deputy editor Fintan O'Toole had joined in on the attack upon Kevin Myers, later pulled a review of his book about his 25 years at the Irish Times by leading writer and former editor of the Sunday Independent, Anne

Harris. The Myers incident demonstrated that once cancelled by the mob, you are to remain so, regardless of the facts.

In an interview for my YouTube channel Counterpoint, I asked Kevin Myers, "As somebody who's for decades involved the heart of Irish media, what do you see now? What's of concern to you?" He responded thus:

> *"I see wasteland. I see an abject, supine media obeying the religious orders as if from a pope on all matters, to do with everything in the world, to do with political correctness, to do with transgenderism, a fiction we'd never heard of 20 years ago, uniformity on beliefs about global warming and about the peace process. I'm not saying all of these things are right or wrong. What I am saying is that the media in Ireland does not cover these issues and allow a debate of any kind. We are back to, if you like, Ireland of the 1950s, which none of the audience will remember and I barely do, because I was a child at the time and I wasn't living in Ireland. But we know about the 1950s, what a sterile time it is now, and we have recreated that sterility in this epoch of a secular pope and a secular orthodoxy to which all people must submit without discussion and without debate."*[1]

The link between the virtual and the actual was inevitable, it is a result of the changing nature of social systems. In a world where reputations are increasingly managed and displayed online, digital perceptions have a direct impact on real-world outcomes. Employers, fearful of public relations disasters, are eager to cut relationships with persons deemed problematic. Because of their history online, certain people are seen as a potential risk factor to organizations and employers. Online

1. https://youtu.be/WOViRfzAAmI

narratives influence social groups interactions, which are reshaped based on digital reputations and profiles. Furthermore, both traditional and new media have an amplifying effect. Stories about internet cancellations make for compelling entertainment, satisfying the public's insatiable desire for drama and controversy. This media spotlight guarantees that digital crises spread beyond their original channels and into the public consciousness, amplifying their real-world impact. The effect is double, the real-world consequences become new material for digital media.

As the tendrils of cancel culture reach farther into the everyday world, a crucial question arises: Is this a justifiable tool for social justice, or is it a sign of mob mentality?

As stated earlier, some proponents claim that cancel culture holds people accountable, especially when established systems fail. It is viewed as a way to level the playing field, offer a voice to the marginalised, and to achieve change. But we cannot ignore the fact that it can also be a lethal weapon, frequently used without nuance or due process, the new guillotine of mob justice such as that which plagued the French Revolution. However severe the results, jumping to conclusions has unintended repercussions, suffocating free expression and instilling fear. The absence of proportionality is another source of concern. Does a ten-year-old mistake justify contemporary retribution? Can individuals change, and if so, should their pasts be held eternally against them? .

Culture has not yet understood and assimilated modern technology: we still do not know what to do with all of these new gadgets. We do not know their long-term effects and what kind of people they will mould. Not so long ago, the online and offline spheres seemed so distinct. As it grew in size and importance, the digital realm naturally became commercialised, politicised and integrated into the everyday world. It's a complex entanglement that has blurred previously defined boundaries, resulting in social change that we have not yet properly understood. The intersection of our online and offline lives has profoundly altered our view of identity, reality, truth, and even the nature of human bonds. These are difficult sociological and philosophical topics, that must, paradoxically, be discussed in the spaces that produced them and be made part of everyday consciousness and discourse.

To realise the extent of this intertwining, we must first remind ourselves of the original, pre-online world. Historically, human life took place in villages, town squares, at family dinners, in classrooms, coffee shops, and on playgrounds. There were, of course, technologies for indirect communication, mainly using writing or telephone calls. When the digital space initially arose, it was a distinct entity—a unique frontier accessed by bulky computers, then cell phones, where individuals could participate in a different type of interaction, frequently using pseudonyms disconnected from their physical identities. When interaction is anonymous and does not affect a person's identity and reputation, it is quite a different story to when you must be transparent and identifiable. However, as technology advanced and digital platforms proliferated, these realms began to converge.

Initially, the digital realm was an abstraction, a virtual environment distinct from the physical world. With the growing spread of the internet and accessible computers, now people no longer simply "use" digital technologies, but live in a seamlessly interlinked offline-online reality where they can hide and snipe behind faceless profiles without fear of being held accountable for anything they say. Physical spaces—

whether public, private, or institutional—are regulated by long-standing cultural conventions and codes of conduct. In comparison, the digital environment was a new and wild frontier: untamed, unexplored, and marked by lawlessness in its early days.

Smartphones, portable technology, digital cameras, and other devices mediate a greater share of our daily interactions, enabling us to maintain social bonds. The massive data repositories on the Internet became more than just binary information stored in an ethereal cloud; they are now extensions of human identities. Each click, like, share, or tweet helped to build digital avatars that were reflective, if not totally representative, of the people behind the screens.

Reputations, which were traditionally based on face-to-face encounters and concrete achievements, play a vital role in one's digital imprint and tailored profile. Employers don't simply look at resumes; they also search for the associated social media profile. Romantic desires are validated by online searches, and digital histories influence views and decisions. Similarly, internet contacts and exposures progressively shape consumer behaviours, political attitudes, and moral perspectives. Movements born in the digital realm—whether it's a hashtag calling attention to societal inequities or a viral film exposing an urgent issue—are no longer limited to the screen. They flow onto the streets, affecting policy, causing institutional change, and altering public opinion. The Arab Spring, the #MeToo movement, and numerous climate change efforts demonstrate the power of digital mobilisation and its concrete effects on the actual world.

This blurring increases the ease of spying and privacy invasions. The barrier between what is public and what is private is becoming increasingly erased. The users of these platforms and social applications are encouraged to publicise themselves and sign away their privacy. With facial recognition technologies, data brokers, and sophisticated tracking algorithms, things that happen in the digital domain suddenly can have immediate, often unexpected implications in the actual world. Your phone probably knows you better than you do. In contrast, a person's actions in the real world—captured by CCTV cameras, smartphone recordings, or IoT devices—can become fodder for digital inspection, resulting in online ostracism, cancellation, and can lead to legal consequences. As academic institutions, governments, and civil society deal with this new reality, there is an urgent need for rigorous multidisciplinary research, more public awareness, and practical solutions.

The sociological, psychological, legal, and ethical implications of this convergence require a thorough investigation. Traditional borders and frameworks, whether related to jurisdiction, identity, or rights, must be reassessed in light of this digital-physical convergence. This task cannot be left to academics and experts, it requires widespread introspection and thinking. This rethinking ought to be realised in culture and its conclusions shared with a global community. The roles of technology designers, platform architects, and policymakers must be examined, and their work judged. As architects of this integrated universe, they are responsible not just for the practical efficiency of digital instruments, but also for the social consequences of their creations. It is vital to approach design with critical thinking and a caring ethic, prioritising human bonds and social repercussions over technological or commercial gains.

12

IGNORANCE

"War is peace. Freedom is slavery. Ignorance is strength."

— GEORGE ORWELL, *1984*

POLITICIANS, leaders and bureaucrats strategically utilise ignorance to consolidate power, control public perception, and preserve social structures. This manipulation can take various forms, as ignorance is a diverse landscape. Most commonly, the deliberate spread of incorrect or misleading information can be used to influence public opinion and garner support for specific political goals. When complete ignorance cannot be relied on, political leaders can rally support for their plans by instilling uncertainty and doubt.

Governments and political leaders tend to withhold crucial information from the public, deliberately leaving individuals unaware of truths that could weaken their authority or ignite revolt. Politicians and bureaucrats can convey policies and concerns in unnecessarily complex language, making it difficult for ordinary citizens to understand and engage with them. This obfuscation can inhibit informed debate and allow legislation to be passed that benefits only a few. It also gives governments plausible deniability, as it avoids direct statements. When voters lack information or are overwhelmed by the complexities of political problems, they naturally become apathetic or disengaged from the electoral process. Disengagement can lead to lower voter turnout and civic participation, a symptom of democratic erosion, which happens slowly over long periods of time. Although harmful, this form of ignorance is not necessarily a product of political machinations. Often, ignorance is an unfortunate phenomenon that arises out of a lack of interest, time and opportunity and can be taken advantage of by those in the know.

The innate ignorance of inexperienced voters is routinely exploited during political campaigns through the use of fearmongering, simplistic slogans, and emotional appeals . There is also an elitist mindset that sees the electorate as an uneducated mass incapable of making rational or reasonable decisions. Holding political leaders accountable requires a well-informed electorate. This does not necessarily involve elite education and advanced degrees, but transparency and open debate on the part of the politicians themselves, which is rarely forthcoming. Ignorance limits our ability to critically examine the acts and policies of officeholders, when we don't know what is going on, we inadvertently allow corruption and ineptitude to thrive.

The deliberate concealment or distortion of historical and cultural information can marginalise one group while legitimising the supremacy of another. Unequal access to decent education can prolong ignorance among these marginalised groups, restricting their chances for political and economic growth. This imbalance has the potential to perpetuate pre-existing power structures and social hierarchies, especially when political elites keep control of the narrative and stifle opposition. Ignorance, like most things, is unevenly distributed in society. Ignorance of economic policies and their ramifications can be used to enact policies that benefit the wealthy and powerful at the expense of the public. A lack of awareness of economic concerns can stifle effective debate and opposition to exploitative policies. People are generally aware when their economic situation is worsening, even though they might be ignorant of the larger trends and laws at play.

Combating ignorance is critical for promoting civic involvement and empowering citizens. Access to accurate and thorough information is critical for responsible citizenship. Education systems and media outlets are, in theory, supposed to play important roles in distributing knowledge and encouraging critical thinking. However, governments rarely prioritise transparency and accountability by providing citizens with equal and easy access to information about their policies, choices, and actions. Transparency would allow for informed participation in the democratic process, something the elites accept only hesitantly and up to a point. As previously noted, the mainstream media and social platforms are not objective or neutral spaces to encourage the flourishing of discussion and the spread of information that goes outside of the currently accepted narrative.

Addressing ignorance through public education, transparency, and civic engagement is fundamental to building a healthy, functional democracy in which citizens can make informed decisions and hold their leaders responsible. This is exactly why ignorance has become an instrument in the totalitarian toolkit.

There have been several academic attempts at conceptualising ignorance and examining its importance. Ignorance studies is a diverse and growing interdisciplinary project that investigates ignorance, its sources, effects, and function in society, politics, science, and culture. These studies seek to comprehend not only the absence of knowledge, but also how ignorance is created, perpetuated, and strategically applied. Ignorance studies also investigate how gaps in scientific knowledge are handled or exploited. This involves discussing the role of uncertainty in scientific research, the boundaries of scientific knowledge, and how technological advancements can both lessen and produce new forms of ignorance. Examining ignorance via cultural and historical lenses entails understanding how specific types of knowledge or ignorance have been valued or marginalised over time. This can entail investigating historical events, cultural taboos, and the effects of colonialism and imperialism on knowledge production.

Research into ignorance can help shape public policy by emphasising the significance of transparency, education, and access to information. It can also indicate how policy decisions are influenced by what is known, and what is purposely hidden. By understanding the role of ignorance in education, educators can create curricula that promote critical thinking while also raising awareness of knowledge limitations and gaps. Most importantly, ignorance studies can help analyse the influence of media in promoting or countering ignorance. This includes investigating the effects of fake news, media bias, and the digital divide on public comprehension and awareness. This is an interdisciplinary field, covering not only how ignorance is created, sustained, and used to help us grasp the significant impact of what we don't know about various facets of life, from personal decision-making to global policy. It also promotes a more complex understanding of ignorance, not just as a lack of knowledge, but also as a significant and frequently strategic force in social, political, and cultural settings.

Totalitarianism is heavily reliant on the ignorance of its people to maintain power and control. In this context, ignorance is more than a lack of understanding; it is an intentional construct produced and maintained by the regime to stifle dissent, control public perception, and forestall threats to its rule. Historically, by controlling the flow of information through all the important institutions of the media, literature, and art, they ensured that only the state-approved narratives were available to the people. This prevented citizens from accessing opposing opinions or essential information that could undermine the regime's authority. By constantly bombarding the people with biased or incorrect information, these governments shaped public perception and sustained a skewed version of reality. Once these regimes fell, a veil was suddenly lifted from the population.

Totalitarian governments also frequently rewrote or suppressed history to fit their narrative. Controlling historical knowledge allows a regime to remove any references to past failures or crimes, preventing people from learning lessons that could motivate resistance. All governments do this to some extent to make themselves look good. It becomes a patriotic duty to forget the crimes and follies of the past. However, totalitarianism can do much worse, and go much further than this. The use of a secret police and arbitrary detention fosters terror. People are kept in the dark about the scope of these activities and their legal rights, discouraging them from challenging the government or seeking justice. All you know is that you could be arrested for anything at any time, for no apparent reason. Public forums, assemblies, and other forms of collective debate are strictly restricted to constrict the flow of ideas and guarantee that public discourse adheres to the regime's guidelines. Education systems in totalitarian regimes propagate a skewed history, to indoctrinate, rather than to educate. Educational curriculums are altered to emphasise the regime's ideology, eliminating critical thinking and encouraging unquestioning obedience. Independent intellectual inquiry and academic independence is discouraged and becomes non-existent. Scholars, educators, and students who oppose the regime's policies face persecution, jail, or worse. Unsurprisingly, totalitarian regimes have historically feared novelists, poets and artists. Because the regime is so reliant on ignorance, education of any form becomes a threat to its foundation.

Knowledge is power, and the power is in the hands of the leaders of these regimes and their chosen few. It becomes a cult of personality, where their leaders are portrayed as infallible and omnipotent. You may be ignorant, but *The Leader* knows everything. This fosters a psychological reliance on the leader and prevents critical examination of their activities. As power is centralised, ignorance is dispersed. If knowledge is power, ignorance becomes a factor of powerlessness. The asymmetry is necessary if the unjust hierarchy is to endure.

Agnotology is the study of culturally produced ignorance or doubt, particularly the dissemination of incorrect or misleading scientific data. It investigates how ignorance is intentionally created and maintained, which is frequently for ideological or political reasons, and how knowledge is concealed, corrupted, or manipulated to satisfy a variety of goals. ***Agnogenesis***, on the other hand, is the purposeful creation (genesis) of ignorance or malicious doubt. The term agnotology was coined by Robert N. Proctor, a professor of the history of science at Stanford University, and linguist Iain Boal. It is derived from the Greek word ***agnosis***, meaning *not knowing*, and *-**logia***, *speech* or *science*. Therefore, agnotology is the discourse about, or science of, ignorance. Agnogenesis has a similar etymology: the last part of the term, -genesis, is derived from the Greek word ***génesis***, which means origin, source, birth, or creation. Agnotology is not a philosophical thinking about the nature of ignorance, it attempts to show the sources of artificial ignorance in society.

Knowledge is power, as Francis Bacon wrote centuries ago. Therefore, if knowledge and power are closely related, ignorance is crucial to induce powerlessness. The State uses agnogenesis as a means of legitimisation, not only to creating false consciousness in its citizens but also to prevent and silence any knowledge that threatens its hegemony. Corporations practice agnogenesis in the form of corporate propaganda (or *marketing*) in pursuit of profit.

Ignorance is most often seen by ordinary people as something to be corrected, yet ignorance is widespread, manifold, elusive and remarkably significant at times. We understand it as a kind of natural absence or a void, where knowledge has yet to spread. Some things we can learn or discover through research. Sandford Professor Robert N Proctor, as a historian focusing on the history of medicine and technology, through his research on cancer (*The Cancer Wars: How Politics Shapes What We Know and Don't Know About Cancer*, 1995) and the tobacco industry (*Golden Holocaust: Origins of the Cigarette Catastrophe and the*

Case for Abolition, 2012), identified certain phenomena that demonstrated the need to study ignorance as a deliberately produced commodity. The paradigmatic case of ***agnogenesis***, the technical term he uses for the creation of ignorance, is the tobacco industry.

In December 1953, the executives of major tobacco companies met in New York to discuss how they could suppress the damage caused by research linking smoking to lung cancer and other ailments. A year earlier, *Reader's Digest* - then a leading public source of medical information - published an article entitled: *Cancer by the Carton*. After the article appeared, cigarette sales plummeted for two years, the first recorded decline in a century, except during the Great Depression (1929-1933).

Working closely with John Hill, the founder of the public relations firm Hill & Knowlton, the industry crafted the *Frank Statement to Cigarette Smokers* and paid for it to be published in 448 newspapers on January 4, 1954. To humanise the industry, the statement included signatures from the highest-ranking tobacco executives in the country, and reassured Americans that: "*we accept an interest in people's health as a basic responsibility, paramount to every other consideration in our business*." Furthermore, they promised that, "*we always have and always will cooperate closely with those whose task it is to safeguard the public health*."

Their *Frank Statement* was a deception, the first step in a coordinated, half-century-long campaign to deceive American smokers about the catastrophic effects of smoking and to avoid public policies that could harm sales. Revealed later, industry documents showed the executives' repeated duplicity. The industry desperately wanted to prevent, or at least delay, changes in public opinion that would allow for a cascade of legislative, regulatory, and legal efforts that could jeopardize their sales and profits.

Among the many published documents from the Brown & Williamson company there is one statement that perfectly and perhaps overly honestly describes the intentions behind, and methods used for agnogenesis within the tobacco industry: *"Doubt is our product since it is the best means of competing with the 'body of fact' that exists in the mind of the general public. It is also the means of establishing a controversy."*[1] The exact author of this statement is not known. Why are these internal documents available to the public? In 1998, six million secret documents, comprising over 35 million pages, became available to the public due to legal proceedings. The documents came from the national and international offices of seven cigarette manufacturers operating in the United States and two affiliated organisations: Philip Morris Incorporated, R.J. Reynolds Tobacco Company, Brown & Williamson Tobacco Corporation, British American Tobacco Industries, Lorillard Tobacco Company, American Tobacco Company, Liggett Group, Tobacco Institute, and Council for Tobacco Research.

The documents were written by company scientists, consultants, lawyers, executives, and other employees - as well as external organisations closely associated with the tobacco industry, such as public relations firms, advertising and law firms, and research laboratories. The horde includes letters, memos, telegrams, emails, and research reports; strategic, political, and organisational plans; organisational charts, consultant lists, invoices, and copies of paid checks;

1. This statement, and many others like it, is available at: https://www.industrydocuments.ucsf.edu/tobacco/docs/#id=psdw0147

testimonies in courts and before legislative bodies; advertising, marketing, media, and public relations strategies; and several other categories.

Cipollone v. Liggett in the 1980s was the first lawsuit to uncover internal documentation which revealed the hidden face of the tobacco industry. In 1994, while the Brown & Williamson cigarette company (owned by British American Tobacco) was preparing a list of internal documents in anticipation of new lawsuits, an employee handed over approximately 4,000 internal documents to researchers at the University of California, San Francisco, who quickly recognised what the documents revealed.

Over the next decade, prosecutors' attorneys in dozens of lawsuits filed against American tobacco manufacturers knowing what documents they wanted to address. Based on these documents, they made allegations stating that tobacco companies knowingly created a dangerous product; that although they knew tobacco was dangerous, they failed to warn the public, even at times denying the danger; that they increased the strength of nicotine in cigarettes while denying that nicotine is addictive; and that they deliberately targeted minors below the legal smoking age. Since 1994, numerous states have sued the tobacco industry for fraud - hiding from the public what the companies know about their product - and to recover the costs incurred by those states in caring for sick and dying smokers.

Although the tobacco industry still exists and employs various other tactics and survival strategies, its methods of agnogenesis is considered a closed case. It is difficult to find a place where agnotology is mentioned without this formative example. By studying contemporary agnogenesis (climate change, the pandemic, online surveillance, etc...), we can find many identical or similar methods to the tobacco industry, using public relations firms, and even the same false professionals or bribed scientists. The industry of denial and doubt has become quite profitable and established.

Ignorance is not only a political matter – it is also economic. Knowledge may be priceless, but ignorance is not. There is a clear price for both smokers (their health) and the tobacco industry (however much they paid to the public relations companies). Ignorance, or doubt – as the statement says, is a product. It has a use and a price. It is important not to limit this concept and discovery to just corporations. Similar things are carried out by almost every social organisation and by certain individuals: states, international organisations, institutions, bureaucracies, politicians, scientists, etc... For the tobacco industry, and many others like it, ignorance (just like research) is a worthwhile investment.

It should be clear at this stage that ignorance is beneficial for totalitarianism. Since it is manufacturable, and more common than we realise, it poses a growing threat to our freedoms. As will also be clear, it is not just state censorship we have to watch. We cannot point to a single factor to explain the rise of totalitarianism. The state itself cannot impose it. It requires support from the culture, public, scientists and economy. This is precisely why ignorance is manufactured inside of all of these spheres.

Linsey McGoey, sociologist and author, discusses agnotology in her book, *The Unknowers*. She explores how industries and interest groups deliberately manufacture doubt and uncertainty to serve their own agendas. Like Proctor, McGoey argues that ignorance is not always a natural absence of knowledge but rather an intentional creation of embedded interests to maintain power and control. McGoey emphasises how certain industries, such as tobacco and pharmaceuticals, have strategically used misinformation campaigns to sow doubt about scientific consensus and delay regulatory action that could harm their profits. She also highlights the role of political interests and corporate influence in shaping public perception and policy decisions through the promotion of ignorance.

McGoey's work underscores the importance of critically examining all sources of information and the need to question the motives behind efforts to obscure or distort knowledge. She calls for greater transparency and accountability in public discourse to combat the spread of ignorance and promote informed decision-making. McGoey describes scenarios where ignorance is used to evade the consequences of revealed wrongdoing. She uses the term, "Strategic Ignorance," to describes attempts to evade accountability for previous activities. It involves mustering, manufacturing, or misusing unknowns in the wider environment. Strategic ignorance is intentional; it creates or exaggerates unknowns to gain support for future shady activities, rather than just avoiding responsibility for previous mistakes. The strength of her book lies in the many supporting arguments across diverse themes from history and contemporary society. The deceptive practices of American oil baron John D. Rockefeller, Adam Smith and his representation in the history of economics, the history of the British Empire, Grenfell Tower... all of these diverse examples are explained remarkably well and serve to show how *mundane* manufactured ignorance is. Strategic ignorance deeply affects our common sense, history and political consciousness. Other useful ideas from the book, besides strategic ignorance, include ignorance alibis, oracular power, useful unknows, elite ignorance, micro-ignorance and macro-ignorance. These concepts can be incredibly helpful in describing and understanding our ignorance-filled world. They also help us communicate complex reality to each other in a relatively simple way, without ignoring crucial aspects of it.

McGoey has a humanistic way of approaching the inevitability of ignorance. She is not fatalistic about its prominence, nor does she believe that we can completely circumvent it. Human nature does not include omniscience; ignorance is a lasting part of it. This anthropological fact can have many political repercussions. McGoey accepts this epistemic limitation and sees it as an argument *for*, not *against,* democracy. The political utility of ignorance can be used for democratic and egalitarian means, not just authoritarianism and totalitarianism. Ignorance leads to many uncertainties and doubts, which have only increased with the rise of science. We must ultimately accept ignorance as a fact of human nature, we cannot be blind to its utility and effects. As McGoey notes:

> *"... there are enormous financial rewards in harnessing and magnifying the uncertainty and unknowns around us to achieve different financial and reputational advantages.*
>
> *Powerful individuals thrive on strategic ignorance and the deliberate exploitation of uncertainty."*[2]

Some people benefit from ignorance more than others. Determining the uses of ignorance, and not its immense scope,

2. (McGoey 2019, 6)

is crucial for us here. It is not surprising that McGoey also draws on Arendt in order to argue for the political uses of ignorance. Arendt is not only a kindred spirit in this approach, she is also an example of a scholar who perpetuated ignorance about British imperialism. McGoey rightly identifies Arendt's mistake and sees it as an example of micro-ignorance perpetuating a myth about macro-ignorance. Arendt does agree that "*the British Empire was acquired in a fit of absent-mindedness*" in her *The Origins of Totalitarianism.*[3] This does not undermine her overall argument and assessment of totalitarianism, but it is worth going into detail.

The myth that Britain stumbled into being an empire claims that British imperialism was not an intentional or planned undertaking but rather the result of a series of fortunate events and chances. This suggests that Britain's imperial ambitions were not part of a coherent or coordinated strategy; rather, they arose haphazardly throughout time as a result of expansions motivated by individual players, economic interests, or military conquests. This approach ignores the possibility of a planned and systematic nature of British imperialism. In doing this, it relies on macro-ignorance, and vast amounts of it. While it is true that Britain's empire evolved gradually and was shaped by a range of reasons, such as economic interests, military might, and individual efforts, the British government and governing elites maintained a planned imperial agenda.

The quote that suggests the British Empire was acquired in a fit of absent-mindedness is often attributed to historian Sir John Seeley, in his book, *The Expansion of England* in 1883. In it, he says: "*We seem, as it were, to have conquered and peopled half the*

3. (Arendt, The Origins of Totalitarianism 1976, 132)

world in a fit of absence of mind." In truth, the expansion of the British Empire was fuelled by a mix of strategic planning, commercial interests, military conquests, and ideological objectives. The British government and ruling classes avidly pursued imperial expansion by colonisation, annexation, diplomacy, and military action, often with due regard for geopolitical circumstances and national interests.

While there may have been moments of opportunism or improvisation in specific imperial ventures, portraying the acquisition of the British Empire as absent-mindedness ignores British imperialism's intentional and systematic nature, as well as its profound impact on the colonies and the world at large. This myth is used to construct what McGoey calls an "Ignorance Alibi". It is a way of denying guilt and avoiding repercussions.

13

AGNOGENESIS IN IRELAND

THE POST-COLONIAL ELITES in independent Ireland heavily influenced the country's social and political organisation, reflecting puritanical beliefs, economic conservatism, and a distrust of freedom. The government, insecure and tied to the Church, expanded the influence of religion over education, health, and social care, granting it unprecedented authority. The Church and State collaborated to present Ireland as a religio-political entity with a moral mission into which a type of clerical fascism took root.

They employed various methods to suppress dissent and maintain their reputations, including denial, censorship, and demonisation of perceived threats. Children in reformatory and industrial schools, drawn from marginalised sections of society, suffered neglect and abuse, perpetuated by the Church-run institutions with State complicity. Despite overwhelming evidence, Church and State denied this gruesome reality to uphold their image. The failure to address these issues stemmed from a newly forged myth of moral superiority and a disregard for the rights of the vulnerable. Unhappily the Irish media and the population, complicit in this myth, failed to hold authorities accountable, prioritising national pride and stability over justice.

This issue has been well studied and documented by retired Professor of Criminology, Anthony Keating. He has written extensively on similar topics, but the focus here is on *The Ideology and Mechanics of Ignorance: Child Abuse in Ireland 1922–1973,* which is chapter four in the book *Ignorance, Power and Harm* by Alana Barton and Howard Davis. Keating gives a short, but poignant, overview of the topic and connects the agnotological framework to a close and chilling reality. He shows how agnogenesis happens at the cultural, institutional and state levels.

The issue of child abuse in Irish institutional care, primarily run by Catholic religious orders, has led to a cultural and political shift in the Irish Republic, undermining the traditional power and control of the nation's religious and political elites, particularly the Catholic Church. The public final recognition of the abuse of Ireland's children in the 1990s was met with shock and anger, but the reality was, the abuse took place in plain sight of Ireland's people, and responsibility for the brutality extended far beyond the Church.

Ireland's membership in the European Union and a major scandal involving the country's beef industry contributed to public demands for greater openness. By the late 1990s, it became politically desirable for the Irish political classes to break with the draconian enforcement of secrecy that had been a feature of the political functioning of the State since its establishment in 1922. The Church and State had formal powers and moral leverage in determining what was a acceptable for public consumption and comment, making Ireland a victim of a state-enforced culture of denial, until the introduction of the 1997 Freedom of Information Act.

Keating describes how the children held in Ireland's institutions and reformatory schools posed two distinct challenges for Church and State: The Irishness of these children and the reality of their lives as "moral dirt". The abuse was not only sexual but also included starvation and forced labour. Both Church and State ignored and suppressed evidence implicating them in these abuses, in furtherance of reputation, in defence of wider ideological-religious fantasies regarding the Celtic-Catholic virtue of the Irish Free State, and more prosaic political and economic considerations.

The Irish Free State in the 20th century was governed by the moral authority of the Church, which acted above the law on issues of morality. This authority was particularly felt by children from poorer backgrounds and those considered sexually dangerous. The burden of this moral authoritarianism fell disproportionately on the poor, as the elites and middle class had the social and economic capital to avoid scrutiny. The national character was, of course, exemplified by the nation's *finest*. The Church was focused and acted against the poor majority, who became scapegoats for imperial immorality, a remnant of British rule.

The Irish Free State came into being in 1922 after a protracted guerilla war against Britain. The new government faced a fragmented national infrastructure and was quickly engulfed in a civil war. The Catholic faith of the majority of the citizens offered the truest sense of cohesion during the post-colonial identity formation period. The Church's abundant resources ensured a powerful role for the Church in the governance and direction of the State, something that the traumatised populace could not resist.

In a period of uncertainty and disorder, the Church offered the nascent state legitimacy, and the State offered the Church a chance to imbed itself into the fabric of the State and corridors of power. This arrangement would determine the Irish State for much of the 20th century and leave lasting scars on the lives of many. Large numbers of children died at the hands of the Church during this period. It is no wonder that Benedictine monk and writer Mark Patrick Hederman described Ireland during this period as a "*concentration camp*".[1]

The Irish Catholic Church had a rigidity when it came to doctrine and scepticism when it came to the integrity and freedom of its flock. It focused on maintaining social conformity and national holiness. This involved a pessimism over the population's ability to resist temptation without the Church's help. Since the Church became the sole moral judge of the Irish Free State, it could make declarations unopposed. To oppose the Church meant opposing the nation. It meant being un-Irish. Additionally, the Church sought to create a national myth; it was Ireland's unique mission to provide a beacon of purity and virtue in a world sullied by sinful materialism.

This myth was accepted by a devout section of the populace, making national Catholicism and religious nationalism inevitable. However, national myths are viable only so long as they serve as proof of national strength and virtue. The elite in Ireland maintained a strong culture of ignorance, particularly regarding sexual matters and the institutional treatment of

1. https://web.archive.org/web/20170909191104/http://www.nytimes.com/2011/02/13/magazine/13Irish-t.html?pagewanted=2&hpw

vulnerable children. This ignorance played a central role in the cognitive dissonance required to resolve tensions between the visible realities of daily life with the political-religious scaffolding that supported the nascent state. Both Church and State understood the importance of maintaining the conditions necessary to reject or ignore any counter-hegemonic tendencies to maintain this acceptance. The State saw itself under permanent attack, not a ridiculous belief considering its history, and used any means it saw fit to ensure its survival.

The themes used to illustrate and counter the dangers to Ireland's mission, as outlined by Keating, were primarily based on three motifs: warfare, disease, and evil. This religiously inspired national myth has its roots before the Irish Free State. The founding text used in the institutionalisation of this myth is Bishop Spalding's *The Religious Mission of the Irish People*, published in 1880. The themes of the myth were used to create an atmosphere of fear and rejection of anything associated with modernity. This included non-religious books, movies and fashion. Engaging with such foreign imports was seen as a betrayal of the Irish race and Catholic faith. Any form of liberalism was spun to be a form of Imperial oppression due to its association with Britain. The narrative use of these motifs provided powerful overt and subliminal tools in the fight against alternative views of the underlying morality and material existence of the independent Irish State.

The Church lobbied the State with ease in order to enact its desired legislation. This included draconian literary censorship, fighting secularism and lawfare campaigns against perceived transgressors. This political strategy had a broad reach; it used journalists, politicians, clerics, newspaper vendors, social workers, parents and even judges. Everyone was subject to legislative action or social alienation if they dared to oppose the power grab by the Church.

The abuse was a clear failure of the state and its close partnership with the Church. The failure to protect and nurture all the Nation's children needed to be kept from the public, as it flew in the face of religious scriptures and the promise made in *The Democratic Programme* of the First Dáil, the founding assembly of the aspirant Republic. In the case of the children in the industrial and reformatory schools, this promise was completely disregarded. It is clear that both Church and state understood the vile nature of these issues. To protect their domestic and international reputation, they engaged in an equally vile agnogenesis process that stunted Irish culture, politics and society.

The Irish Free State was founded by a religious elite who drew inspiration from the intellectual development of nationalism and the nation-state in the 19th century. This era also saw the conceptualisation of the *Nation* as a living entity. A living organism needs to perpetuate itself. This organic conception of the nation made fertility, sexuality, children and childhood crucial to the national interests. These areas led to concerns among the emergent post-colonial elites following years of degradation under the British. The nation needed to be revitalised. Hence the strictness around family, and taboos on sexuality.

The elites sought to control the national image through legislation, suppression of information and social and economic pressure. Censorship was at the heart of this strategy. In 1923, the government rushed through legislation providing a nationwide censorship of films. The Catholic Church was not satisfied; it wanted literary and journalistic censorship as well. In 1925, pressure was brought on the Minister for Justice, Kevin O'Higgins, by the Irish Vigilance Association of Ireland, the Christian Brothers and Catholic Newspapers to suppress the availability of what they called "*evil literature*". The Committee of Enquiry on Evil Literature (CEL) was established in 1926. They placed a large emphasis on the control of press freedom and reporting. Legislation based on the CEL's recommendations was presented as a Bill in 1928, following a campaign of direct action by Catholic vigilante groups.

Irish journalism generally was either silent on the issue or supportive of the censorship. Ireland faced "censorship by anticipation", with many editors refusing to confront difficult issues. Sadly, this issue has persisted in some forms. The censorship extended beyond journalism, with two key reports intended for public consumption kept from public scrutiny due to their perceived political danger. The 1926 Report of the Inter-Departmental Committee of Inquiry on Venereal Disease and the Carrigan Report, which investigated child prostitution in Dublin, were considered dangerous to Ireland's reputation.

The Carrigan Committee unearthed evidence of extensive child sexual abuse in Ireland. When news of this reached senior politicians and the Catholic hierarchy, the decision was made to liquidate the Report and its potential negative impact on Irelands society and reputation. The Report contained numerous sweeping charges against the state of morality in Ireland, and the Department of Justice believed it should not be made public. The existence of such a report shows the issue was not about a complete lack of investigative ability and concern of children. Some people knew, but they were suppressed by the might of both Church and State. These censorship practices led to a culture of silence and a lack of investigation into the plight of the nation's children.

The Artane Industrial School, run by the Christian Brothers from 1870 until its closure in 1969, was a brutal institution where many children were beaten, raped, and even murdered. The boys spent much of their time performing unpaid manual labour, from which the Christian Brothers benefited financially. Abuse was commonplace and unpunished. The only thing that the inexperienced staff had to fear was relocation to another facility run by the Christian Brothers. The poor treatment of children in such schools was largely due to the poor quality of staff, often selected by the Church. Many members of religious orders and those employed in the schools were hostile to the children's welfare and drawn from the ranks of those deemed unsuitable to work in mainstream schools.

The Irish State's indifference to the quality of personnel employed to work with these children was also abusive. Between 1922 and the 1960s, the State paid little attention to the schools, leaving the religious orders to run them as they saw fit. However, by the 1960s, even members of the State hierarchy were concerned about the activities in some of their schools. An inspection report written by a Department of Education inspector relating to Artane demonstrates the propensity of civil servants to minimise the poor conditions they encountered. It took another 10 years for the Irish State to take its first tentative steps towards improving the system after the report of the Kennedy Committee in 1970.

This overview of Irish history illustrates how the state, institutions and culture works together to ignore, forget and minimise actual harm. To protect its reputation, the government employed denial, suppression, censorship, and demonisation of anything that didn't conform to its narrative. Children in reformatory and industrial schools, drawn from the poorest segments of society, were stigmatised and received inadequate care in substandard institutions. These schools, run by orders closely tied to the State denied abuses perpetuated by unsuitable staff to maintain the institutions' and the state's credibility. In this atmosphere, the populace failed to hold the authorities accountable for abuses occurring in plain sight, contributing to a structural disregard for human rights.

There is no better way to describe this mode of religio-political governance than clerical fascism, or "clero-fascism". Fascism is almost synonymous with totalitarianism; not an unfitting description of the Church's centralisation of power and overreaching. This form of totalitarianism was not unique to Ireland, clerical fascism has a rich history in Europe. It is an ideology that blends aspects of fascism with the widespread authority of religious institutions, especially the clergy. It first appeared in the early 20th century in Europe as fascist governments looked to religious organisations for support and cooperation to establish their hold on power and further their nationalist objectives. Their cooperation was aided by common enemies, such as liberalism and communism. At its core, this cooperation arose as a rejection of modern individualism and secular values. Many examples show that Ireland is not unique in this way.

Although itself secular, Mussolini's dictatorship in Italy forged a tight partnership with the Catholic Church to solidify its hold on power. In exchange for the Catholic Church's support of

Mussolini's fascist government, the Lateran Accords of 1929 between Mussolini and Pope Pius XI recognised Vatican City as an independent state and gave the Church considerable control over education and other social issues.

Francisco Franco's reign in Spain, also referred to as Francoist Spain, was a fascist dictatorship that controlled the country from 1939 to 1975. With the help of the Catholic Church, Franco's administration was able to further its traditionalist and nationalist goals. There was a strong influence from the Catholic Church on education, social policy, and moral standards, and a close relationship between the Spanish State and the Church.

During World War II, the Independent State of Croatia (NDH) was governed by the Ustashe regime, headed by Ante Pavelić. The dictatorship was deeply racist and nationalist, and adhered to a strict interpretation of Catholicism that was in line with its own fascist ideology. Serbs, Jews, and other minorities were oppressed and exterminated by the dictatorship which frequently had the backing of Catholic clergy.

Portugal was ruled by António de Oliveira Salazar's Estado Novo, a corporatist, authoritarian, and fascist state that existed from 1933 until 1974. The Catholic Church, which the administration had a tight connection with, was crucial to upholding social order and advancing the regime's agenda.

Clerical fascism in all of these examples entailed the cooperation of religious organisations and fascist governments in the advancement of nationalist, authoritarian, and frequently oppressive agendas, with religion serving as a weapon for control and repression of dissent. As with all political systems and doctrines, there is a spectrum. We do not have to equate Ireland with a staunchly fascist state to see the workings of clerical fascism. It is a matter of degree. Any amount of clerical fascism is too much.

14

POLITICAL EMOTIONS

If we want to truly understand political dynamics and how public opinion can be manipulated, we must also study the function of emotions, yet emotions are often left out of both academic and everyday discourse about political matters. It is almost as if admitting the role of emotions somehow automatically undermines an argument or cause. This dogma, or rather prejudice against emotions, is highly dangerous – as totalitarian projects use emotions to gain control and have historically paid attention to them.

Anxiety is a clear example of an emotion exploited for political gain, for example, Professor Mattias Desmet highlights how anxiety underpins mass formation. There are a range of emotions and emotional reactions that people and groups have in connection to certain political circumstances, personalities, ideologies, and social movements. These feelings are very important in forming public opinion, motivating political action, and determining political behaviour. To fully appreciate the complexities of political dynamics and the manipulation or influence of public opinion, we must factor them in. Pride in one's nation, patriotism, is one of the most obvious and possibly one of the strongest political emotions. Evoked during national holidays, often through flags and anthems, patriotism ignites a sense of national solidarity and identity. For example, patriotic feelings are displayed proudly on Independence Day in the United States, which strengthening a feeling of belonging and pride in the country. Every country has its own version of this, with Ireland's uniquely global parades on St Patrick's Day, March 17th. National symbols, visual and audible, bring together millions of people under the banner of a single nation. Such feelings strengthen the social fabric against outside dangers and support government actions.

Fear and anxiety are often triggered by perceived threats. These feelings are also politically significant and have great potential to promote particular actions or defend policies. For instance, popular support of strict security protocols and military operations has been greatly aided by the fear of terrorism, most notably the Homeland Security Act 2002 which was triggered by 9/11 in the USA.

Economic anxiety can greatly influence voter behaviour, pushing voters towards parties or politicians who guarantee job security and economic stability. Outrage and anger have similar political significance. Many times these intense feelings are the result of dislike or animosity towards political leaders, laws, or societal injustices. Social wrath can spark large-scale demonstrations and calls for structural reform. Similar rage at political corruption can produce anti-establishment feelings, which in turn strengthen support for movements that oppose the status quo.

On the other hand, constructive political feeling that arouses faith in the possibility of social or political change can drive behaviour. Political campaigns can use hope to mobilise people as they paint a picture of a better future, such as Barack Obama's *Hope* campaign. The UK Brexit campaign also used hope, however it was perverted by untruths about trade deals, improved national finances and border controls and concealed the impact of exiting the world's richest regional economy absent any deal.

Optimism is equally important in environmental movements, where belief in a sustainable future spurs support for environmental laws and renewable energy projects. Political emotions of compassion and empathy motivate humanitarianism. These feelings frequently result in support of more just and inclusive laws. Positive political emotions often work to bolster solidarity, they can influence large political projects and social cohesiveness. Love of one's neighbourhood leads to local political involvement and grassroots activity. It ignites care for the immediate and close-by. This has long been the core political teaching of Christianity. Historically, worker solidarity has also propelled labour movements and the unionisation movement, which promotes better working conditions and equitable pay.

Negative political emotions including contempt and resentment, feed both elitist and anti-elitist political beliefs. These emotions usually spawn from unjust benefits and inequity possessed by particular groups. For instance, resentment of the affluent elites can fuel populist movements that support economic redistribution, opposing the concentration of power and money. Equally important, contempt leads to a hatred of the powerless by the powerful. Contempt is crucial in understanding the pervading elitism present in society. Contempt and resentment are forms of hatred, a powerful emotion that drives many people to extreme actions.

Shame and remorse for past deeds or present injustices can motivate politicians to make amends, apologies and reparations. Official apologies and reparations have resulted from national shame over historical occurrences, notably Germany's reaction to the Holocaust. Political leaders who feel shamed personally could support social changes to correct wrongs and stop them from happening again. Remorse can be cathartic, as it helps a country accept and overcome shame and guilt.

From these examples you can see that emotions highly influence political behaviour. They encourage involvement, mould views, promote group identification, and can be used to change public perception. People may vote, protest, or become involved in activism out of anger, hope, or pride. We form opinions and understand political facts based on emotions. Stronger group identity and cohesiveness brought about by shared emotions result in more well-organized political activities. Furthermore, media and political leaders routinely use emotions to promote ideas or solutions.

Complete control over every facet of public and private life, which is the hallmark of totalitarian governments, is impossible without mastering political emotions. If we consider ourselves purely rational beings we leave ourselves blind to emotional manipulation for political ends. The manipulation of emotions is one of the best instruments totalitarian regimes employ to keep and strengthen their hold on power. Totalitarian leaders stifle opposition, promote loyalty, and guarantee citizen compliance by knowing and taking advantage of emotional reactions. Fundamental tactics used in the manipulation of emotions in totalitarian regimes includes fearmongering, chauvinism, scapegoating and utopianism.

The strongest emotion used by authoritarian governments is fear. Through the widespread instillation of fear, authoritarian regimes guarantee compliance and stifle opposition. Frequently, the threat of violence, monitoring, and the arbitrary exercise of power serve to feed this dread. In George Orwell's dystopian novel *1984*, for instance, the thought police's constant threat guarantees that people follow the Party's orders. Examples from real life include the Soviet Union's Stalinist purges, which sent millions of people to labour camps or to be executed, generating an atmosphere of fear and widespread terror that suppressed even the thought of opposition. Comparably, Nazi Germany eliminated political opponents and terrorised the general public by using the Gestapo and concentration camps like Dachau.

Governments deployed a fear of covid, despite its tiny fatality rate, to lockdown societies where populations traded freedom and informed consent for a feeling of safety. In practice, the human immune system and the progressive weakening cycle of the respiratory virus did more to defeat covid than all the countermeasures, many of which were constructed on dubious claims including masking, social distancing and covid vaccines.

Extreme nationalism, chauvinism, and a feeling of superiority over other countries are common ways that totalitarian governments control emotions. Propaganda exalting the history, leaders, and alleged future of a country helps to accomplish it. Such regimes promote allegiance to the government as equal to patriotism, thereby establishing an emotional link between the state and its people. For instance, the government of North Korea has created a widespread personality cult around its leader using public displays, media, and education to implant a steadfast feeling of patriotism and devotion. Under Mussolini, fascist Italy also displayed this intense nationalism as the government encouraged the idea of a Roman Empire resurgence to bind and motivate the people. In these regimes, the state is identified with one political party, and that party is personified by one leader. One man becomes the face and mind of a whole nation. Disobedience to this leader then becomes a form of national treason.

Creating scapegoats is yet another emotional manipulation strategy employed by totalitarian governments. Regimes can bring the people together to deflect attention from internal issues by focusing their fear, rage, and frustration on a shared adversary. Scapegoating involves blaming a person or group for social problems to justify their persecution and likely extermination. Adolf Hitler's Nazi government infamously blamed Jews for the economic and social issues that followed the First World War. Similar persecution of intellectuals and alleged counter-revolutionaries by Mao Zedong's government during the Chinese Cultural Revolution was his excuse for accelerating the advancement of communism.

During the Covid era, the unvaccinated were identified, targeted, demonised and condemned throughout the political and media establishments with patently false claims about being reckless spreaders of the virus, grounded in the equally false claim that vaccines stopped transmission and infection. This was a blatant lie. The majority did not question or oppose this lie, and, according to Professor David Hughes, it advanced society to at least step four in Stanton's ten steps to genocide, before covid dissipated naturally.

Though hatred and terror are powerful instruments for controlling emotions, totalitarian governments also take advantage of positive emotions such as optimism and utopianism. These governments may win over their people with promises of a utopian future or significant social progress. In this approach, propaganda is very important; it presents the policies of the dictatorship as steps towards a better future. As evidence of progress, the Soviet Union under Stalin, for example, promoted the concept of creating a socialist paradise by pointing to technological and industrial accomplishments. Despite general hardships, the public supported the Five-Year Plans because they were seen as enormous steps towards a developed and egalitarian society.

To successfully control emotions, totalitarian governments tightly regulate information. Through their control of the media and suppression of opposing viewpoints, totalitarian regimes mould the public narrative. With this power, they may stifle any counter-narratives that would encourage empathy or critical thinking while magnifying feelings like fear, pride, and hate.

In authoritarian settings, public rituals and displays are another way that emotions are controlled. Protests, parades, and open executions are all effective means of arousing feelings in the people and preserving the authority of the dictatorship. These occasions, which are sometimes accompanied by deep emotional experiences, foster a sense of togetherness and a unified goal. The participants of the Nuremberg rallies in Germany were made to feel powerful, loyal, and proud of their country. In modern North Korea, public celebrations honouring the Kim dynasty and military parades are intended to inspire wonder, respect, and loyalty to the government. These are well-established methods that predate modernity. Their contemporary implementation should not surprise us as they rely on our enduring human nature. Spectacle takes precedence over everything else in these political rituals and displays. Emotions are seen as solely individual experiences in traditional psychology, however there is a sociology of emotions which examines how emotions are influenced by and contribute to social structures, cultural norms, as well as interpersonal relationships . This discipline studies how emotions are created, felt, and controlled in various social contexts and how they impact institutions and social behaviour. The study of totalitarianism benefits especially from an understanding of the sociology of emotions since, as we have seen, emotions are essential to the upkeep and operation of totalitarian regimes. Emotions are not simply biological or psychological, they have a cultural component. At a funeral, for instance, showing grief is seen as appropriate; at the same time, expressing joy is seen as strange and *uncultured.* Similarly, it is socially expected to feel happy at a graduation ceremony or national holiday. It should be noted that not all emotional norms are of equal value and strictness. Perceived emotional norms regulate the public expression of emotions and influence our own experience of them. Emotions also have an economic dimension, emotional labour, so named by sociologist Arlie Hochschild, is the act of controlling emotions and expressions as part of one's job description. This idea emphasises how people frequently control their emotions in order to perform the duties of their jobs, as when a customer care agent keeps a happy face even when they are upset personally, or how call centre staff remain stoic in the face of rage and abuse from customers. Emotional labour can involve either hiding emotions or exhibiting them, regardless of how a person actually feels. The abilities and resources people employ to successfully regulate their own and other people's emotions are referred to as emotional capital.

Totalitarian governments, by definition, aim to dominate not only the political and economic domains but also the emotional lives of their subjects. Emotions are purposefully controlled to uphold social order, quell opposition, and support the ideology of the state. Studying totalitarianism requires knowledge of the sociology of emotions, since it exposes the methodical use of emotions to support these regimes. Sociologists learn about the control and resistance to control in totalitarian regimes by examining how emotions are culturally interpreted and publicly displayed in these settings.

Resistance to a regime can be greatly heightened by feelings like hope, unity and even righteous fury. Knowing how these feelings arise and are controlled can help one understand the circumstances in which resistance movements take off and prosper. The sociology of emotions can also guide us towards democracy and greater freedoms, as well as emotional maturity. Recognition of the emotional aspects of political life allows us all to create solutions that meet the material as well as the emotional demands of people living under totalitarian governments. Let’s begin with anxiety, as it has featured much in the work of Mattias Desmet as a foundation to the human proclivity to generate mass formations.

Anxiety and Fear

According to Stanley Rachman, anxiety can be defined as

> *"...the tense, unsettling anticipation of a threatening but vague event, a feeling of uneasy suspense. It is a negative affect so closely related to fear that in many circumstances the two terms are used interchangeably; like anxiety, fear also is a combination of tension and unpleasant anticipation."*[1]

Like many other authors, Rachman distinguishes anxiety from fear. The two are closely linked and belong to the same cluster of enduring emotions. The distinguishing component seems to be the object of the fear or anxiety.

Fear arises as a response to a recognised threat, such as from a large rat or from oncoming heavy traffic on a narrow lane. The intense situation or dangerous object triggers a sense of urgency, significantly increasing our level of alertness and readying us for action. Fear is characterised by this distinctness; it diminishes when the threat, or the appearance of one, is gone. It is influenced by sensuous stimuli and can be logical or illogical. Phobias are the scientific name for irrational fears, where the object of the threat does not justify the fear that is experienced. Fear is an unpleasant, but useful emotion, we can see its evolutionary benefit. Together with anger, sadness, and happiness, fear is a primary emotion that we share with all mammals. Anxiety, however, is more complex and can be, characterised by an internal struggle to determine the source of an uncomfortable tension, or expected event. It has no clear sensuous stimuli. Anxiety has a diffused nature, it can lack a specific object, is unpleasant and it persists. Since there may not be a clear object of anxiety, we cannot escape from it or try to eliminate the threat because is no rat or truck

1. *Anxiety*, p. 3

for us to evade. Due to its unclear subjective experience, it is not easily distinguishable from fear while experiencing it.

Anxiety is closely linked to unpredictability, risk and lack of control. It is a condition of increased alertness and expectation, rather than an immediate response to a threat or dangerous situation. Anxiety can be a nebulous or overloaded concept with a rich history in existential philosophy and phenomenology. It is linked to existential notions of freedom and finitude. It also has a somewhat paradoxical nature; namely, it can be objectless, yet it points towards our death,

Fear is characterized by its intensity, brevity, and the fact that it is triggered by specific stimuli, but anxiety is formless, enduring, and consistently present at a lower degree of intensity. Fear is defined by distinct boundaries and is limited in scope, but anxiety lacks well-defined boundaries and is challenging to measure in terms of duration. Anxiety is not a subordinate manifestation of fear and can be more challenging to endure, as it is unpleasant, disconcerting, all-encompassing, and exhausting. Severe and long-lasting anxiety can cause significant impairment and physical harm. At a lower intensity, fear and anxiety can manifest as concern, hesitation, reluctance and shyness.

Anxiety is regarded as a uniquely human phenomenon, according to the philosophical existentialist tradition. Different existentialist thinkers, from Kierkegaard to Sartre, have emphasised that anxiety is a fundamental characteristic of human existence. The Danish philosopher, Kierkegaard, first introduced the differentiation between fear and anxiety. He postulates that anxiety is characterised by an absence of a distinct object; it is a form of fear that is not directed towards anything in particular. Anxiety has a crucial function in the intricate process of self-identification, and it exposes a fundamental antagonism in humans, between finitude and infinitude. For Kierkegaard, this antagonism was tranquillised only through genuine faith, a direct relationship to God. Later, existentialists abandoned this religious framework, however, the existential problematisation he identified proved to be enduring.

The German philosopher Martin Heidegger, who was the teacher and lover of Hannah Arendt until she had to flee to America, developed an interesting understanding of anxiety and its place in human existence. Heidegger examined the theme of moods and how we experience the world through them. His account can be difficult to grasp within the context of existential philosophy, however, it is worth examining this approach, due to its wider influence. Heidegger suggests that anxiety is a mood, not an emotion, and is separate from fear. He also problematized its objectless nature and its relation to death – , or to nothingness. Heidegger does not treat anxiety as an emotion, a mood is something quite different, and it is existentially important. Neither subjective nor objective, a mood has to do with our existence in a world we feel is separate to us, yet to which we are forever bound . Before we think or feel, we are already attuned to the world in a specific way through our moods. Anxiety, then, is not just one fleeting emotion among others, it is a deeper feeling – a mood – that underpins our other experiences. If we want to understand anxiety as a mood, we must dig deeper and examine not just the emotions and thoughts we currently have, but what lasting structures underly them.

Anxiety, for Heidegger, is a fundamental and basic mood that cannot be reduced to fear or fright. Heidegger's philosophy, unlike psychology and sociology, does not see anxiety as low intensity fear. He says that anxiety is fundamentally different from fear – where fear always has a specific object that threatens us in some way. Fear seizes the person and confuses them as they try to free themselves from it. Fear can appear in different forms: as alarm if it is sudden, as dread if it is unfamiliar or as terror if it is both sudden and unfamiliar. We fear fear itself. Fear is unpleasant and worrying. It signals we are in some kind of danger, potentially. Anxiety may not be a specific worry about something or for something or someone. Neither is it necessarily unpleasant. It has no dangerous object. This indeterminacy and lack of object is the essential feature of anxiety. Heidegger is very vivid in his descriptions of anxiety, he says, while anxious, everything familiar to us seems to slip away. The physical things in our world do not literally disappear, rather, they lose their original meaning to us. They seem to be slipping away because we cannot make sense of them to orient our life around them. They remain there as empty husks, without their everyday meaning, or importance. They cease to be part of our world, which for Heidegger, is a system of interwoven meanings and not a physical realm.

Heidegger says anxiety reveals and opens up "the nothing" within, a sense of complete meaninglessness of existence, which is frightening to those who comfortably cling to the *status quo*. Some people are disturbed by new possibilities, whether they are political or psychological. Anxiety is natural and necessary, it stops us from sleepwalking through life. It reminds us that things can be different; that our world is frail and can change at any moment.

Anxiety can be experienced on a spectrum, where at it's strongest effect, it reveals and opens up "the nothing". It seizes and overwhelms us; in anxiety, we are left speechless. The creeping nothingness around us causes us to engage in idle chatter as we try to break and cover up the empty silence. Anxiety shows us there is something missing, the world does not have to be the way it is now, it does not have to be there at all. It is an expression of our own ultimate possibility: death, but also the nothingness inherent in the world.

While being anxious, the individual is faced with the possible impossibility of their existence, or their own impending death. Anxiety deprives a person of the possibility of self-understanding through the world, as it taints all forms of their public interpretation. It destroys the comfort of conformism in everyday life. An anxious individual finds themselves in the midst of the indeterminacy of nothingness and nowhere, no longer at home in the world. They feel uncanny because their previous sense of self and structures of meaning are revealed to be empty. The complete insignificance that manifests in nothingness does not imply the absence of the world, but means that worldly beings become entirely insignificant in themselves. Anxiety does not lack an object, its subject matter is the perishing and disappearance of all beings, including the human being.

Heidegger's philosophy of anxiety aspires to break out of everyday inauthenticity and the tendency to skip over our fear of death. When we are inauthentic we are not experiencing the fullness of our lives. We observe the death of other people and experience the accompanying grief, but the mechanism of our own death is a mystery. We can be fearful of people, events or objects that might bring us to that point, but the experience of death itself remains inaccessible, until we actually die. He says that anxiety is the indicator of the possibility of our death.

Heidegger’s phenomenological and existential account of anxiety has many interesting points, but we must not let it undermine psychological theories of anxiety that do see anxiety as a form of fear and that try to address it clinically. Existential anxiety is not pathological, although it can be disruptive to everyday life. This does not mean that there are no pathological and treatable forms of anxiety.

Irvine D. Yalom draws on Heidegger in his examination of death anxiety. In particular, he draws on Heidegger's understanding of authenticity and death, where death is the impossibility of further possibility. Yalom analysed how death anxiety covertly shows up in our everyday decision-making, especially when faced with important decisions that require us to choose one possibility over another. As Yalom states: "*Every yes involves a no*".[2] He feels that anxiety in this case, is actually the low-intensity fear of missing out. No matter what we choose, we will miss out on something. We do not only have anxiety over the complete impossibility of further possibility, but also about the relative losses of possibility. As in Heidegger, we experience anxiety when we are faced with the loss of potential ways of leading our lives.

Yalom approaches anxiety from an existential psychotherapeutic perspective. He draws on philosophers like Epicurus, Kierkegaard and Heidegger in order to contextualise his clinical and personal experiences. Death anxiety can be both overt and covert. Overt death anxiety is a disturbing awareness of our own finitude and coming end. It can happen to anyone, not just people who are faced with danger and the real possibility of death. Yalom points out that overt anxiety about death is often mistakenly assumed to be a mask for something else. Covert death anxiety can take hold of us when

2. *Staring at the Sun*, p. 58

we least expect it. It can appear symbolically in our dreams. Heidegger suggests that it is always there, sleeping within us.

Yalom agrees with Heidegger in that we can accept anxiety and use it to live an authentic life. He also agrees that anxiety of death is not some mental illness or obstacle to life, but an existential feature of human existence. Anxiety can save us from conformism and meaninglessness. Death anxiety is a direct, non-conceptual, way of encountering little deaths before it is too late. The awareness it brings can be integrated into much more authentic and meaningful living. Yalom states: "*Death awareness may serve as an awakening experience, a profoundly useful catalyst for major life changes*".[3]

Like all emotions, anxiety can be contagious. Sociologists such as Anthony Giddens and Ulrich Beck have studied the social aspect of anxiety and its place in Western modernity. Anxiety is a typically modern emotion, influenced by risk and uncertainty, according to Beck, and by reflexivity and loss of trust according to Giddens. In modern societies, the idea of risk management plays a crucial role in creating anxieties about the future. Beck argues that the modern focus on risk is driven by a desire to eliminate randomness and uncertainty through rationalisation and planning. Modernity is progress towards greater control and less natural chaos. According to Beck:

> "*Risk may be defined as a systematic way of dealing with hazards and insecurities induced and introduced by modernization itself. Risks, as opposed to older dangers, are consequences which relate to the threatening force of modernization and to its globalization of doubt*".[4]

3. *Staring at the Sun*, p. 30
4. *Risk Society*, p. 21

Anxiety develops as a consequence of the increasing demands of modernisation. It is not mere fear over catastrophe and danger, anxiety is a consequence of ignorance, as much as it of the information age. It seeks to manage risk through comprehension and knowledge, which is connected to our innate desire to govern unpredictability.

Risk, unlike previous natural threats, is not merely a vague threat but is calculated, evidence-based, and probabilistic, involving the anticipation of potential catastrophes. Modern statistical methods have created a stronger emphasis on security, safety and certainty. These have become, graspable ideals. Their absence makes us anxious because we know that they are achievable.

Beck also discusses the political significance of anxiety, using risk as the basis of political action. Previous political movements mobilized people through a utopian project, but today's risk centred society cannot afford utopianism. This is anti-dystopian. Beck explains the situation: "*The dream of class society is that everyone wants and ought to have a share of the pie. The utopia of the risk society is that everyone should be spared from poisoning*".[5] Anxiety, when used as a political emotion, steers social discourse towards the management of risk, not towards the realisation of ideals.

British sociologist Anthony Giddens has addressed the modern prevalence of anxiety through his examination of the modernisation project, with an emphasis on reflexivity. Giddens has explained how trust in scientists and experts relies on an asymmetry of knowledge between them and the laypeople. He points out that a preoccupation with the

5. *Risk Society*, p. 49

uncertain future and thus with safety, elevates the notion of risk in society. Trust becomes necessary in the functioning of highly complex societies. It is necessary due to the layperson's inability to actually verify the expertise, leading to a reliance on expert systems. Confidence in expert systems, since it is not really grounded in evidence and understanding, can be easily shattered by dramatic events and ensuing collective emotions. The loss of trust in systems that are deemed to be necessary causes many negative states and emotions, one of them being anxiety. As with Beck, anxiety is connected to a loss of certainty and safety.

Giddens draws from psychoanalysis to examine the unconscious dimension of anxiety and its origins in childhood. He states: "*Anxiety has its seeds in fear of separation from the prime caretaking agent (usually the mother), a phenomenon which for the infant threatens the very core of the emerging self and of ontological security more generally*".[6]

Anxiety is always with us. It has been so from the start. Giddens also elaborates on how anxiety can lead to hostility, as a reaction to the pain of abandonment and hopelessness.

Not only is society at risk; we do not know what it will look like in the near future due to economic, ecological and technological factors. We also do not know who we are as individual people, and we are anxious in the face of our freedom. Giddens writes in *Modernity and Self-Identity* "*If basic trust is not developed or its inherent ambivalence not contained, the outcome is persistent existential anxiety*".[7] In extreme cases, this anxiety becomes dread. The modern self requires trust and

6. *Modernity and Self-Identity*, p. 45-46
7. *Modernity and Self-Identity*, p. 100

certainty in order to confront the many possibilities of modernity.

These theories and accounts of anxiety and fear present a confusing, and even contradictory picture. The way Heidegger characterises anxiety could be enough to discourage further interest. However, we should not allow philosophical and scientific jargon to dissuade us from trying to understand basic human realities. What Heidegger seems to be saying, presumably, is that anxiety is inherent in human existence – it is not something wholly negative. Being a conscious and finite being in a world makes us anxious. Finitude implies the inevitability of death, but also of freedom! We do many things to counter and hide this anxiety because it upsets our comfortable and familiar lifestyle.

We fear both our death and our freedom, so we shun anxiety because it makes us aware of these possibilities. The culture of docility despises anxiety exactly for this reason, it promotes an inauthentic life where we ignore death and abandon our freedoms. Heidegger's interpretation espouses simple truths with political consequences. The important learning with respect to the topic I am covering here, is that flight from anxiety can leads us into the embrace of political monsters. Next on the list is shame, a driving force in the establishment of Nazi Germany in the last century.

Shame

Sociologist Thomas J. Scheff is credited with making important contributions to the sociologies of emotion, social bonds and mental health. Understanding the connections between feelings and social interactions has been made possible in large part by his work. Scheff's theories have shed light on how social settings both form and are shaped by emotions, therefore affecting many facets of human behaviour and social systems. He claims social bonds are strengthened and weakened through certain emotions. For example, an understanding of empathy and pride is essential to comprehending social interactions and relationships. Scheff claims unresolved feelings can cause mental health problems and social isolation. His writings stress the need to identify and work with emotions in order to preserve positive social relationships.

Scheff's work cleared the path for additional study and investigation in this field by highlighting the significance of emotions in social interactions and in political regimes, such as totalitarianism. His contributions have also influenced therapy and mental health treatment, influencing therapeutic techniques and promoting a more sympathetic and emotion-focused approach to therapy.

He has a lot to say about shame. For instance, he sees shame as a basic emotion that influences relationships and social behaviour. In *Bloody Revenge: Emotions, Nationalism and War,* Scheff defines shame as a basic social emotion that develops when people believe they are being judged poorly by others, or when they fall short of their own expectations.

Shame is intimately related to a person's sense of self and social identity and a potent force that controls behaviour and preserves social order. People who feel ashamed usually have a disturbance in their social networks, often feeling they have broken expectations or social standards, and is cut off from the group.

Scheff presents the idea of the shame-rage cycle, where unresolved shame can cause violent behaviour and social unrest. This cycle also sustains social isolation and conflict. Deeply ashamed people, for instance, may respond defensively or with animosity, which would further isolate them from others and exacerbate their original shame. They feel that their social bonds are threatened and respond in a way that actually damages them.

Shame is more freely recognised and handled in various cultures, which might help people process and resolve their emotions. Conversely, people may find it more difficult to manage their emotions in societies where shame is seen negatively or even suppressed, which can have long-term psychological and social repercussions. An inability to accept shame is a sign of emotional immaturity, and it can be individual as well as cultural.

Scheff sees pride as a complicated feeling with both good and bad aspects. Pride may inspire people to pursue goals and uphold high standards and can also boost self-esteem. Conversely, too much or inappropriate pride could breed conceit and societal unrest. Pride, much as shame, is essential for the formation and upkeep of social bonds. Pride can positively strengthen social ties and promote a feeling of belonging when it results from sincere accomplishments and acknowledgement from others. Social bonds are heightened, for instance, when people feel proud of their contributions to a group and are acknowledged.

Scheff contends that social harmony depends on a balance between pride and shame. Too much pride can breed conceit and hostility, too much shame can cause withdrawal and social isolation. Politically, excessive pride leads to chauvinism, whereas shame to atomism or disassociation. Retaining good social bonds requires a balanced approach where people may experience and express both emotions appropriately. This requires a level of emotional maturity.

In applying his theory to World War I and the subsequent rise of Hitler, Scheff shows how humiliation leads to shame, which culminates in a need for catharsis through bloody revenge. The prideful German nation, brought to its knees by the loss and peace treaty, experienced excessive shame and could not find a healthy outlet for it. Hitler was an individual prone to humiliation and shame, according to Scheff, and he offered the German people a restoration of their pride and trust in social bonds.

Desmet, identified anxiety as a crucial emotion that led to the atomisation and isolation of the period. Shame was equally, if not more, important. The mass formation can arise only after social bonds have been annihilated by shame. Anxiety, in this case, is an acknowledgement of the damage that shame has done. The two emotions feed on each other and reinforce the decay of social bonds. Scheff does well at pointing out how these cycles are not inevitable; excessive shame does not have to lead to excessive pride. National humiliation is not a highway to national chauvinism or vice versa. There are healthier alternatives for societies. Totalitarian leaders are quick to deny this, their only response to humiliation is bloody revenge so we must not fall for this simple and flawed reasoning. This brings us to hatred and contempt.

Resentment, Hatred and Contempt

Hatred is a strong and often harmful emotion that can greatly influence politics, social cohesion, and policymaking. Hatred may be caused by old grudges, unfair economic conditions, cultural conflicts, perceived threats and political oppression. It is difficult to conceal hatred as it leads to various forms of hostility. At worst, it is expressed as overt aggression in the form of violence. Usually it is repressed and appears through acts of *passive aggression.* At best, we confront our feelings of hatred and attempt to dissolve or sublimate it.

Identity politics, in which groups define themselves in opposition to others, and hatred often go hand in hand. Politicians and political movements use hatred to get people to support them, bring people together within their own group, and make the other-groups look bad. This is clear in nationalist, religious, and racial conflicts where hatred of "others" is used to bring people together and strengthen group identity. Hatred is often spread with the help of political rhetoric, the media, and propaganda. Politicians and the media use disparaging words, stereotypes, and false information to make people hate each other. It's clear this is the case when certain groups are blamed for major problems in society, making people angry and resentful.

Hatred has a big effect on how people act in politics, including how they vote, get involved, and most importantly, on violent behaviour. Psychologists who study politics and society look at how hatred can make people support dictators, take part in violent protests, or commit hate crimes. For example, it is known that economic downturns make people more hateful and support hateful parties. The sense of despair and insecurity caused by worsening economic conditions makes people more suspicious of other groups and willing to engage in witch-hunts and scapegoating.

Hatred breaks down social unity and can cause society to break-up. However, it can also inspire a sense of solidarity among those who hate. Generational hatred between groups solidifies social disorder and makes it difficult to agree on basic political issues and work together. This hateful split undermines democratic institutions and even makes popular governance dangerous, as hateful groups can use political institutions to hurt each other.

Many societies and governments do try to deal with and lessen hatred. Laws against discrimination, rules against hate speech, and school programmes that teach tolerance and acceptance are all examples of policies that make an effort to reduce hatred. Of course, these attempts are focused on lessening the social harms of hatred, and do not necessarily address the many sources and potential legitimacy of this emotion.

In the past few years, the rise of extremist political movements in many countries has been linked to the spreading of hate. Most political leaders regularly use people's worries about the economy and their fears of otherness and change. Since this emotional manipulation is so widespread, it is difficult to determine its overall outcome and effect. What is clear is that emotional manipulation can lead to diverse forms of hatred; people can be made to hate on mass other cultures, immigrants, rich, minority groups and even themselves. Hatred can be a galvanising source of political energy, but it can also easily become a destructive force endangering the whole of society.

The Rwandan Genocide of 1994 is a clear example of how politics can use hatred to cause terrible violence. Political sociologists have studied how political leaders used racial tensions and old grudges to stir up hatred and plan large-scale violence against the Tutsi minority. During the same period, Yugoslavia was also undergoing civil war and ethnic cleansing, motivated by both economic hardships and political use of hatred. In both cases, whole societies and ethnic groups were subject to systematic hateful campaigns and terrible extermination.

There are many different theoretical frameworks that seek to explain the political significance of hatred which offer competing explanations for a very complex and familiar emotion. There is no need to go into detail about them or to select a single one, the important point is to keep in mind the inherent complexity of this seemingly simple emotion.

Throughout history, powerful leaders and political movements have used hatred as a political tool to gain more power, change public opinion, and push social and political agendas. Hatred is quite flexible and can be used for different things in different political situations. It can even be good in the short term, as it can fuel positive change, but bad for society in the long term if it is not successfully diffused and addressed in a healthy way.

Creating common enemies is universally implemented by political leaders and movements to get people to work together in support . The enemy could be a political rival, a religious or racial group, or a country on another continent. In this case, hatred can be used to achieve goals, but it often comes at a great cost. In wartime, for example, political leaders rally their supporters, strengthen national identity, and get more people involved in the war efforts by directing collective anger and hatred at a specific target. In the case of World War II, we are well aware of the damaging hatred spread by the Nazi regime. However, the Allies utilised hatred as well, depicting the Germans, Italians and Japanese as barbarous people prone to violence. In an act of terrorism, the Allies fire-bombed a defenceless Dresden, a civilian target, turning it into a firestorm to killing its firefighters and first responders and, inflicted great numbers of civilian casualties.

Hatred can be used to blame certain people or groups for problems in society, which takes the focus off of mistakes made by those in power. This strategy creates a distraction that enables leaders to avoid responsibility by putting the blame on someone else. For instance, when the economy is doing badly, immigrants are often blamed for taking jobs and resources, which takes attention away from problems with the way the economy is built. Hatred can also be used to defend harsh actions and policies. When a group is seen as a threat, it can be dehumanised and harsh actions against them are justified by the greater need to keep society safe. During World War II, the internment of Japanese Americans is an example of how fear and hatred led to extreme actions being taken against a certain racial group.

Totalitarian governments often use hatred to silence political opposition and dissent. Regimes create hate in their people for their opponents by calling them traitors, or enemies of the state. This isolates their opponents and hurts their credibility. Nazi Germany used this strategy by making their political opponents, everyone from communists to centre-right monarchists, Jews, Slavs and other minorities, look like they were threats to the Aryan race and the country.

It's important to know the differences between contempt and resentment when looking at political feelings and how they affect people. When you feel contempt for someone you think they are less important or not deserving of respect. It is often marked by moral judgment and a sense of superiority. People, groups, or even whole institutions can be treated with contempt. When it comes to politics, contempt makes it harder for people to get along and respect each other. For instance, elites may look down on the working class and think they are stupid or behind the times. This can lead to policies that don't take into consideration their needs and wants.

On the other hand, resentment also comes from thinking that someone is being unfair, and appears in the form of anger and bitterness towards people who you think have hurt you or your group. These are often people who are above you in the social hierarchy. Where there are imbalances of power and social injustice, resentment often grows. When it comes to politics, hatred, in its many forms, can be a strong motivator for working together and resisting. In the United States Civil Rights Movement, the anger that marginalised groups felt towards systemic discrimination led positively to social movements and calls for change.

Policies that are based on contempt are likely to ignore the rights and needs of people who are seen as less important. Even though hatred can cause division, it can also bring people together who have similar problems, leading to group efforts for social change. Contempt, in particular, has an elitist tone and promotes solidarity among the elites. When the ruling class treats the people badly, it can make a lot of people lose hope and stop caring about politics. If you don't do anything about your anger, it can lead to social unrest and questions about the legitimacy of political institutions. Hatred can be a powerful way to get people to work together, distract them, give them a reason to do something, or shut them down, but it also poses serious threats to social harmony and political stability.

Contempt and resentment are both forms of hatred. We should think of it as a vertical spectrum, where contempt is the hatred that the powerful feel towards the powerless, whereas resentment is the hatred the powerless feel towards the powerful. Contempt is hatred combined with disgust, whereas resentment is hatred combined with envy. These definitions have their limitations, but they give us an approximate and working image of these emotions. The German philosopher Friedrich Nietzsche discussed resentment in many of his colourful philosophical works. Nietzsche's work on resentment, or *ressentiment* in French (the term he uses), is a central theme in his critique of modern morality, especially in *On the Genealogy of Morality* and *Beyond Good and Evil.* Nietzsche explains how he believes moral values are formed in the mind, and he says that hatred is the main cause of what he calls, "slave morality". People who are weak and abused have this kind of morality because they are deeply angry at those who have power and privilege. Slave morality is the opposite of "master morality", which is made by strong people and is based on values like pride, strength, and nobility. As Nietzsche saw it, qualities like meekness, humility, and sympathy come from a place of weakness and repressed envy.

Nietzsche thought weak and oppressed people could not directly take action against those who hurt them out of anger. Instead, they make a moral framework that devalues the traits of the powerful and praises their own. This flipping of values is a way for people who are weak to feel better about themselves than the people who are above them. Nietzsche also says that the idea of *good* in slave morality comes from the traits that weak people have that strong people don't. He believed that slave morality involves routinely lying to oneself. People who follow this moral system tell themselves that their virtues of meekness and humility are better by nature, instead of realising that these traits come from powerlessness. If you lie to yourself, you end up with a hypocritical stance where moral strength is presented as a weakness.

A self-proclaimed aristocrat, Nietzsche criticised all the progressive movements of his time, this included both socialism and liberalism. He thought that the democratic and egalitarian movements of today are examples of slave morality. These movements were supposedly motivated by hatred and a desire to weaken the strong and strengthen the weak. Nietzsche concluded that this made society less strong because the average people made it harder for exceptional people to stand out. He believed that "master morality" is creative, full of life, and driven by a desire for power, while "slave morality" is reactive, devoid of life, and based on resentment.

The introduction of the idea of ressentiment into ethical discourse by Nietzsche is a strong attack on the psychological basis of modern morality. Nietzsche challenged the common understanding of moral values by connecting them to the hatred that powerless people feel. These supposedly good values, like sympathy and humility, can be used to hide weakness and limit human potential. His call for a re-evaluation of values is an interesting and important part of the history of modern philosophy. It makes us think about the moral and cultural frameworks that shape our society in a critical way. We do not, of course, have to completely agree with Nietzsche . His dismissal of what he calls "slave morality" is shocking and unjustified, to be precise, he identified a form of hatred as the origin of supposedly virtuous behaviours. I believe Nietzsche's mistake was concluding that all sympathy, humility, meekness and forgiveness is based on hidden resentment. His view was reductionist. We can accept resentment as a potential source of false virtues, but not the only one. He didn't cover the impact of contempt.

When you feel contempt for a person or a group you think is less important or deserving than you are, you tend to treat them badly. Their troubles and suffering are simply worth less to you, they might even deserve it. When it comes to politics, contempt can mean different things. People in the political elite have a tendency to look down on people from lower classes or groups that are struggling economically. For the elite, their struggle is a sign of their innate inferiority, this was the prevalent response of the British establishment to the Irish Famine. Their contempt for the Irish was disguised in religious terms as divine providence or God's will for a peasant, landless people, dismissing the obvious point that their apartheid policies had caused widespread poverty and risked the catastrophe that unfolded. The contempt continued after the Irish War of Independence into the formation of Northern Ireland with an engineered non-Catholic majority and suppression of civil rights.

Hatred divides people, contempt breeds resentment, and vice versa. When politicians and their supporters look down on their opponents, it leads to a sense of superiority that stops people from talking to each other in a constructive way. This vertical polarisation makes society more divided, making it harder for people to work together and agree on things. The most important thing is to have someone less fortunate than you to hate. This creates and almost comical situation where powerful elites hate managerial elites, who hate white-collar workers, who hate the blue-collar workers, who hate the poor who, hate the immigrants. Hatred ends up being a reinforcement mechanism of social stratification.

Leaders often use contempt to distract people from their actions, as their ire is focused on the people below them, instead of those above them.

Both contempt and resentment can influence politics, but they do so in different ways and often from different directions. The elite often look down on their citizens, seeing them as less important than them, however even the average person has contempt for people who are they believe are somehow below them. A lack of basic respect, stemming from a contemptuous elite, can make people even more resentful, which can lead to more division and possibly eventual physical conflict.

Anger directed towards the elites can lead to disdain for the current system, this can be a driving force for movements that want to change the regime. This raises the question as to whether politics based on hate is legitimate. Emotionality is still seen as the direct opposite of rationality and as an obstacle to sound judgment. When we call someone emotional, we may think of them as irrational, however this is not necessarily true. This dogma is perpetuated through the constant linking of emotionality and conspiracy theories.

People often create and believe conspiracy theories because they are angry about what they see as injustice or unfair treatment. When people are angry, they try to figure out why they are suffering and unhappy, which can lead them to believe stories that blame certain people or groups for their problems. Conspiracy theories often offer a simple way to make sense of complicated social and political situations by giving what seem to be logical reasons for problems and wrongs. Conspiracy theories, in this case, serve as a channel for emotion, particularly hate. We are not flawed because we are emotional, instead, emotions are a way we deal with being finite; we never know enough, never have enough control and can never escape our ultimate end. Emotions are a way of recognising these basic facts in a deep and essential way. Rationality only confirms the importance of emotions, as modern sociology, neuroscience and psychology confirm. When someone is angry, they want to find what or who is to blame for their problems. Emotions motivate us to look for the truth and be curious about the world.

Today's societies are complicated and constantly changing. It is not always easy to discover exactly what causes social ailments and economic problems. These problems are often made easier by extremist ideologies, spectacular science and simplistic conspiracy theories, which give appealing but wrong explanations. People may believe these simple stories when they are angry at systems or authorities which they feel are unfair. Joy, hope and pride can also make people unwilling to accept that the institutions and authorities they are emotionally attached to are acting in a malevolent way. Overly patriotic and chauvinistic people are almost always unable to accept that their countries have engaged in covert operations, propaganda, assassinations and unjust wars. Their pride prevents them from accepting any criticism of their government. The same is true for people who get attached to celebrities, admiration makes them furious and zealous defenders if any crimes and sins of their beloved star are revealed.

Many of the fantastical conspiracy theories involving reptilian, aliens and shapeshifters originate from an unhealthy mixture of paranoia and hate, creating an enemy where no obvious enemy can be found. In the 1950s, many people in the US were angry about what they saw as communist influence in government and society, leading to the idea that communists had infiltrated important institutions, causing the infamous *Red Scare*, during which many people were wrongly accused and punished. The negative effects are still visible in American society, as most people are afraid to strongly criticise the US government for fear of being labelled as traitorous communists or, God forbid, un-American. So what is the counterbalance?

Comedy as a Solution

Humour, satire and the laughter of the crowd provides cultures universally with special means to challenge authority, voice disapproval, and promote community that go beyond traditional political discourse. Many comedians highlight social issues as form of political resistance. Politicians and policies can be powerfully criticised through humour. It is no accident that comedians first lead the counternarrative challenging covid taboos. Comedy reveals the inconsistencies and absurdities of those in authority, it deconstructs the falce façade of seriousness and infallibility that politicians, scientists and bureaucrats rely on. It does this by reminding us that politicians too, are human. Being human, of course, comes hand-in-glove with absurdities and oddities. In Gaelic society, the Bard occupied a revered and feared position, whose praise or condemnation in story, poetry and song, could decide the fate of kings and their succession. We need to go back to those ways of thinking.

Rip off Republic was a four-part TV series comprising of one-hour live stand-ups that I co-wrote. It was filmed for television at the Helix theatre in Dublin in the early autumn of 2005 and set new Irish TV audience records for factual entertainment. That the Irish Government bristled at the blend of facts, pithy observations and humour helped drive viewership ever higher, culminating in a unique 55% national viewing audience. Such was the reaction it created among the public, senior politicians demanded an urgent Government committee hearing for its presenter and u-turned only after learning that 85% of all the facts deployed came from Government agencies. The Taoiseach of the era, Bertie Ahern described me as a *'non-factual person'*, coded language for a liar. It didn't work, the public mood which had first belly-laughed, turned quickly to derision when they perceived an orchestrated personal attack on the messenger. Responding to the programme, a gleeful public, sensing Government unease, flooded one of its departments with thousands of envelopes full of nappies to express their desire to have the protectionist 1987 Groceries Order scrapped. It worked; shops could then pass through bulk discounts to consumers on all groceries without facing prosecution by the Director of Consumer Affairs.

Traditionally, late-night comedy shows and political cartoons employ humour to expose the inadequacies and hypocrisies of politicians, bringing difficult subjects closer to the general audiences. Laughter helps us deal with social and political concerns, it works as a psychological release that instantly raises our mood and helps us bond with others. Laughter is a momentary respite and also a means of processing challenging reality. It can also be used as an indirect way of expressing subversive political thoughts in repressive environments. Laughing together creates a sense of community. Political humour frequently appeals to groups with similar beliefs, aspirations or complaints, therefore strengthening their sense of communal identification. Social movements can be strengthened, and activists opinions validated by this feeling of solidarity.

Comedy has a rich and ancient history as an essential component in political and cultural life, most especially satire that criticises powerful people, organisations, and social mores with irony, sarcasm, and mockery. In ancient Greece, the Dionysian festivals may have been the origins of such comedy.

These festivities honoured Dionysus, the god of fertility, wine, and festivities through poetry, dance, and musical performances. The caustic and bawdy humour that was common in the rites helped to establish more regimented comedy styles.

Many credit the great 5th-century BCE playwright Aristophanes with developing Old Comedy, a form distinguished by its use of chorus, political satire, and fanciful narratives. In *Lysistrata*, *The Clouds*, and *The Frogs*, among other plays, he skilfully blended comedy with social and political criticism. Aristophanes attacked Athenian politics, society, and intellectual life through inflated characters and ridiculous circumstances, frequently focusing on well-known individuals like Socrates and the politician Cleon. Greek comedy regularly touched on political subjects and attacked institutions and public personalities, to undermine policies, reveal corruption, and make fun of foolish politicians. Greek comedy also went beyond politics to examine social concerns such as gender roles, social tensions, and everyday life.

Satire affects public opinion of political events and personalities by highlighting the ridiculousness and simplification of complicated problems and underground comedy has been essential to subversion and resistance under totalitarian governments. Through the effective and memorable phrasing of political topics, it can raise awareness of what is going on behind the scenes. Not so funny has been the rise of premeditated mobs emoting on social media, so let's deal with the cry-bully next!

The Cry-Bully

At its core, the term *cry-bully* melds the characteristics of a cry-baby, someone who portrays themselves as helpless, the victim, with those of a bully; one who aggressively imposes their will onto others. This uniquely modern fusion results in an individual who habitually positions themselves as the aggrieved party while simultaneously employing aggressive tactics to silence, marginalise, or even persecute others, particularly those they perceive as threats to their narrative or self-image. One might ask, how does such an incongruous blend of vulnerability and aggression coexist within a singular psyche?

The digital realm with its echo chambers, selective visibility, and amplified emotional responses, fosters the perfect environment for the cry-bully to thrive. As we have previously seen, online platforms, in their pursuit of sustained user engagement, prioritises content that elicits strong emotional reactions, inadvertently spotlighting and even rewarding these behaviours.

The roots of this social behaviour can be traced back to the broader human need for both validation and control. Historically these two needs have often manifested independently; one might find solace in the community's empathy or assert dominance over their environment. The digital ecosystem offers individuals an intoxicating blend of both sympathy and power. When perceiving a slight, whether it is real or imagined, the cry-bully responds with a well-curated narrative of victimhood. This narrative, often amplified by their chosen online echo chamber, garners waves of support and validation. Riding this wave of collective indignation, the cry-bully then transitions from the defence to offence, lashing out at their perceived oppressor with a ferocity often disproportionate to the original grievance.

Platforms such as X, Facebook, and Instagram, with their vast user bases and algorithm-driven content dissemination, inadvertently become amplifiers for the cry-bully. Here, the cry-bully lurks, typically presenting as an anonymous account with a fake name whose sole function it appears, is to persistently bait and attack known persons until they get the response desired, they are blocked. They then display the blocked notice on their feed as evidence of the righteousness of their attack and present it as an assault on 'free speech'! A post depicting personal distress can quickly gather momentum, attracting likes, shares, and comments. This digital affirmation not only validates the cry-bully's sense of victimhood but also mobilises a faceless digital army, ready and willing to champion their cause, often without delving deeply into the nuances or facts of the situation.

For example, a female journalist attacks criticism of her writing on the basis that it is misogynistic, garnering vast support from the remnants of the #MeToo sisterhood; few, if any, of whom will bother to read either the article or the criticism. They rush to attack the male, pale and stale villain, attempting to cancel him. This digital army, driven by righteous indignation and often armed with partial or skewed information becomes the cry-bully's weapon, targeting those labelled as aggressors. The targets, often taken aback by the sheer magnitude of the online onslaught, find themselves vilified, their voices drowned amidst a cacophony of outrage.

The rise of the cry-bully carries significant implications for societal discourse, particularly in realms like academia, politics, and culture. Ideas and discussions, once the lifeblood of progressive societies, risk becoming stifled as individuals fear the potential backlash from the ever-vigilant cry-bully. The space for nuanced dialogue shrinks, replaced by polarised shouting matches where emotional resonance trumps factual integrity. Moreover, genuine victims of oppression or injustice may find their voices diluted or even hijacked by cry-bullies.

As the lines between genuine grievance and strategic victimhood blur, society becomes desensitised to real issues, viewing them with undue scepticism due to the misgivings of past cry-bully incidents, while fearful of being caught in the maelstrom. This leads to a collective stilled silence. Political apathy and appetite for spectacle go hand in hand. Grievances become something to be talked about online and are not treated as real issues in need of a political solution.

Addressing the cry-bully phenomenon requires a multi-pronged approach. First, as digital consumers, there's a pressing need for a more critical engagement. Before jumping onto an outrage bandwagon we ought to pause, research, and understand the broader context of any given situation. Empathy, while a noble sentiment, should be tempered with scepticism. Algorithms that blindly prioritise emotionally charged content need recalibration, ensuring that depth, nuance, and authenticity are equally valued. Attention is a valuable resource; we should not throw it around carelessly.

Recognising the difference between genuine victimhood and manipulative tactics, understanding the implications of one's online actions, and cultivating an environment of mutual respect are foundational to curbing the rise of the cry-bully. Emotional maturity is not something we value as a society. We must acknowledge the existence and influence of our emotions whilst behaving as responsible adults. The two are not at odds. Ensuring that discourse remains open, respectful, and informed is not merely an academic endeavour, but a pressing existential necessity. The cry-bully, in all its complex duality, is a stark reminder of the delicate balance between validation and aggression, between listening and shouting, and between genuine grievance and strategic victimhood.

The duality of the cry-bully is a marker. Their shield, representing their claim to victimhood, grants them moral authority and immunises them against critique. After all, how can one assail someone who is already 'hurt'? Surely the victims of injustice cannot be perpetrators of injustice, can they? This dogma serves as a protective barrier that allows them to amplify their grievances, often rallying sympathetic voices to their cause. The weapon, on the other hand, is the aggressive assertion of their pain, marshalled to silence, suppress, or even cancel the original transgressor. Far from being passive, the cry-bully actively seeks validation for their stance, employing emotive narratives, selective evidence, and occasionally, outright distortion. The anatomy of the incident unfolds as a cascading series of events, spiralling outwards, drawing in bystanders, influencers, and sometimes, even institutions.

Sensing the rising tide of interaction around the incident, the platforms' algorithm spotlights the controversy, pushing it onto trending lists and recommendation feeds. This heightened visibility attracts a larger audience, further fuelling the fire. As the incident gains traction, two polarised camps often emerge: one decrying the perceived injustice and rallying behind the cry-bully, and the other, either defending the initial trigger or condemning the tactics of the cry-bully. The grand spectacle of the digital colosseum is underway, the audience picks their sides, and the gladiatorial combat of opinions commences.

Beyond this observable sequence of events, subtler, more insidious undercurrents are at play. A cry-bully incident is not merely a spontaneous eruption of feelings; it's emblematic of deeper societal fissures. The digital age, with its relentless barrage of information and stimuli, has eroded the traditional gatekeepers of information, leading to a democratisation of narratives. While this has its merits, enabling marginalised voices to rise, it also paves the way for manipulation, distortion, and the entrenchment of echo chambers. The anatomy of a cry-bully incident, therefore, is a microcosm of the larger societal shifts we're witnessing. The confluence of genuine grievances, the human need for validation, the manipulative potential of digital platforms and the breakdown of traditional modes of discourse all come to a head in these incidents.

Corporations and businesses are not immune to the lure of the victimhood narrative. When faced with valid criticism regarding unethical practices, environmental concerns, or other issues, some corporations have adopted a stance of being unfairly targeted. By portraying themselves as victims of 'cancel culture' or agenda-driven activists, these corporations seek to shift a particular narrative. The real issues are sidelined and the discourse revolves around whether or not the company is being unjustly attacked. Such tactics often rally support from unsuspecting consumers and divert attention from the genuine concerns at hand. Boeing and Nestlé, for example, by abusing the mechanics and patterns established by the cry-bully try to continue to endanger hundreds of lives and still manage to present themselves as victims. Boeing was heavily criticised and closely watched after the deaths of 346 people in two 737 Max planes. Investigations showed the plane's design had major flaws, and there were also problems with Boeing's safety procedures and governmental oversight. As a reaction to the criticism, Boeing took the position that the regulators and media were unfairly picking on them. They said it was facing problems that had never been seen before, and that the attention on its mistakes was taking away from the complexity of the aviation business. Their story tries to shift the focus from Boeing's specific safety and regulatory failures to a larger discussion about how hard it is to keep safety up in a high-tech, highly regulated business. In this way, Boeing hopes to lessen the damage to its image and win back the trust of the public and investors.

Nestlé was criticised for using up local water supplies in drought-stricken areas, making it harder for people to get this essential resource. Nestlé said that campaigners were unfairly going after the company because they don't understand how committed they are to sustainable water management. The company said it is being unfairly blamed for bigger problems like water shortages even though it follows all the rules and helps the local economy. This story moves the discussion away from Nestlé's actions to the bigger issue of water management. Nestlé wants to be seen as a good corporate citizen who is being unfairly attacked by campaigners.

Higher education institutions, once revered as bastions of free thought and discourse, are not immune to the cry-bully. Faculty members or students who voice unpopular or contentious opinions, face a potentially significant backlash, then, the waters can get muddied when after making provocative statements, the instigators adopt the role of victims, claiming academic suppression or infringement on their freedom of speech. This muddling of lines can lead to institutional actions, protests, and larger debates about academic freedom, yet the core issue often remains unaddressed: Was it genuine victimhood or a calculated move to gain attention or deflect criticism?

Digital activism has brought about some positive change. It allows people to express their support for causes and criticise power from the comfort of their homes. However, as we have seen, there's a dark side to it. Some individuals, recognising the power of the digital mob, have fabricated incidents or injustices, casting themselves as victims to gain attention, support, or even financial aid. When these fabrications are revealed, they not only harm the individual's credibility but often cast a shadow on genuine cases of injustice, making it harder for real victims to find support. While technology has amplified voices and democratised access, it has also introduced challenges with which society is still grappling.

Social media has become an essential tool for politicians to reach and engage with their constituents. One particularly intriguing phenomenon involves politicians who, after launching scathing attacks or making polarising comments, position themselves as victims of media bias, or public misunderstanding. Take for instance, a hypothetical senator, whom we shall refer to as Senator Slick; he makes a controversial statement about a minority group. As anticipated, this elicits backlash from activists, the media, and fellow politicians. Instead of addressing the concerns or clarifying his statement, Slick doubles down, alleging the media is unfairly targeting him, that he is being silenced, or that his words are being taken out of context. Slick's core base rallies behind him, viewing him as a martyr facing unjust persecution. The original problematic statement becomes obscured as the narrative shifts to Slick's victimhood. This manipulation of digital sentiment not only deflects criticism but often galvanizes a politician's support base, making it a recurring strategy in the digital political playbook.

Celebrities often find themselves under intense scrutiny. However, there are instances where celebrities, after initiating controversies or engaging in questionable behaviours, pivot to portray themselves as victims of excessive public scrutiny or media misrepresentation.

The nature of contemporary media consumption, characterised by rapid news cycles and sensationalism, often gravitates towards polarised narratives. Cry-bullies, with their inherent dichotomy, provide compelling stories. However, the lens of media, depending on its orientation, can either amplify the narrative or challenge it. The danger is that, in the quest for virality or engagement, the nuanced realities of such situations may be overshadowed by more sensational, simplified versions. Striking a balance is hard work: policies must protect genuine victims while discouraging manipulative behaviours. Reactive measures, such as disciplinary actions or platform bans, are just one facet; proactive strategies, including education on digital etiquette, empathy training, and fostering inclusive environments, are equally important.

While the cry-bully phenomenon poses intricate challenges, it also presents an opportunity—a call to action for society at large. It demands a deeper introspection into the nature of online interactions, the sanctity of genuine victimhood, and the imperatives of justice. As the digital era matures, the onus is on society to discern, understand, and judiciously respond to the nuances of the cry-bully conundrum, ensuring that genuine voices of distress are heard, while manipulative tactics are recognised and addressed.

Tackling the cry-bully phenomenon will probably require a multi-pronged approach, intertwining pre-emptive measures, immediate interventions, and long-term educative efforts. Vigilance as to the crybully's *modus operandi* is paramount, recognising the telltale signs—such as the swift transition from offensive behaviour to defensive posturing, the frequent reliance on emotional manipulation, and the consistent portrayal of oneself as a perennial victim even in the face of contradictory evidence—are the early warning signals.

15

CLIMATE CHANGE

THAT BOTH CLIMATE and pandemic scares were identified as conduits to drive towards global governance as far back as the 1950's is a cause for continued concern. The continued politicisation of science and trillions of dollars in grants and funding, has, much like the Covid pandemic, distorted pure science into propaganda. There is vast money and power to be gained from creating fear and anxiety globally; that is abundantly clear from this book so far. It is simply a statement of fact that we have been living in a sustained propaganda war about climate change for at least five decades, characterised by the requirement of the popular media for hype which is elevated further by extreme activists.

The truth is that there is no scientific evidence anywhere near the burden of proof required to qualify as a scientific theory, which states that human derived CO2 is the driver of climate change, to the exclusion of all major contributors, notably solar cycles and irradiance, oceanic cycles and volcanic activity. Increasingly, more and more science is being published that questions the link between what appears to be moderate warming since about 1850, which was the end of the mini ice age that commenced in the 13th century, linking it to CO2. The issue is that rising temperatures drives CO2 growth and greening, and not the other way around. This does not rule out the fact that we *are* in a warming period, and it is possible that human activity is a contributor, but other major factors are at play. The notion that we can tax our way to zero carbon is a dangerous fallacy.

The Intergovernmental Panel on Climate Change (IPCC), a scientific group overseen by the United Nations, produces a regular report which has been held as one of the most authoritative and comprehensive sources of information on climate science. The IPCC report is typically published in several volumes, each concentrating on a different aspect of climate change. These studies are apparently based on a thorough evaluation of peer-reviewed scientific literature and feedback from thousands of scientists throughout the world. The primary goal of the UN IPCC report is to offer policymakers and concerned citizens an impartial and evidence-based evaluation of the risks and probable consequences of climate change.

The UN IPCC reports make cursory mention of other causes besides human activity, including solar variability, but do not investigate them. Their models are focused on human activity as the primary culprit. The IPCC reports track greenhouse gas (CO2), methane (CH4), and nitrous oxide (N2O) from fossil fuel combustion, deforestation, and industry, claiming that these are 'clearly known' to increase the greenhouse effect, and they conveniently exclude solar fluctuations, volcanoes, and natural variability. The term *'well-known'* is fascinating.

We're also informed that there is a strong scientific consensus that 97% of experts agree about the anthropogenic causes. The 97% ratio comes from 2013 research by John Cook, who analysed abstracts from 12,000 scientific papers which included the words "global warming" and "climate change", categorising them depending on their viewpoint on human-induced climate change. It sounds compelling until you look at how many periodicals simply stated their opinions, then the number drops to 3,896. When you look at how many explicitly stated that human action was directly to blame, the number of papers drops to 64. That's 64 papers out of the 12,000 cited. This 97% slogan is politics, not science, and was calculated using just the abstracts from these publications. Most of the papers were considered implicitly favourable if they just discussed climate change, or global warming, without expressly indicating their view on the issue. Here are some of the criteria for identifying implicit support:

1. *Papers on how climate change and global warming affect natural systems, ecosystems, and species.*
2. *Papers on how human actions, such as greenhouse gas emissions, impact climate and temperature change.*
3. *Papers addressing the impact of climate change on society, including mitigation and adaptation options.*

Anthropogenic (human derived) climate change is the dominant global paradigm in the propaganda campaign, affecting policy, rousing public opinion, and driving states to take immediate action. This paradigm, replete with scientific, political, and ethical intricacies, shapes current discourse, managing the demands of ecological protection, economic pragmatism, and public welfare. However, like many other areas of discussion, the narrative of climate change is frequently affected by a consensual majority, as evidenced by the prevalence of the ongoing oxymorons regarding *'scientific consensus'* and *'settled science'* and which drowns out voices that challenge the established paradigms or provide alternative interpretations.

Thankfully, there *are* many scientists challenging this paradigm, here we focus on a few of them. Increasingly they are forming into groups and releasing studies for peer review that, collectively, cause us to question the zero-carbon strategy as both scientifically correct, socially acceptable and economically viable. In particular, the most recent book from Climatologist Dr Judith Curry is a voice of informed reason and commonsense, recommending a multi-disciplinary way forward in addressing the challenges of what she calls, *"wicked science."* Dr Judith Curry, whom I interviewed on Counterpoint[1], is a climatologist and former professor at the Georgia Institute of Technology. She is best known for her work on climate variability, climate models, and the intersection of climate science and politics. Her findings and criticism of mainstream science are presented in her newest book, *Climate Uncertainty and Risk.* She has criticised the politicisation of climate science and urged for increased transparency and open debate within the scientific community.

As I have said, she isn't the only voice; there are many, including Patrick Moore, a co-founder of Greenpeace who later distanced himself from the organisation. He brings a perspective that often clashes with mainstream climate science. Moore's views are rooted in his extensive understanding of the geologic time scale, directly challenge the

1. https://youtu.be/hKEy8zM8Rhg

anthropogenic climate change narrative. He argues climate change is not primarily caused by humans, and emphasises the lack of scientific proof to back global warming claims, urging for a more nuanced discussion that considers natural climate variability

These intellectuals, each with their distinct vantage points, challenge the mainstream climate narrative, urging for a more nuanced and diversified discussion on climate change. They represent a faction of the intellectual scene that calls for a re-evaluation of prevailing climate theories, an openness to alternate hypotheses, and a pragmatic approach towards climate action. Their critiques, experiences and propositions are met with resistance, underscoring the essence of diverse dialogues in shaping robust and well-rounded climate policies.

Dr Patrick Moore, Nuclear Pragmatist

Patrick Albert Moore is a Canadian industry consultant, former activist, an early member and past president of Greenpeace in Canada, which he left 1986. Moore has roundly criticised the environmental movement for what he sees as scare tactics and disinformation, saying that it has "*abandoned science and logic in favour of emotion and sensationalism*".[2] He claims that increased carbon dioxide in the Earth's atmosphere is beneficial, that there is no proof that anthropogenic carbon dioxide emissions are responsible for global warming, and that even if it were true, increased temperature would be beneficial to life on Earth

Patrick Moore's political journey is marked by a significant

2. http://greenspiritstrategies.com/the-environmental-movement-greens-have-lost-their-way/

transformation from a pioneering member of Greenpeace to a pragmatic environmentalist advocating for evidence-based solutions. Initially drawn to Greenpeace's impassioned activism in its nascent days during the 1970s, he was an integral part of its early campaigns, embodying the radical ecological fervour of the time. Moore's endeavours at that time were aimed against nuclear testing, and he achieved international recognition when he was arrested for protecting a baby seal from a hunter's club. His dedication was not just peripheral; Moore was at the core of Greenpeace's activism, serving as the president of Greenpeace Canada for almost a decade and a director of Greenpeace International.

The early 1970s were an important time for the development of environmental activism. Amidst the backdrop of nuclear tests, whaling expeditions, and growing concerns about pollution, Greenpeace emerged as a radical force, challenging governments and corporations alike. Patrick Moore was not just a witness to this transformative era; he was an active participant, shaping and being shaped by the events of the time. As one of the co-founders of Greenpeace, Moore's initial involvement was characterised by a deep-seated passion for the environment and a belief in direct action. Greenpeace's early campaigns, from sailing into nuclear test zones to confronting whaling ships, were audacious and often fraught with danger.

But as Greenpeace grew in size and power, things started to change within the organisation. In the middle of the pressures of global activism, the group, which began as a grassroots movement, began to question its own identity. Moore's work on some projects started to move away from science-based activism. A point of contention was the focus on emotional messages, which sometimes came at the cost of accurate facts. Moore's increasing disappointment wasn't a sudden realisation; it came to him over time. Among other things, he started to wonder what the group thought about nuclear energy and genetically modified organisms (GMOs). Greenpeace took a strong stand against these ideas, but Moore saw subtleties, difficulties, and possible benefits that he thought were being overlooked.

He began discerning a divergence between his beliefs centred around understanding ecological complexities and seeking balanced solutions versus the trajectory Greenpeace was embracing. His nuanced approach began clashing with the radical ethos of Greenpeace, prompting his departure from the organisation. As global warming transitioned from a scientific hypothesis to a public concern, Moore parted ways with Greenpeace in 1986, intending to demonstrate to the environmental community that pro-nuclear environmentalism was a viable stance. His advocacy for nuclear energy as a pragmatic solution to reducing carbon emissions highlighted his transformed outlook, often at odds with mainstream environmental narratives. For example, he believes that a carbon zero footprint would be akin to a mass suicide for humanity.

Today, Moore's advocacy extends to chairing the Clean and Safe Energy Coalition under the Nuclear Energy Institute, where he vociferously critiques what he deems an extremist anti-nuclear environmental movement. His criticisms, particularly towards groups like the Sierra Club and Friends of the Earth, have not always been well-received, garnering him labels like traitor from his former Greenpeace colleagues. Moore's transformation is emblematic of a growing sentiment among some environmentalists who believe nuclear energy must be considered in the discourse on renewable energy alternatives, a stance that has caused fissures in the environmental movement.

When people talk about the environment, nuclear energy is one of the most divisive issues. For many, the word itself brings up memories of Fukushima and Chernobyl and the terrible things that could happen during meltdowns. Still, Patrick Moore thinks that the narrative about nuclear energy is full of false information, misunderstandings, and sometimes outright lies. He used to once agree with Greenpeace's strong resistance to nuclear energy. Moore looked into nuclear energy not because he was an unwavering supporter, but because he wanted to learn more about it. He knew that nuclear power had its own problems, like how to deal with waste material and the chance of accidents happening.

He did, however, see a side of nuclear energy that was often hidden by fear and false information. Contrary to what most people think, nuclear power plants leave behind very little carbon. Modern reactors are also much safer and more efficient than the ones that came before them thanks to improvements in technology. Nuclear energy is something he thinks can help solve some of the world's most important problems. As the world's population and energy needs grow, it is not possible to rely only on sustainable energy sources like wind and sun. Because it can provide steady, base-load power, nuclear energy could be a key part of making sure that all countries have enough energy.

Still, there are a lot of things that stand in the way of accepting nuclear energy. The way people think about nuclear power is still a big problem, thanks to decades of anti-nuclear efforts and high-profile accidents. Moore thinks that changing the narrative is necessary. We shouldn't just talk about the risks; we should also talk about the possible benefits, like a cleaner world, fewer greenhouse gas emissions, and a reliable energy source for future generations.

One of Moore's main issues with the climate change narrative is that the story of climate change is oversimplified. Moore's view on climate change comes from a deep appreciation for how complicated Earth's natural systems are. In particular, he agrees that human actions have changed the climate, especially the rise in carbon dioxide levels. But he also stresses how important it is to understand that the climate system is naturally variable. The climate on Earth has historically gone through periods of warming and cooling, caused by things from solar radiation to volcanic activity. Focusing on carbon dioxide as the only cause ignores the many other factors that affect the temperature of the Earth. For example, water vapour, which is the most common greenhouse gas, isn't given enough attention in most conversations. In the same way, ocean currents are often forgotten, even though they play a key role in controlling world temperatures and act as huge heat reservoirs.

Moore also questions the idea that all of the effects of a warming world are bad by default. Concerns have been raised about rising sea levels and extreme weather events, however, a warmer environment could have benefits, such as more arable land and longer growing seasons in some places. He says it's important to look at the problem from both sides, understanding both the problems and the opportunities. He also dislikes how the climate change debate has become so divided, that people who disagree are often shut down or called *deniers*. He thinks that we can only make real progress when we listen to different points of view, have productive conversations, and make choices based on strong, real-world evidence.

Moore's background in ecology and years of working in forests has given him knowledge about how important they are in the Earth's ecosystem. Forests, which are often called the *"lungs of our planet"*, keep the ecosystem in balance. They don't just store carbon; they are complex environments full of life that affect local climates and are complex ecosystems in themselves. Trees breathe, taking in carbon dioxide and releasing oxygen, they keep the atmosphere balanced. Moore says, the connection between trees and carbon is more complicated than this simple exchange. As trees grow, they store carbon in their biomass, which keeps it locked away for decades or even centuries, meaning that they take in more carbon than they release.

In addition to storing carbon, forests are very important for keeping water cycles in balance. As natural sponges, they soak up rain and slowly release it back into the ground. This keeps rivers and streams from flooding and makes sure they do not dry up. This is vital for the aquatic life and also for the humans. Moore talks about forest succession, which is how a forest environment changes over time, from the first pioneer species that move into a new area, to the mature community that settles down. He says that these changes are necessary to keep species alive. Different stages of succession offer opportunities for different species to live, keeping forests alive and full of a diversity of life. Biodiversity is a crucial component of ecosystem health. Moore doesn't just see trees as important for the environment, he also talks about the economic and social aspects of forests, especially the connection between forests and native people. For many native groups, forests are more than just places to live; they are deeply connected to their culture, religion, and ways of making a living. Moore has argued that biological knowledge and cultural knowledge should work together to make sustainable forest management.

About 31% of the world's land is covered by forests yet Moore says that even though forests are strong and resilient ecosystems, they can be hurt by both natural and man-made factors. The health of these environments can change drastically due to wildfires, pests, diseases, and deforestation. However, they can quickly adjust to new environmental conditions and if managed correctly, can grow back quickly. Disturbances like wildfires can be part of a tree's natural life cycle, encouraging new growth, leading to more biodiversity and resilience.

Moore supports long-term forestry methods that combine protecting the environment with commercial interests. He suggests logging can be a healthy activity that helps the economy without hurting the health of the forest if it is done in the right way. Sustainable logging methods, like selective logging and clear-cutting with replanting, keep trees healthy so they can grow back and continue to provide benefits to the environment. Moore also supports afforestation and reforestation, to create forests on lands that have been cleared of trees by farming practices.

Moore's knowledge of marine ecology and his support for environmentally friendly practices give us a full picture of the delicate balance of the oceanic ecosystem and how human activities affect it. The oceans, which cover more than 70% of the Earth's surface, are full of mysteries and wonders that have fascinated people for thousands of years. In addition to being beautiful to look at, oceans keep the planet's temperature stable, support many types of life, and feed billions of people. Oceans are much more than just huge bodies of water, from tiny plankton to the huge blue whales, they are complex environments full of life. The oceanic environment receives its energy and nutrients from the complex interactions between predators and prey that make up the marine food web. Any change in this balance, whether it's caused by natural events or by people, can have a domino effect on marine species.

Overfishing is one of the biggest issues in marine ecosystems. Population growth, eating habits and new technologies (such as radars to find shoals of fish), has put more pressure on fishing areas. Moore stresses how important it is for fisheries to be healthy, fishing is an important part of the economy and provides jobs for millions of people. Some fishing methods such as trawling or using drift nets, are not sustainable. Not only do they kill off fish stocks, but other species that are not needed, known as bycatch, ends up in the nets too. This random killing of marine life throws off the delicate balance of the marine food web, endangering the ecosystems we rely on. Solutions include sustainable fisheries and marine protected areas (MPAs), which are designated parts of the ocean where human activity is restricted. Moore thinks that MPAs are more than just ways to protect wildlife; they are investments in the future. Protecting important areas and letting fish stocks recover is how MPAs ensure fisheries become good for both the marine ecosystem and the people who depend on it.

But overfishing isn't the only problem the ocean environment has to deal with. Pollution, mainly plastic trash, is becoming a bigger problem. Ocean pollution from one part of the world can have effects in other parts that are thousands of miles away. We need to work together, come up with new ideas, and become dedicated to protecting the health of our oceans in order to solve this world problem. Moore shows a world that is rough and tough at the same time. Marine ecosystems are under massive stress because of human activities, but they also have a huge capacity to recover and replenish themselves . We can make sure our oceans continue to thrive and support life on Earth for future generations by using sustainable methods, making laws that are based on facts, and work together around the world to make it happen.

Many people think that renewable energy will solve all of our environmental problems, but Moore's ideas show that not all renewables are the same. He agrees that green energy sources are important. Most of the world's renewable energy comes from wood, which is mostly used for heating and cooking in developing countries. A big part of the world's green energy comes from hydroelectric power, which also plays an important role. Moore, on the other hand, has doubts about wind and solar power. Even though they are very famous in environmental circles, they only make up a very small part of the world's energy output.

One of the main problems with wind and solar energy is that it is not reliable. The wind and sun aren't always around, they are not as stable as other energy sources, such as hydroelectric power. It is not practical for a society to run its most important facilities, like hospitals, workplaces, and schools, on energy sources that might not be available when it is cloudy or there is no wind. And these energy sources are expensive. Using Germany as an example, Moore shows how the prices of different types of power generation vary from each other. Even though they receive a significant amount of money through funding, wind and solar energy are still much more expensive than traditional sources like coal or nuclear power because they require an intricate infrastructure and batteries that accumulate excess energy for later use.

Moore criticises green energy sources, yet he knows green energy can be useful in some situations. For example, solar energy can be helpful when you're not connected to the main power source and the only option is a diesel generator. Still, Moore says that renewable energy sources like solar and wind might not be the magic bullet that many people hope for when it comes to meeting the world's energy needs on a global scale. The switch to cleaner power is the most important thing we can do to build a sustainable future.

Moore has a vision of a world where our energy needs are met without harming the environment and new ideas and technology work with nature. Nuclear energy would play a role, along with other tools, such as underground heat pumps These systems use the earth's steady temperature to heat and cool buildings in a way that uses little energy. Geothermal heat pumps are a more environmentally friendly way to heat and cool your home than standard systems that depend on the weather and can use up a lot of energy. When it comes to protecting the environment, Dr Moore thinks these pumps are a great example of how new technologies can change the way we use energy, reducing our energy consumption, instead of meeting increasing demand in new ways.

In the last few decades, urbanisation has sped up at a rate that has never been seen before. Cities, which used to be small towns, have grown into huge metropolises with millions of people living in them. These cities may be amazing works of human creativity and are often seen as signs of progress, but they leave big marks on the environment. Villages and smaller communities have been usually presented as environment-friendly havens, as opposed to large, polluting cities. Cities consume large amounts of resources quickly. Energy, water, and other resources are needed to facilitate large numbers of people living in a small area. Tall buildings and complicated transportation networks often hurt natural ecosystems and habitats. Cities produce inorganic trash, pollute the environment, and releasing greenhouse gases into the air. From an environmental point of view, modern cities are global malaise that destroys the planet.

However, cities also have an opportunity to lead the way in being environmentally friendly. For example, a city's well-designed public transport system can make people much less likely to drive their own cars, which can greatly lower emissions. In the same way, green areas, vertical gardens, and green roofs in cities not only make the city look attractive, but they are also important for storing carbon, keeping the temperature stable, and protecting biodiversity. The density of cities allows for solutions that are not applicable in sparse villages.

Dr Moore stresses how important it is to see urbanisation not as a problem but as an opportunity. Cities can go from being a detriment for the planet to a benefit with the right planning. He imagines cities where environmentally friendly practices are built into their designs. There are many options, from buildings that use renewable energy sources and are energy-efficient, to garbage management systems that focus on recycling and reducing waste. Not only does incorporating green technologies matter, but also making sure that urban growth doesn't hurt the natural environment. To ensure urban growth doesn't hurt the environment, we must protect natural areas like habitats, water bodies, and green fields.

Through his work, Moore offered us an unconventional example of environmental consciousness and activism. Although his ideas and policies align strongly with his values, he is seen as a walking contradiction. People struggle to classify Dr Patrick Moore because the politics around environmental issues have become so dogmatic and polarised. Moore has seen through this politicking and political division; he cares only about the actual issues and potential solutions. If only we all could think in the same way.

Dr Judith Curry Challenging Climate Response

Dr Curry is a distinguished climatologist and former chair of the Georgia Institute of Technology's School of Earth and Atmospheric Science. In 2023, she published *Climate Uncertainty and Risk, Rethinking Our Response* to shake up the conversation around climate by questioning its assumptions and proposing a fresh perspective.

She was extensively interviewed on my channel, Counterpoint, where she addressed the significant uncertainties that exist in climate science. She feels the debate over climate change is far from settled, and argues that the science is more complex and uncertain than often portrayed, and believes our current understanding of the climate system is incomplete, therefore we cannot predict future climate changes accurately.

Curry emphasises that despite decades of research, the climate system's non-linear and chaotic nature means that new complexities continue to emerge. Factors such as ice sheet dynamics, under-ocean geothermal heat flux and atmospheric chemistry processes add layers of uncertainty to climate models. This persistent uncertainty challenges the reliability of these models and, by extension, the policies based upon them.

One of Curry's central critiques is the overreliance on climate models which she says are fraught with limitations and uncertainties. She highlights the myriad of choices that go into constructing a climate model, including decisions about model resolution, the complexity of sub-models, and parameterisations for various processes. These choices result in a wide range of models, each with different sensitivities and outcomes. The variations among different models often stem from local interests and specific aspects of climate simulation, leading to fragmented and sometimes conflicting results.

Curry quotes climate modeller Reto Knutti, who humorously but pointedly critiques the field: "*People build the most complicated model they can think of, include everything, then run it once on the largest computer with the highest resolution they can afford, then wonder how to interpret the results.*"

Curry categorises the imperfections in climate models into several types:

1. *Framing and Context Inadequacy*: Errors and uncertainties that arise from the exclusion of certain real-world processes, such as solar indirect effects.
2. *Structural Uncertainty*: Uncertainty in the model's functional form, including which subsystems to include and the equations used to represent the physical system.
3. *Technical Uncertainty*: Implementation issues, including solution approximations and numerical

errors when translating continuous laws into discrete grid points.

4. *Parameter Uncertainty*: Uncertainty in the constants and parameters used, especially those related to sub-grid scale processes like clouds and precipitation.
5. *Input Uncertainty*: Uncertainty in the initial conditions and external forces that drive changes in the climate system.

The greatest uncertainties, Curry notes, are associated with the parameterisations of clouds and precipitation. She identifies the "*Butterfly Effect*" and the "*Hawkmoth Effect*," which highlight how small changes in initial conditions or model structure can lead to vastly different outcomes, complicating the interpretation and reliability of model predictions. She advocates for a plurality of climate models developed and utilised for different purposes and believes that the current path, dominated by the UN Intergovernmental Panel on Climate Change (IPCC), might not be the best approach for many decision-support issues. Instead, she calls for exploring alternative frameworks and innovations in theoretical and model development.

She also questions the effectiveness of emissions targets aimed at limiting global warming to below 2 degrees Celsius. She compares these targets to highway speed limits, arguing that slight deviations might not be dangerous, but significant ones could be. She points out that variations in global temperatures are linked to natural cycles, like the Atlantic Multi-Decadal Oscillation, which can impact future warming predictions.

Dr Curry explains that not accounting for these natural cycles in predictions risks overestimating future warming. For example, the Atlantic Multi-Decadal Oscillation (AMO), a natural variability mode in sea surface temperatures, is expected to shift to a cold phase, potentially offsetting some warming effects for the next two to three decades. She also highlights the potential impact of volcanic eruptions and solar activity on climate and notes that large volcanic eruptions can lead to temporary cooling, while changes in solar activity can influence long-term climate trends. These factors, often underrepresented in models, add another layer of uncertainty to climate predictions.

Historical data show that periods of high volcanic activity, like the "Little Ice Age", significantly impacted global temperatures. Similarly, solar activity, which follows approximately 11-year cycles, has its own influence on the climate. Dr Curry argues that understanding these natural influences is crucial for more accurate climate predictions.

She doesn't shy away from discussing the political dimensions of climate science. She argues that the United Nations Framework Convention on Climate Change (UNFCCC) and the IPCC have mischaracterised climate risk by focusing too narrowly on CO2 emissions and downplaying natural climate variability. This, she believes, has led to policies that might not be effective or optimal for addressing climate challenges.

Curry calls for a more balanced view that considers the full spectrum of scientific uncertainty and risk. She argues that the current approach of setting emissions targets and relying heavily on climate models oversimplifies the complexities of climate change and may lead to suboptimal policies. She advocates for a broader, more inclusive approach to understanding and addressing climate change and stresses the need to consider a wide range of scientific opinions and recognise the ethical and political dimensions of climate issues. By doing so, she believes we can develop more effective and resilient strategies to cope with climate risks.

Curry proposes "climate pragmatism" as a more effective strategy. This approach prioritises "*no regrets*" policies that avoid options with controversial or uncertain benefits. Climate pragmatism emphasises understanding what we do not know and reducing the role of public policy in favour of more flexible, multi-level approaches. This bottom-up decision-making process allows for incremental policies and more responsive actions to local conditions and market signals.

Curry touches on the broader implications of politicising science, arguing that the torquing of climate science has led to an oversimplified narrative. This narrative drives a "*predict then act*" strategy that may not be suitable for complex issues like climate change. She points out that this approach has resulted in systematic biases and neglected broader societal vulnerabilities.

Her standout theme is the need to rethink how we manage climate risk. She suggests adopting a risk management approach more aligned with other complex issues, such as public health and national security. This means being more realistic about what we can predict and control and preparing for a range of possible futures rather than betting everything on a single outcome.

Drawing parallels with the Covid-19 pandemic, Curry discusses how both climate and pandemic risks are systemic and impact interconnected global systems but that the immediate and visible threat of a pandemic contrasts with the gradual and distributed risks of climate change. She argues that the urgency often associated with climate change should be re-evaluated in light of these differences.

Curry challenges the idea that humanity can control the climate, suggesting that our efforts might be better spent on adaptation and resilience rather than attempting to control a highly complex and unpredictable system. She argues that much like the responses to Covid-19, the pursuit of control in climate policy may lead to unintended consequences and reduced societal resilience.

Curry criticises the tendency to catastrophise climate change, arguing that it leads to polarised politics and unrealistic expectations. She suggests a more pragmatic approach, focusing on incremental and achievable goals would be more effective. This includes addressing immediate and pressing issues like energy poverty and developing resilient infrastructure.

She advocates for "*climate pragmatism*," which emphasises practical and flexible solutions over grand, centralised plans. This approach encourages localised decision-making and a focus on tangible, incremental improvements. By prioritising policies that offer clear and immediate benefits, Curry believes we can make meaningful progress in addressing climate risks without falling into the trap of alarmism and overreach. She introduces the concept of "*wicked science*," a transdisciplinary approach that integrates natural sciences, engineering, social sciences, and humanities to tackle complex societal problems like climate change and argues that addressing these "*wicked problems*" requires acknowledging the limitations of control, embracing uncertainty, and fostering open dialogue and collaboration across disciplines.

Dr Judith Curry's book, *Climate Uncertainty and Risk: Rethinking Our Response*, is a thought-provoking read that challenges conventional climate science wisdom. Her call for a more nuanced, flexible approach to climate risk and her critique of current models and policies offer valuable insights for anyone interested in the future of climate science and policy. Whether you agree with her views or not, Dr Curry's work is sure to spark meaningful conversations and encourage a deeper examination.

16

ROBERT F KENNEDY JR. AND GLOBAL HEALTH

Robert F Kennedy's two recent books are structured more like prosecutions. This is unsurprising given his career as an environmental lawyer. These also have the advantage of been researched and edited by renown experts, including Professor Francis Boyle.

The Real Anthony Fauci (Bill Gates, Big Pharma, and the Global War on Democracy and Public Health published in 2021, followed in 2023 by *The Wuhan Cover-Up and the Terrifying Bioweapons Arms Race,* covers the ground in detail like no other. The latter has 63 chapters that build the evidence and concludes with the WHO, which attempted to landfall a global health technocracy at the World Health Assembly (WHA) in June 2024. This is the event which gave rise to the Killarney Declaration in Appendix I. In giving an open public lecture five weeks before the WHA, in Cork April 25th called *Breaking the Silence,* I relied upon the painstaking research evident in both works to put a timeline together and tell the arc of the story. Nobody left the room over the 1.5 hours of my lecture.

In essence, RFK's books are about regulatory captivity by the pharmaceutical industry in the United States. The forensic material and notation in these lawyerly masterpieces I believe cannot be bypassed, whether claiming expertise in the area or in abusing the lawyer as a misguided anti-vaccine advocate. He is not. He is instead anti-unsafe vaccines.

The movie *Pain Hustlers* on Netflix, staring Emily Blunt, Chris Evans and Andy Garica premiered at the Toronto International Film Festival on Sept 11th 2023, tells the story of Insys Therapeutics. Its executives received criminal convictions in the USA coincident with the outbreak of Covid in January 2020, from laws used to prosecute mob bosses. The film is an exposé of some of the darkest parts of the Pharma industry, finding common cause with Kennedy's book.

Robert Francis Kennedy Jr's career began as a young environmental lawyer taking a blizzard of lawsuits on behalf of fishermen along the toxic Hudson River. His legal work, in and out of court, pitched him against powerful polluters, gave him a deep understanding of poisonous heavy metals, including mercury. The Hudson is now one of the least polluted large waterways in the Northern Hemisphere.

Time and again mothers kept showing up at public meetings asking Kennedy to look at their children. The children were diagnosed with autism, the prevalence of which has surged. Vaccine manufacturers sought and got indemnities through the Regan administration to continue to bring vaccines to market. RFK makes no scientific link between metals in vaccines and autism, but notes that scientific studies have found that mercury, once common in vaccines, didn't magically exit the human body as claimed, but can jump through the blood-brain barrier to settle in the human brain.

Mercury is an accumulating poison, so it doesn't leave the body, and it grows over time.

He needed to seek proof that vaccines targeted successfully at specific diseases did not cause damage elsewhere to human health, notably to immune systems. He found no such evidence despite claims to the contrary by Anthony Fauci, Director of the National Institute of Allergy and Infectious Disease (NIAID) and Chief Medical Advisor to the US President 2021-2022. When he confronted Dr Fauci during the Trump administration, the head regulator promised to produce the studies to prove vaccine safety tests were done but failed to deliver them.

RFK's stance on public health policies, especially those concerning vaccines, is rooted in a profound respect for individual rights and freedoms. He champions the principle of individual autonomy, which he believes is a cornerstone of a democratic society. He believes every individual ought to have control over their body and health decisions and that such decisions should be made with full knowledge and understanding of the consequences, and without external coercion. This is the first principle of the Nuremburg Code. Kennedy's emphasis on informed consent is not just a theoretical stance; it's a call for transparency and openness in the realm of medical interventions. Informed consent, a foundational principle in medical ethics, ensures that individuals are provided with all relevant information about a medical procedure, including its potential risks and benefits, allowing them to make an educated decision. He argues that for consent to be genuinely informed, there must be a free flow of information, devoid of biases or external influences.

His concerns about certain vaccines, particularly those that have undergone rapid development and approval processes, stem from this principle of informed consent. Kennedy calls for a more transparent, rigorous, and open evaluation of these vaccines. He believes that only through such a thorough examination can individuals be provided with the complete information they need to make informed choices.

He is deeply concerned about what he perceives as a growing trend to stifle dissenting voices in public health discourse. For a society to thrive, he argues, there must be room for open dialogue, debate, and even dissent. Suppressing alternative viewpoints, especially in a field as crucial as public health, can lead to a narrow, one-dimensional narrative. Such a constrained discourse, in RFK's view, is not only detrimental to individual rights but also to the broader societal interest.

In essence, his views on public health and vaccines are a clarion call for greater transparency, respect for individual rights, and the fostering of an open and inclusive discourse. He challenges us to look beyond mainstream narratives and ensure that policies and practices in public health are rooted in the principles of autonomy, transparency, and democratic values.

A central theme that consistently emerges in his discourse is the profound influence of corporate interests on public narratives and policymaking. This influence, RFK contends, has far-reaching implications, not just for specific industries or sectors but for the very fabric of democratic societies. In the modern era, corporations have grown in power and reach, often rivalling, if not surpassing, the influence of nation-states. With vast financial resources at their disposal and a global presence, large corporate entities have the means to shape public opinion, influence policy decisions, and even dictate the direction of scientific research. Kennedy's concern is that this corporate influence often goes unchecked, leading to a scenario where profit motives consistently overshadow the broader public interest.

He has also expressed concerns about the role of mainstream media in shaping public perceptions and narratives. In his view, the media landscape has undergone significant transformations, with a few conglomerates now dominating vast swathes of the information ecosystem. This concentration of media power, Kennedy argues, has implications for the diversity of voices and perspectives that reach the public. He has consistently highlighted the symbiotic relationship between corporate interests and mainstream media. Media outlets often rely heavily on advertising revenues from large corporations. This financial interdependence, he suggests, can influence the content that these media outlets produce.

What makes RFK a notable dissenter is how he has deployed his skills litigating complex cases against polluters into building meticulously researched and compelling exposes in his two recent books, released during the pandemic era. These are legally uncontested contemporary works characterised by meticulous research and may be set to become works of historical significance.

He believes that improvements in water, nutrition, housing and engineering, together with attention to physical health, has had a greater benefit when dealing with many common diseases than vaccines. The Spanish Flu 1918-1920, was attributed to the H1N1 influenza virus and thought to have reached a third the of world's population, with a death toll in the tens of millions, was caused, not by the virus, but from the bacterial pneumonia it triggered, today easily treated with antibiotics.

He has raised questions to Dr Anthony Fauci head of the National Institute of Allergy and Infectious Disease (NIAID) during Trump's presidency about the collateral impact of mandated vaccines on human health, including potential harms to human immune systems and that have not been scientifically addressed. For continuously raising these concerns he has been labelled anti-vaccine. He is Chairman and Founder of Children's Health Defence and in October 2023, he entered the US presidential election as an independent candidate squeezed between the Republicans on one side and the Democrats on the other.

In *The Real Anthony Fauci*, a tome that covers over 450 pages, RFK lays out how the leadership of US Health regulators are captive to the powerful US pharmaceutical complex. His case flows into *The Wuhan Cover Up*, which builds the case further and culminates in the WHO changes to its International Health Regulations (IHR) and its new Pandemic Treaty, disguised as a framework convention, much like how UN climate conferences are modelled. These both were scheduled to make landfall for a meeting of the World Health Assembly (WHA), the governing council of the WHO in June 2024.

When reading this material for the first time, be prepared to be shocked because little or none of it has passed through the captive filters of Mainstream Media (MSM) editorial boards. Almost all of the content of his book is suppressed on social media platforms by the same forces that suppressed repurposed drugs, informed consent and your personal freedoms.

Anthony Fauci, who recently retired after a career that spanned 40 years in US public health regulation, was the former head of the National Institute of Allergy and Infectious Disease (NIAID). In the first book, RFK outlines the *modus operandi* of Fauci, deploying the NIAID budget among health scientists, the Professional Investigator (PI) marketplace of US drug development. The NIAID largesse acts as a subsidy to the pharmaceutical producers to incubate an assembly line of profitable drugs to treat the symptoms of diseases monitored by the NIAID. RFK describes how PIs operate like clans loyal to drug producers including Pfizer, Glaxo, Merck, Sanofi, Johnson & Johnson etc.

Drug companies dish out contracts to PI's via research institutes, medical schools and hospitals ranging up to $10k per patient and drug trial with skimming to "academic overhead" running up to two-thirds of the payments. He alleges that drug companies court loyalty through legalised bribes in the form of speaking fees, expert witness reports and testimony, offering first class travel to exclusive resorts for conferences. The system is biased against repurposed drugs and non-pharmaceutical remedies as those that are patent-expired are cheaper. *The Real Anthony Fauci* recounts the first pivotal meeting between Dr Anthony Fauci and Bill Gates over two decades before the Covid pandemic in Gates' 40,000 square foot Seattle mansion at Lake Washington under the auspices of discussing TB. In Dr Fauci's own words at the private meeting in the library, Gates said, "*Tony, you run the biggest infectious disease institute in the world. And I want to be sure the money I spend is well spent. Why don't we really get to know each other? Why don't we be partners?*".[1]

1. https://www.nytimes.com/2021/03/03/podcasts/the-daily/coroanvirus-

In 1998, the US Department of Justice and 27 State attorney generals filed an antitrust suit against Microsoft for illegally supressing attempts by consumers to install competing software on its PCs. Microsoft was fined, and Bill Gates criticised by the Judge who described Gates as having an arrogance that emanated from uninterrupted power and success and a Napoleonic self-concept. He described the billionaire's testimony as "*evasive and forgetful*".[2] Two decades later, the erstwhile Microsoft monopolist and billionaire's foundation now accounts for one Dollar in every five of the WHO budgets. He is the biggest private investor in the pharmaceutical industry and the most powerful actor in the PPR industry worldwide.

In the first book, RFK painstakingly recounts examples of phony pandemics. In 2005 the Bird Flu is a standout. The British data modeller Neil Ferguson, funded by Gates and Jeremy Ferrar of the Welcome Trust, predicted Bird Flu would kill up to 150 million. It killed under 300 by 2009. The inept Ferguson of Imperial College, would continue to provide models, including one for Covid where in 2020 he predicted 2.2 million deaths in the USA propelling the White House, advised by Dr Fauci, to justify lockdowns.

In 2002, Neil Ferguson projected 136,000 deaths in the UK from foot-and-mouth disease, for which 11 million cattle and sheep were slaughtered. The total human deaths were 177. In 2009, he predicted 65,000 deaths in the UK from Swine Flu, it killed only 457.[3] In 2009, despite worldwide seasonal flu deaths of 145 over eleven weeks, the WHO in secret meetings

vaccine-bill-gates-covax.html?showTranscript=1

2. *The Real Anthony Fauci,* p. 283
3. Chapter 11 is completely dedicated to an overview of phony pandemics.

declared a Class 6 global pandemic and altered the definition of a pandemic by removing the requirement for 'mass deaths around the globe'. The declaration fired nation states to load up on H1N1 flu vaccines. Henceforth, pandemics became about infectability, instead of being based on fatality and morbidity data. No minutes of this crucial WHO meeting which so altered the global public health response, nor who attended it, has ever been released, despite requests to do so.

After closely examining the behaviour of Dr Fauci at NIAID over a prolonged time and across several events, RFK identifies the Fauci *modus operandi*;

1. Hype up fears of an imminent pandemic, incriminate a pathogen, exaggerate its transmissibility by stoking hysteria, warn of its mutant strains and surges and spook the public into a state of anxiety.
2. Next broadcast substantial changes to lifestyles, to protect lives and keep changing these to keep the public and the politicians unbalanced.
3. Soon as possible inflate the prevalence of the virus with bogus amplification of PCR tests and exaggerate death data.
4. Attack counter science, such as the Great Barrington Declaration, which challenged the efficacy of Lockdowns.
5. Trample over informed consent as between GPs and patients, there can only be one universal solution.
6. Dismiss repurposed drugs, such as Ivermectin and natural compounds such as Vitamin D for respiratory viruses, losing weight and getting fit.
7. Focus attention and resources only on profitable new

vaccines and drugs even when dangerous and ineffective.

8. Openly champion big Pharma as the only solution and use Emergency Use Authorisation (EUA) to fast-track lab to jab.
9. Cite only experts that can be trusted, disguising conflicts of interest and publish in medical journals opinions that favour the zoonic origin narrative, while dismissing the real origin from gain of function in bioweapon labs.
10. Only fund research that reinforces the narrative, contrary to the scientific method and, see the management of the message as of superior importance to the truth of it. Speak often and with authority, repeating the message.

RFK's central finding from his team of researchers into the material is this:

> *"Over the two decades since the anthrax attacks, an immensely profitable new industry known as Pandemic Preparedness and Response arose from the 'public-private partnership' composed of private vaccine investors like Bill Gates; pharmaceutical, Big Tech and surveillance companies; military intelligence and public health agencies; and the media. This new arm of the medical/military-industrial complex has made monumental profits for private companies and justified the erection of an intrusive and repressive surveillance infrastructure, enabling the systemic dismantling of constitutional rights and imposition of repressive social controls. The feedstock for this new industry is pathogens and particularly viruses that can be manipulated by both science and propaganda. Attractive and perennial preoccupation of PPR managers has been the creation of an archive*

> *of the world's viruses with weapons potential. The ostensible purpose of this archive/library is to anticipate pandemics and create vaccines. Serious sceptical scientists regard these virus collection efforts as an elaborate hoax to monetize and extort deliberately orchestrated public fears of pandemic danger that doesn't actually exist. The most cynical critics suggest that these archivists can provide a reservoir of pathogenic microbes to fuel a steady stream of future pandemics upon which this PPR industry thrives".*[4]

From the time of Mongol invasions, disease has been used as a bioweapon by catapulting rotting corpses into besieged cities to spread plagues and weaken defences. In 1347, the Mongols hurled plague-infested bodies over the walls of the port city of Caffa, which is today Feodosiya on the Black Sea, in Crimea. Some historians point to this incident as the source of the Black Death pandemic as ships from the besieged city returned to Italy, spreading death to a third of the European population over the following four years and killing 25 million. In 1763, British forces besieged at Fort Pitt, present day Pittsburgh, devastated the coalition of native American tribes that arose against their rule in the Great Lakes region by passing smallpox-infected blankets among them.

In World War I, modern bioweapons were deployed in earnest including gas attacks in trench warfare. This led to the 1925 Geneva Protocol, which banned the use of chemical and biological weapons. It was signed but ignored by Japan which initiated secret bioweapons research which it deployed against China in 1937, and carried through World War II, until its eventual defeat. At the end of the war, Japanese and German

4. The Wuhan Cover-Up, p. 223

bioweapon scientists were quietly invited to join the US bioweapons research in operations that came under CIA control. US bioweapons research was first established at Fort Detrick, in Frederick, Maryland as early as 1940, becoming the US Army Biological Warfare Laboratories three years later.

Two decades later, the US Army would deploy defoliants such as Agent Orange during the Vietnam War 1961-1971 that included the highly toxic compound dioxin, a persistent organic pollutant, eventually banned by the Stockholm Convention in 2001. The USA, which argued that the Geneva Protocol of 1925 did not cover defoliants during the Vietnam War, signed but has not ratified the Stockholm Convention.

The Biological Weapons Convention, effective from March 26th, 1975, was signed by 185 nations including the USA, prohibits the research, manufacture, development and stockpiling of offensive biological and toxin weapons. The convention, however, allows research and development into pathogenic microorganisms for peaceful, defensive purposes such as the production of vaccines, these are the so-called gain of function enterprises. This is the dual-purpose loophole, through which a coach and four has been driven to spawn the hugely profitable global bioweapons complex. It was most evident during the run up and response to Covid-19.

In the first Gulf War in 1990, the US military injected US troops with an anthrax vaccine. Years earlier, the US had shipped weaponised anthrax and botulinum toxin to Saddam Hussein. In 1997, the US Secretary of Defence attempted to inject the entire military against anthrax but was stopped by order of Judge Emmet Sullivan of the District Court in Washington; *"The women and men of our armed forces put their lives on the line every day to preserve and safeguard the freedoms that all Americans cherish and enjoy. The United States cannot demand that members of the armed forces also serve as Guinea pigs for experimental drugs".*[5] According to John Hopkins Medicine, Gulf War Syndrome is the term used to describe unexplained illnesses occurring in veterans of the 1991 Gulf War. The most common symptoms include fatigue, muscular/skeletal pain, cognitive problems, skin rashes and diarrhoea. A report released by the Institute of Medicine (IOM) in 2013 estimates about a third of Gulf War veterans suffer from chronic multi symptoms that cannot be medically explained. Possible causes of Gulf War syndrome include chemical warfare agents, particularly nerve gas or pyridostigmine bromide used to pretreat against nerve agents which was given as a preventative measure to soldiers likely to be exposed to chemical warfare agents. Psychological factors such as post-traumatic stress disorder may also have been having an impact given the high rates of accompanying psychiatric disorders. Other chemical agents such as smoke from oil well fires, pesticides, depleted uranium or exposure to solvents and corrosive liquids have also been identified as possible causes. It has been estimated that more than 200,000 U.S. troops have suffered from Gulf War Syndrome (GWS), and it may be connected to the anthrax vaccines that were administered before the court injunction.

In the run up to the Covid 'Pandemic', Moderna, a US pharmaceutical company with revenues close to $7bn in 2023 and which trades on the Nasdaq as MRNA, patented spike proteins for coronavirus vaccines in 2016, some six years after its foundation. Officially called ModeRNA to 2018, Moderna is led by Stéphane Bancel who owns 7.3% of the company. He would later appear at a press conference at the World

5. https://www.cbsnews.com/news/judge-us-cant-force-vaccines/

Economic Forum in January 2020, with Jeremy Farrar, chief of the Wellcome Trust. This trust is the fourth wealthiest charitable endowment in the world, with assets over €30bn today, a 1936 legacy by pharmaceutical magnate Henry Welcome. Bancel was formerly the CEO of French biotechnology multinational, bioMérieux which built Wuhan's BSL-4 laboratory in China.

At Davos 2020, Farrar stood in for the Chief of the World Health Organisation, Tedros Adhanom Ghebreyesus, who was too busy with unfolding events in China to attend the WEF annual conference. Farrar and Bancel jointly announced the global pandemic to the audience of Davos billionaires chaired by WEF chief Klaus Schwab. Farrar served on the British Government Vaccine Taskforce with Sir John Bell, the Oxford Regius Professor of Medicine under whom he completed his doctoral and who chairs the Gates Foundation's Global Health Scientific Board. Farrar left Wellcome Trust to be appointed Chief Scientist at the WHO in 2023, a position from which he can make the scientific case to call for a Pandemic Health Emergency of International Concern (PHEIC). This can then be declared by the WHO Director General, Tedros Adhanom Ghebreyesus. Farrar is identified by RFK as one of the key actors in covering up the bioweapon origin of the spike protein that constitutes Covid-19 from the Wuhan lab.

Farrar has a close personal relationship with Dr George Gao, Director of China's Centre for Disease Control. Their friendship goes back to their doctoral days in Oxford in the early 90's. In October 2019, while attending Event 201 in New York, which simulated a coronavirus pandemic co-hosted by Bill Gates and the WEF, Gao's contribution to the simulation included a demand for US social and mainstream media to be pressured to censor any lab leak story.

Covid-19—A Timeline

To better understand the actual course of the Covid-19 pandemic and what happened to us during that hectic period, it is necessary to reconstruct a timeline. September 2019 seems like the correct moment to begin charting recent events as the US Republican congressional investigation in 2021 concluded that the lab leak occurred sometime before September 12th, 2019. This is also supported in my Counterpoint interview with Professor Francis Boyle, from June 2024. In addition, RFK places the first covid infections circulating in Wuhan into September 2019 involving lab workers, including Ben Hu senior assistant to Shi Zhengli, the primary gain of function researcher at the Wuhan Institute of Virology. In September 2019, the Chinese Government raided the Wuhan Lab to remove viral sequences from its online database. Hu was hospitalised in November 2019.

Also during September, 2019, when the Chinese experts at Wuhan would have known of the virus circulating, the Gates Foundation bought into a little known RNA biotechnology company called BioNtech, with $55m at a pre-IPO price of $18. A little over six months later, the billionaire wrote an op-ed in the Washington Post on March 4th 2020, "*The new approach I'm most excited about is known as an RNA vaccine*". Five days later on March 9th, Italy went into national lockdown.

- March 17th 2020: Ireland cancelled it's St Patrick's day festivities and Irish President Michael D Higgins signed emergency measures into law on March 20th. The country went into full lockdown on March 27th, banning all "non-essential" travel with a stay-at-home order, thus commencing Europe's longest lockdown.

- BioNtech, which had partnered with Pfizer to develop its Coved-19 vaccine, experienced a dramatic share price surge as the emergency use drugs rolled out across the world. The Gates Foundation offloaded its shares after two years, in November 2021 for $1,300m. This is the same month Bill Gates admitted that the vaccine wouldn't block transmission, but the investment did perform by delivering a return of over twenty-three times the original investment , in a little over two years.
- Known colloquially as *Bat Woman,* Shi Zhengli at Wuhan Institute of Virology (WIV) was the recipient of NIAID funding and funding by the US Agency for International Development (USAID), which describes itself as the world's premier international development agency, the catalytic actor driving development results, including preventing the next global pandemic. This funding was routed to WIV through the EcoHealth Alliance, headed by British-born zoologist Peter Daszak, after President Obama intervened following multiple lab leaks to stop bioweapons research on US soil in October 2014. The US President declared a moratorium on gain of function research in the USA on "*novel potential pandemic pathogens*" causing consternation among grantors and grantees, threatening to shut off the movement of lucrative funds.
- One of the most vocal was Dr Ralph Baric, PhD, described as a master of cloning RNA viruses and a prolific gain-of-function researcher at the University of North Carolina-Chapel Hill. NIAID awarded Baric

$21.7m in 2012 for a five-year study into the immunogenetics of biodefence pathogens, and $10.58m the following year for a separate 5 year study into novel genes encoded by RNA and DNA viruses.

- Baric ignored the Obama moratorium on the grounds that his studies were underway before it commenced, and he continued genetically manipulating coronaviruses including one recovered by Shi Zhengli from horseshoe bats. RFK claims that Baric trained his Wuhan lab counterparts in the secrets of genetically engineering pandemic corona viruses after filing a patent in 2015 on engineering spike protein which he had developed.[6] This is the same year Baric jointly published an article with Zhengli in Nature Medicine.
- Based on later evidence from a colleague, 2015 was the year Peter Daszak of the EcoHealth Alliance pitched the CIA's venture capital arm, In-Q-Tel, a presentation about identifying predictable patterns in disease emergence. This was identified by Daszak's former vice president and senior scientist, Andrew Huff PhD to RFK, when Daszak began functioning as a CIA asset to spy on the Chinese.
- October 2019, a month after the Gates Foundation investment in BioNtech, Bill Gates and former CIA deputy director Avril Haines, who was to become the Director of National Intelligence and President Biden's coronavirus adviser, hosted Event 201 in New York. They played a game which simulated a worldwide coronavirus pandemic that killed sixty 60 million people. It was sponsored by John Hopkins

6. Chapter 32 of *The Wuhan Cover-Up* examines Ralph Baric.

Centre for Health Security, in partnership with the World Economic Forum and the Gates Foundation.

- November 17th 2019: the South China Morning post reported a case of Covid-19 affecting a 55-year-old male in Wuhan. On December 30th, China officially attributed a severe outbreak of pneumonia in Wuhan to "*a mysterious new coronavirus*" and twelve days later announced its first death.
- January 11th: the SARS-CoV-2 genetic sequence was internationally released. A few days later, both China and the WHO denied there was a human-to-human transmission, a position that didn't last long, and Wuhan went into full lockdown.
- Jan 26th: Anthony Fauci at the NIAID described the Wuhan virus as *'very, very low risk'*. The next day, Peter Daszak of EcoHealth Alliance confirmed that funding from Fauci at NIAID went to Chinese coronavirus scientists who had identified that SARS-related CoVs can bind to human cells.
- Near the end of January 2020, the WHO declared a PHEIC. On the next day, Jan 31st, US President Trump banned travel from China. This is the same day that scientists in New Delhi published a preprint paper stating that the viruses spike proteins had unique genetic insertions. The Indian scientists came under pressure to pull their paper, which they did.
- February 1st 2020: Farrar held a secret teleconference with Fauci and other scientists to discuss the possible lab origin of Covid-19. It was followed by a Fauci email which said; "*suspicion was heightened by the fact that scientists in Wuhan university are known to have been working on gain of function experiments to determine the molecular mechanisms associated with bat viruses*

adapting to human infection and the outbreak originated in Wuhan".

- Feb 3rd: Zhengli and other Chinese scientists published a note stating that Covid-19 was a natural spillover from wild bats. Three days later, after a short investigation which included a zoom meeting with Fauci, the National Academy of Sciences Engineering and Medicine (NASEM) wrote to the White House with no mention of the possibility of a lab leak. This is the same day Peter Daszak penned a letter to The Lancet ridiculing the lab leak as a conspiracy theory, heavily supported by endorsements from his associates.
- February 7th: Major General Chen Wei took over the Wuhan Institute of Virology and on the 11th of February, Fauci met Ralph Baric privately, a scientist he would later claim, under oath, to be unsure of ever meeting.
- February 19th: The Lancet published the Daszak letter which had been signed by 27 associates but it was entirely silent on their conflicts of interest, which is standard protocol, so that readers can assess motive and bias.
- In March, the Chinese authorities blamed Covid-19 on a US bioweapon or on imported fish.
- April 28th: Chinese doctor Li-Meng Yan informed the American media that the source of the deadly pandemic was the Wuhan lab.
- May 2020: a study was released attacking hydroxychloroquine efficacy in treating Covid-19. It would later be retracted, but not after being deployed by the compliant media to attack repurposed drugs. Ivermectin was also attacked as a '*horse dewormer*',

despite its widespread use large parts of the world. Emergency Use Authorisations could not be granted for vaccines if existing medicines could be shown to deal with the virus.

- In the first quarter 2021, the US State Department launched a widespread investigation into the origins of the virus, but US intelligence officials killed it quickly. In March 2021, the Munich Security Conference, a favoured meeting event for the intelligence community, hosted another pandemic simulation that gamed a Monkey Pox pandemic. Similar to Event 201 in October 2019, it was amazingly prescient because in July 2023, the WHO declared a monkeypox public health emergency, upgrading it in 2024 to a PHEIC, an international emergency
- August 2021: the Director of National Intelligence Avril Haines, reported back to President Biden following his request to reopen the investigation into covid origins. She concluded a *'low confidence'* in the theory that the virus emerged from in a natural zoonotic event.
- October 2021, EcoHealth admitted to Zhengli's huge success in infecting humanised mice with lab engineered coronavirus.
- December 1st 2021: the WHO tabled an international treaty on Pandemic Preparedness and Response,
- September 14th 2022, Politico, the Washington-based digital newspaper, published its investigation revealing Bill Gates funded and coordinated his pandemic response through the Bill & Melinda Gates Foundation (BMGF), the Coalition for Epidemic Preparedness Innovations (CEPI), the Global Alliance

for Vaccines and Immunisation (GAVI) and the Wellcome Trust.
- December 2022, the WHO, which receives its largest private donations from the Gates Foundation (BMGF) announced the appointment of its new Chief Scientist starting in May 2023. This was to be Jeremy Farrar, who was stepping down as chief of Wellcome Trust to take up a role where he has the power to declare pandemics.
- November 2022, in a sworn deposition, Anthony Fauci denies ever having met Ralph Baric.
- June 2023, the US State Department investigators confirmed to the Sunday Times in London that three Wuhan institute researchers were hospitalised with Covid-19 in the autumn of 2019, making them the likely source of the pandemic.
- July 2023: the US House Select Subcommittee on the coronavirus pandemic concluded that Doctors Anthony Fauci (NIAID) and Francis Sellers Collins (NIH) had scientists support papers to disprove the lab leak using *'fatally flawed science'*.

With this reconstructed timeline, we are able to better understand the actors in play. RFK pays close attention to the Geneva headquartered, World Economic Forum (WEF) for good reason. Despite the cruelty, health damage and deaths caused by lockdowns, to merely delay the pass-through of a respiratory virus, the policy was lauded by Farrar at the WEF annual conference in Davos when standing in for the WHO Director General, Tedros Ghebreyesus in January 2020. He addressed over three thousand attendees, including fifty-three heads of state, in an audience teeming with billionaires.

The WEF chief Klaus Schwab took the opportunity to press for *The Great Reset*, a model for global governance characterised by tight centralised controls maximising technology including surveillance, and chiming with plans by the Bank for International Settlements (BIS), for central bank digital currency, linked into digital IDs that also double as vaccine passports and can carry personal carbon limits. In his chapter on the WEF, RFK summarised the Great Reset agenda;

> *"Not surprisingly the WEF and its membership will benefit from centralised economies and political systems that facilitate both surveillance of and other state control mechanisms over unruly or democratically inclined global populations. Such protocols treat democracy like an expensive extravagance that impedes their unlimited accumulations of wealth and political power by a technocratic elite. Over the two decades since Dr Fauci and Bill Gates first shook hands in Seattle, WEF and its membership have hijacked public health and climate crisis to give moral gloss to top-down solutions that shift wealth and power to the super-rich and give rise to centralised control of a security state. Proponents call the public health strategy that prepares the path for Schwab's Great Reset 'the biosecurity agenda' or 'Pandemic Preparedness and Response".*[7]

CEPI, the Coalition for Epidemic Preparedness Innovations, was founded by Gates to gather money from the foreign aid budgets of Governments towards pandemic vaccine development. It is led by Richard Hatchett who, when as part of the George Bush administration, was a leading author of the US national strategy for pandemic influenza implementation plan, 2005 to 2006. Hatchett advocated for a militarised,

7. *The Wuhan Cover-Up*, p.380

authoritarian approach to pandemic management. He described how governments ought to impose strict lockdowns accompanied by social distancing and compulsory mask-wearing on citizens, where the path to escape would require taking jabs with novel and inadequately tested compounds, that held zero liability for their manufacturers. In 2017 Hatchett was appointed the CEO of CEPI founded by Gates and in May of 2020, he was appointed to the expert advisory group for the UK government Vaccine Taskforce and a member of Britain's Pandemic Preparedness Partnership.

Coinciding with the Wuhan lockdown, CEPI held a press conference in front of 30 reporters, led by its CEO Richard Hatchett, which also included Farrar. At the Davos press conference, when Hatchett was asked by a Chinese journalist if there was any historical precedent for lockdowns, he replied: *"There is a literature which I would certainly encourage Chinese authorities to review"*. What he didn't say was that the literature to which he was referring were his own studies on the playbook for draconian lockdowns, which had been hotly contested for unsubstantiated claims about the Spanish Flu that ran contrary to long established and tested protocols by WHO and CDC.

Writing in *The Conservative Woman* on August 28th 2022, Paula Jardine summarised the press conference;

> *"There was no need to encourage the Chinese authorities to review the literature. CEPI already had a man in Beijing Dr George Gao the director of China's Centre for Disease Control but also a member of the CEPI scientific advisory panel. The community mitigation approach the Chinese adopted in Wuhan was straight out of [Hatchett's] 2006 US Homeland Security pandemic playbook. The response plan is in reality an American scheme,*

> *with its origins more than a decade and a half earlier and against a backdrop of bioterrorism concerns. Uncle Sam is the wizard behind the curtain, not acting in the West's interests at all".*[8]

PANDA was established in April 2020 by a group of multidisciplinary professionals, who perceived the global reaction to Covid - from lockdowns to mandates - as overwrought and damaging to the point of causing a great tear in the fabric of society. David Bell and Emma McArthur, writing report in 2022 for PANDA, summarised the WHO pivot promoted by Farrar and Hatchett:

> *"The WHO's failure to follow its own pre-existing pandemic guidelines by supporting lockdowns, mass testing, border closures and the multibillion-dollar COVAX mass vaccination programme, has generated vast revenues for vaccine manufacturers and the biotech industry, whose corporations and investors are major contributors to the WHO".*[9]

The WEF support led by Farrar and Hatchet for draconian Chinese lockdowns fits into the interconnection between the Davos billionaire class and China's ruling elite. China has been long courted by Schwab, cultivating relationships with the Chinese Communist party leaders, paving the way for external investment by its members into the vast domestic Chinese marketplaces. This is evident from the Chinese equivalent of Davos, held by the WEF in the Chinese cities of Tianjin and Dalian, bringing together billionaires, politicians, academics

8. https://www.conservativewoman.co.uk/paula-jardine-3-it-was-americas-bio-spooks-who-locked-down-the-west/
9. https://pandata.org/whos-driving-the-pandemic-express/

and media elites. In 2021, the WEF removed the Summer China Conclave page from its website.

RFK makes the claim, supported by the evidence he presents, that by February 2020, actors which included Fauci, Farrar and Daszak, in combination with US Spooks and the editors of Nature Medicine, Nature, and The Lancet, had been working closely with their Chinese counterparts to disguise information from health agencies throughout the world. At the time of writing this book in 2024, the WHO had unpublished plans developed in secret talks to alter the current International Health Regulations and introduce a Pandemic Treaty in the guise of a framework convention. These plans were formulated to be adopted at the World Health Assembly (WHA) meeting in Geneva in early June 2024.

RFK points out that Bill Gates advocates more simulations and drills, all of which are entirely absent of normal public health policy towards respiratory viruses, once advocated by the WHO and the CDC and were based on long established science and practice. This includes bolstering human immune systems with proper nutrition and exercise, loading up vitamin D levels, using repurposed medicines to mitigate the impacts and isolating and protecting those most at risk, including the elderly in nursing homes. The new rigid orthodoxy from Covid-19 does not allow for informed consent, or for doctors to treat patients as they see fit. It instead puts forward a one-size-fits-all response, that coincidentally magnifies corporate and elite wealth and expands state powers of surveillance and control.

This makes no allowance for counter-science. It attacks it like it attacked the *Great Barrington Declaration,* labelling it disinformation and misinformation, and labelling those involved as enemies of the state. It does not admit that lockdowns, masks and social distancing are ineffective in stopping transmission. Instead, the gameplan is to repeat the formula, to double-down. It is for this reason that we should be alarmed that the WHO proposals include national governments to work as part of the great game, gathering pathogens for gain of function research as a part of their natural resource endowment. This strategy establishes a massive expansion and proliferation of the bioweapons complex, involving nation states as the gatherers. The WHO proposals set the scene to generate an open-ended supply line of pandemic emergencies and thus, new supplies of emergency-use authorised drugs, from lab to jab into arms within 100 days, with legal immunity for their manufacturers.

The WHO project proposes to become a vast library of viruses with bioweapon and vaccine potential upon which nation states and corporations can apply gene editing technology to alter the pathogens to create novel organisms which can then be patented. This is a one-stop shop in which nation states and corporations will own both the poison and the antidote. Given the capacity to create grotesque amounts of money for corporations and massive increase in state power from surveillance and control, it is inevitable that an assembly line of pandemic emergencies will be scheduled for humanity.

At the centrepiece of the WHO, changes to the International Health Regulations and its Treaty is the classic playbook from the WEF, the public-private partnership. This is to be the fulcrum of the new global PPR (Pandemic Preparedness & Response) complex, where it will be assisted with digital technologies and led by propaganda grounded in tested psychological operations. These proposals are clearly the landing zone for 21st century totalitarianism, a centralised global governance led by an elite class that believe they know best, where humans are expected to give up personal freedoms and risk their health for the benefit of all, and for the uber-enrichment of the tiny few.

Unless checked, this totalitarianism could eclipse its 20th century predecessor in both intensity and extent. It will be global and biological. There is another future possible, however, where more and more citizens wake up to the plot unfolding before them, reject the ideology that drives it and demand that these elites armed with their bioweapons are held to account. A future where personal freedom is cherished, and our constitutional rights reestablished. It is our choice.

17

FINANCIAL SYSTEM RISK

The Global Financial Crisis (GFC) brought the world's financial system within a hairs breadth of total collapse. The worry isn't what we know, but what we do not know. The debt excesses that caused the GFC may not be over, merely delayed. Economic science is contradictory and doesn't help us find the tipping point. The Keynesians believe in Government fiscal and Central Bank monetary intervention to stave off crises. The Austrian school does not believe in external interventions but lelieves instead in free markets to stabilise prices. The Austrians hold that markets are efficient and self-regulatory and best left to themselves to enact a creative destruction and regrowth cycle.

These ideologies are diametrically opposed. The Keynesians want Government policies to stabilise the economy and mitigate volatility, the Austrians believe that these make downward business cycles worse, that businesses should be allowed to fail so that scarce resources and capital can be pushed to the most efficient, not the least. The Keynesians argue for Government intervention for insolvent companies during recessions to soften job losses, but Austrians would argue that this robs capital from more efficient businesses and job creators.

On inflation, the divide is equally as stark. Keynesians believe in a low, steady inflation rate that encourages economic growth and investment. They think paper currencies can be manipulated through central bank monetary policy, effectively fixing the price of money to stabilise the economy and by adjusting it to the ups and downs of business cycles. On the other end of the spectrum, Austrians believe inflation to be the Darth Vader of outcomes because it destroys savings and currencies which they prefer to be backed by gold or other hard assets, in other words *'sound money'*..

If you've followed that so far, you'll clearly see that Keynesian thinking dominates both Government and Central Bank policies. While Keynesian policies staved off the extra downward forces of depression after the GFC, the concern is that it has created a monster of its own; next to the elaborate computers that drive modelling in the inner sanctums of central banks, they are burning essence, sprinkling holy water and rubbing rabbit's feet. Here is why:

The GFC exposed modern modelling as defunct and put economic science in the dock. Time and again, events in the real world, calculated to be extremely unlikely, keep occurring, including the GFC and the collapse of funds based on the most advanced mathematical sciences. These so-called high sigma events, outcomes which are labelled extremely unlikely to occur, happen much more commonly in nature than the models calculate. It isn't nature that is wrong, however, it is the models.

An event that is extremely rare, say beyond the sixth standard deviation in a normal distribution, is assigned a probability of happening at about twice in a billion opportunities by models, but, the 1998 collapse of the Long-Term Capital Management fund was calculated at over Sigma 10. The LTCM fund which supported $1.25 trillion in derivative positions which was founded by two Noble Prize award winning economists, changed the great game. Its significance was in the immediate intervention by the US Fed to stave off a market crisis from a LCTM insolvency. The Fed lent money cheaply to the Wall Street banks which were exposed to the threatened insolvency, to bail out LCTM, and themselves. The Fed's rescue fostered a unique incentive for Wall Street bankers to increase their own risk taking based on the implicit understanding that the Fed would effectively underwrite big banks from 1998 onwards.

Shortly thereafter, the Dot.com bubble burst. This led the Fed to cut rates and the US Government to send cash to consumers, kickstarting a property bubble. It burst at the GFC when the extreme risk taking by Wall Street behemoths was exposed and led to the insolvency of Lehmann Bros due to its subprime mortgage exposure. Lehmann's supernova in 2008, which was one of the banks rescued by the Fed from big LCTM losses ten years before, delivered a tremendous shock to the financial establishment worldwide. For months the valuation of all banks was up in the air because of the vectors of transmission of default risk from Wall Street banks to insurance funds, pension funds and other banks worldwide. This could not be easily calculated due to how worthless subprime debt had been concealed within higher grade debt and sold as sound credit packages. The concealment was criminal, but no one went to jail.

Ever since the GFC, central banks have used various monetary tools, crushing interest rates to zero, open market operations like cheap loans to shaky banks and quantitative easing where they buy Government bonds and other securities off banks at inflated prices, to flood banks with liquidity.

The economic lockdowns that accompanied Covid-19 raised the game to a new level by lending vast sums money to Governments to pour cash directly into hundreds of millions of consumer bank accounts. The result was the global inflationary surge of 2020-2024. Despite the inevitability of unprecedented money printing and, led by the Fed, central banks including the ECB maintained the fiction that the excessive inflation which took off at the latter end of 2020, was *transitory*.

By the time inflation began to show signs of cooling in 2024 after nose bleeding rate hikes from 2022, rates once at zero and below, peaked at over 5% in the USA and 4% in the Eurozone. Total excess inflation, in other words real losses in money value over the period, is still being calculated, but likely to run close to one Euro and Dollar in every five compared to pre-lockdown.

The legacy since LTCM and the costs of ageing populations is the excessive debt now carried by the global economy, notwithstanding the economic growth it sustained. This, in turn, has created a growing industry of dissenters, sceptics and alarmists, ranging from stock market bears to doomsters and preppers, all contributing to a rising anxiety about the capacity to keep the great Keynesian game going, without torching the financial system.

Following sanctions against Russia including the freezing of its foreign reserves, a plan to challenge the US Dollar as the world reserve currency is afoot from BRICS growing membership. The US has long enjoyed a privileged position of owning the currency through which the majority of global trade is conducted, including the oil market lubricated by the so-called Petro-Dollar. This has given the US economy an almost bottomless capacity to borrow money cheaply from countries, corporations and funds throughout the world, to finance its growth. The Dollar dominance has continued because of the lack of an alternative. This would require the issuer to ditch capital controls surrounding their economies, allowing free capital movement in and out. It is why China, since April 2021, is testing the Digital Renminbi, a central bank digital currency issued by the People's Bank of China.

The BRICS move, the details of which continue to unfold, appears to be aimed at establishing a multi-currency trading platform backed, not purely by economic strength, but by gold and other commodities. It is an open question as to whether it can be done at scale. BRICS original five members, Brazil, Russia, India, China and South Africa – admitted Egypt, Ethiopia, Iran and the United Arab Emirates in 2024 after agreeing to expand the previous year. This brings the total of BRICS+ to nine members and represents a little over 37% of world GDP or about $37 trillion. A trillion is a thousand billion.

A Hollywood-type burst of the global financial system, led by the USA, gets regular treatment from experts selling books, videos and subscriptions. It is a tale I've been following for decades during which, each time, US resilience, ingenuity and cussedness has defied the doomsters. The truth is, no one really knows at what level the fattening debt US debt load reaches a tipping point. What can be said with certainty is that, on this trajectory, it is unsustainable and a crisis would become inevitable. The figures are stark with US debt by end

August 2024 reported on the National Debt Clock of $35.36 trillion representing $268,000 per taxpayer and costing an amount of money to service which will shortly reach $1 trillion per year. This debt is being financed by an economy with a GDP of €28.3 trillion, putting its Debt to GDP at about 125%.

We do know is that the USA enjoys a superiority over all its rivals based on a range of pillars, not just economic might. It has demonstrably robust financial institutions and capital markets that have weathered many crises, its top universities produce very high-level graduates for its professions, its military power and political reach therefrom is vastly in excess of any other country and its appetite for investment in R&D has placed the USA at the forefront of global technology. It also enjoys the benefits of owning the world's reserve currency, the safe haven status, which is demonstrated at each global crisis. In short, the USA, despite its obvious faults, has been in a virtuous self-supporting circle but like all colossus it is vulnerable to the decline of empire.

The question is when and how, and one knows for sure, so with this in mind, how does the global scorecard look? Based on ongoing excellence in diverse data presentation the Vancouver-based *Visual Capitalist*[1] does all the hard work and makes the answers easily accessible to anyone;

- By the turn of 2024 global debt which accounts for governments, households and businesses worldwide reported by the *Institute of International Finance* (IIF)

1. https://www.visualcapitalist.com/all-of-the-worlds-money-and-markets-in-one-visualization-2022/

had reached $315 trillion[2] up from $305 trillion, a quarter of which was owed externally, so owed by borrowers to non-resident creditors.

- By the end of 2022, according to *Trading Economics* the total value of cash, banknotes and coins in circulation was estimated at $8 trillion but when deposit accounts, money market funds and the like are added, the total reached $82.6 trillion. This is the value of M2 money supply at the end of 2022. M1 money supply is all the cash in circulation plus instant deposit accounts and stood at $48.9 trillion, but M2, the broader measure was at $82.6 trillion.
- The total held in gold above ground according to the *World Gold Council* was valued at $11.5 trillion and crypto currency, then going through a dip from a much higher peak the previous year, stood at $760bn.
- Global Real Estate according to *Savills* was estimated at $326 trillion in 2020 of which $259 trillion or 79% was in residential properties, the latter forms part of global household wealth which stood at $463 trillion, a *Credit Suisse* calculation. Global Equities across public stock markets according to the *World Federation of Exchanges* (WFE) stood at $96 trillion and *Forbes* 2022 World's Billionaires lists 2,668 billionaires globally with accumulated wealth of $12.7 trillion.

In his 2023 book, *The Great Taking*, David Webb puts total global wealth higher than Credit Suisse, at $500 trillion, five times annual global GDP which measures the annual value of all output from goods and services.

---

2. Institute of International Finance Debt Monitor May 2024 https://www.iif.com/portals/0/Files/content/Global%20Debt%20Monitor_May2024_vf.pdf.

Global Debt is $315 trillion, lower than global wealth, but when the total notional value of Derivatives is added, it vastly exceeds global wealth. Derivatives, which are contracts between counterparties, also have a market value which reflects the price the market puts on buying or selling the derivatives and this stood at $12.4 trillion according to *BIS* at the end of 2022, but the notional value stood at $600 trillion. This value varies up to two quadrillion in other estimates, or twenty times global GDP.

The Great Taking has been published for free, online at thegreataking.com. It is being made into a documentary to be released in December 2024. You will find a detailed interview with David on my Counterpoint series on YouTube, conducted during Sept 2024. I first met David, an ex-Wall Street fund manager in Sweden, where he now lives, at a three-day conference in October 2023. I read his book on the return flight to Dublin, since that time I've interviewed him privately before integrating his material into public lectures. The content of his book is remarkable, relating to the liquidators call on digitalized securities in the event of the insolvency of a Central Clearing Party. It isn't opinion, it is factual and is fully supported by documentation he acquired through discovery in the EU archives, which had not been previously published, and which has not been rebutted .

Webb points out that in 1994 the US *Uniform Commercial Code* was quietly altered without the fanfare of an Act of Congress, replacing property rights and property owners with contractual rights by entitlement holders. This change coincided with the arrival of the digital age which replaced pieces of paper such as share certificates, with your name on the certificate as the title holder, with contractual rights to call on your property as an entitlement holder.

All very fine, Webb points out, until there is an insolvency of a Central Clearing Party (CCP). In other words, the operator in the intermediation process between you and the centralised and digitalised pool of assets. He has found that the global financial assets pool, in other words pensions, savings and investments, whether segregated or not, is being used as collateral to support credit underpinning the vast global derivatives marketplace which is many times larger than total global wealth. This means that banks security over its credit trumps your claim to your financial investments in the event of an insolvency. Webbs discovery is that the liquidation of a CCP will give bank creditors priority call on the asset pool notwithstanding the fact that the underlying owner believes he or she has an incontestable right of recovery in full of their securities. There is one CCP in the USA and two in Europe, all operating on slivers of capital reserves relative to the scale of financial assets perched above it, so you can see concentration risk lit large.

In short, Webb argues that the global security market is acting as hidden security for banks who clearly are not the originating investor. This is happening without the knowledge and consent of the investor.

In his evidence, *The Great Taking* produces the smoking gun, an exchange of crystal-clear correspondence between a top legal officer of the *Federal Reserve Bank of New York*, Mr Joyce Hansen and his equivalent legal senior at the EU, Mr Martin Thomas dated March 6th 2006. Over several pages the American lawyer responds to the precise questions posed by the European on how the US system works. Anyone can follow it to its conclusions.

Two years earlier, the EU had formed the *Legal Certainty Group* to examine and mimic the US system in the event of such insolvencies. The EU achieved this aim in 2014 in the *Central Securities Deposit Regulation* (CSDR) through an EU Directive. It copied the US model and the two the holdouts in the EU, Sweden and Finland rolled over.

On March 12th 2024, Webb gave testimony to a committee hearing by the Tennessee Senate on his findings, following which, with unanimous bi-partisan support, a bill was proposed to give priority to Entitlement Holders in the event of a CCP insolvency. The following day, Webb advises that a Banking lobbyist threatened the Tennessee State Treasurer with the withdrawal of banks from Tennessee if enacted into State laws. In a hearing the next week under oath, the bank representative repeated the warning that banks would withdraw en-masse from Tennessee and alienate any banks moving in. The warning specifically identified the proposed bill as being bad for the Deposit Trust & Clearing Corporation (DTCC), the US clearing house.

On April 25th 2024 I put the findings of *The Great Taking* to the Governor of the Irish Central Bank for clarity, not knowing that the *Financial Stability Board* (FSB) on the same day was issuing a detailed 31 page report[3] dealing specifically with the insolvency of Central Clearing Parties (CCP), to map out the path to recapitalization by other market participants and to help in the smooth running of the marketplace. Webb's book, published in October 2023 identified wafer thin capital reserves at CCPs, as a severe risk. Neither the FSB paper nor the

3. https://www.fsb.org/2024/04/guidance-on-financial-resources-to-support-ccp-resolution-and-on-the-treatment-of-ccp-equity-in-resolution-revised-version-2024/.

response of the Irish Central Bank address the potential alienation of property from entitlement holders or address the charge that this manufactured outcome is foundational to the derivatives marketplace. It probably is unhelpful that the manner in which it was achieved could be prosecuted under US Racketeering laws on criminal conspiracy.

Here is the unrestricted exchange with the Central Bank of Ireland starting with the email to the Governor's email address April 25th 2024.

> *Dear Governor,*
>
> *At this link you can download a book, https://thegreattaking.com/read-online-or-download the Appendix of which page 69-98 contains a concerning exchange by way of Q & A from senior lawyers at the US Fed and at the EU (Legal Uncertainty Group) in 2006.* (sic)
>
> *The interpretation of this, was outlined in evidence recently by David Webb before the Senate legislature in Tennessee after which it decided to legally reverse the position whereby creditors, mostly banks will not, in the event of a liquidation of financial actors most especially Central Clearing Parties, put themselves before the Contractual Right holders, namely the voluminous investors in financial securities. The claim is that the derivative mountain is secured on these as collateral, hence the slide below.*
>
> *I bring this to your attention because I have put this to leading asset managers but have been met with silence and if it stands up to scrutiny it goes to the very heart of Consumer Protection and of Prudential Supervision, requiring coordinated legislative action at Irish and EU level and public statements issued in connection with same, before any major event unfolds.*

Thank you for your attention and I look forward to learning the position of the Irish Central Bank's legal experts on securities, on this matter.

Eddie Hobbs,

Managing Director

Hobbs Financial Practice Limited

The response arrived June 12th 2024, not from the Governor but from an expert senior officer of the Irish regulator.

Central Bank of Ireland - UNRESTRICTED

Dear Mr Hobbs,

Thank you for your email of 25 April in relation to securities markets, which has been referred to me for consideration.

I would like to assure you that the Central Bank undertakes significant work in relation to supervision and policy development in securities markets. This includes active participation in European institutions tasked with coordinating work in this area, for example, the European Securities and Markets Authority. There is a substantial legislative framework in place at EU and domestic level which includes legislation on Markets in Financial Instruments, Central Securities Depositories, OTC derivatives, central counterparties and trade repositories much of which has been developed in recent years. This legislation is reviewed and updated at prescribed intervals.

As you will appreciate, the Central Bank cannot share legal advice nor disclose confidential details of its work and its engagement with European institutions. Notwithstanding these constraints, it is our aim to be as open and transparent as possible and further

> *detail on our work on securities markets supervision and policy is on our website and regularly discussed with our stakeholders and in public forums.*

I replied the same day June 12th since which, no further information had emerged by mid-November 2024;

> *Thank you for your considered reply and I fully understand that your work must remain discrete and private. I'm also aware of the FSB paper specific to shoring up Central Clearing Parties released in late April, thus showing its attention to this less well-known link in the chain.*
>
> *The central question however requires to be clarified which is, whether or not the digitalised pool of securities is being used by banks as collateral for engaging in derivatives? It is either a true or false claim, can you clarify this point.*
>
> *The matter of solvency of CCPs I understand and see it now being addressed at FSB level, so there it rests.*
>
> *Thank you so much*
>
> *Eddie Hobbs*

The startling revelation is spreading. On Sept 9th 2024 in my interview with David Webb he confirmed that between 10 and 20 US State legislators, evidently convinced by the facts revealed to Tennessee are now working on changes to insolvency laws to thwart the priority claims of the bank behemoths who would stand to gain. This change is to reverse what has been quietly constructed and give entitlement holders priority claims over creditors. Nothing is yet happening in the EU. Until counteracting legislation is brought to bear which gives entitlement holders priority during CCP liquidations it is, at least, legally possible for the assets to be taken. After the interview with David Webb I sent a link for it together with his book and US legal notes, including draft Tennessee legislation, to every member of the Irish Oireachtas, all Irish MEPs and the Irish media. The whistle was blown in Ireland loud and clear Sept 25th 2024 to the establishment. It has been met by silence.

In practice there is a clear blue ocean between legal claims and the capacity to enact upon them if deemed racketeering and theft by hundreds of millions of investors, many of them armed, no matter what the view of the Fed and the powerful banking lobby. It would be helpful if actors and their masters who plotted the change in the US Uniform Commercial Code are exposed and investigated.

AFTERWORD

There is real hope as 2024 closes out, that we may be at a pivot point in the struggle against the rising tide of 21st century totalitarianism. The addition of Robert F Kennedy Jnr to the White House inner team as a health reformer and the clear impact his lectures and interviews have had in reshaping US political discourse is pivotal. Moreover, the arrival of Musk as a champion of free speech is precisely what totalitarians most fear, dispersed engagement and debate outside of channels they do not control. It is a turn in the tide against what can broadly be defined as the 'woke' impulse with its open borders and indoctrination of children in the classroom into critical race theory and gender ideology, both of which are designed to destabilise the roots of society, the family.

Covid was a beachhead to land a global technocracy in the form of the WHO pandemic treaty and, despite WHO attempts to disguise its real intent, it failed to make landfall in Geneva on the June bank holiday weekend. The treaty would have breached national sovereignty and passed unilateral control over every human, plant, animal health and ecosystems to an unelected politburo in the WHO in Geneva, an organisation immune from criminal prosecution, and bought and paid for by pharma money, a fifth of which comes from the Gates foundation.

Still, the WHO attempted to land multiple changes to the 2005 International Health Regulations. This included dropping the term "*non-binding*" over 160 times. That too failed. Delegates left Geneva with a husk of change. It marked a major defeat for totalitarians who see the WHO, the UN and the WEF as instruments and agents of their strategy.

Early May 2024 was the turning point. It was the moment all US Republican Senators signed a letter to President Biden informing him that the WHO plans were offensive to US sovereignty and had to go before the Senate for a two thirds majority before ratification. At least 21 US states followed as their State Attorney Generals intervened against the WHO and, at the time of writing, led by Louisiana many states are tabling laws to reject the WHO, the UN and the WEF within their territories.

The EU Parliamentary elections in the summer of 2024 have pushed the political calculus in Europe to the right, now including Italy, the Netherlands, France, Germany and Austria. The Green agenda is losing steam, as is the madcap idea of getting to net zero fossil fuels in twenty-five years. It is not possible to do this without degrowth and poverty. The flooding of Europe with fake asylum seekers is now being met by the conservative German government with crackdowns as they are fearful of losing even more of their electorate to parties like AFD, from whose base in Eastern Germany its power is growing.

Data and scientific studies, once regarded as heresy are circulating, detailing excess deaths correlated to heavily vaxed countries together with vaccine harm, myocarditis, pericarditis, immune system compromise, clotting and reproductive damage. It is becoming a tsunami within which Japanese doctors have played a pivotal role, its lead oncologist Dr Masanori Fukushima sounding the alarm on surges in turbo cancer, echoed by British Oncologist, Virologist and Immunologist Professor Angus Dalgleish in a Counterpoint interview November 2024[1], where he called for a worldwide ban on mNRA vaccines, due to harm to the human immune system.

The pushback is growing at such scale that is overwhelming the capacity of captive media and fact-checkers. Elon Musk buying Twitter to protect free speech was another milestone, as many platforms including YouTube and TikTok continue to deploy truth-killing censorship algorithms contrived in the early Covid years.

If you are reading this book and hearing this material for the first time, welcome to the struggle. There is no room for complacency, all hands are still needed to the pumps. These hugely resourced omnipresent agents of 21st century totalitarianism will not go quietly and will keep coming back to instil fear, division and mass formations, until we reveal them like the Wizard of OZ as the corpulent small man behind the curtain. This is work done mostly one by one, face to face with your peer group and networks, to break the crusty layer of cognitive dissonance that still entraps those most deeply affected by the propaganda. But don't hesitate to call out individual accountability either, it is no longer 2021-2023 and

1. https://x.com/RealEddieHobbs/status/1856034153755820535

there is no excuse for the weary old tropes and mantras of conditioning, save for a failure of courage and morality by the accuser.

In August 2024 over a glass of wine, a friend asked me what I was doing these days. Knowing him as a critical analyst and a book writing expert, I told him about my findings. Our last conversation about Covid had been three years before, when I'd first outlined my concerns, and clearly had astonished him. Three years later nothing had changed. When he told me that he didn't agree, I simply asked him what he could tell me about the redefinition of a PHEIC in 2009. He knew nothing of it. "*How then*" I asked him "*Can you to know the first thing about what is happening in the international health world about you?*" His typically honest response gave me an idea as to how to conclude this book.

No matter how you slice and dice it, at best, we have allowed global collusion to occur in open sight, without calling it out. This is the very obvious point. The WHO is the agent of those who finance it and those who have colluded behind it, in possible breach of anti-trust laws and laws dealing with corporate conspiracy. At worst, there may be a breach of laws dealing with manslaughter and potentially with mass murder if scientific investigation establishes military grade material in vaccines, a claim that has yet to stand up although it is hotly contested. Nevertheless, criminal matters will arise if it is found that those who colluded knew about and suppressed the danger of vaccines to the human immune system, pressing on anyway, disguising their objectives under the banner of public health concerns.

This book has striven to explain what has happened and what continues to happen to us collectively, by delving into what we can rely upon from psychology, psychological operations, sociology and economics as an explanation for our collective docility. It isn't the only explanation, not when you take it down to an individual level. Given the data, papers, videos and books available and accessible to any enquiring mind, it is clear that there also has been a chronic failure of morality, of critical thinking and of personal courage. That is the blunt truth of it.

It doesn't matter what side of the fence you found yourself on during Covid, what matters is that we, all of us, wake up to the attempts to hollow out our representative democracy, even the basic family unit, free speech and our homogeneity. It is all on the line, those who pursue rigid centralised surveillance and control are not going away. The Mpox PHEIC in August 2024 confirms that an assembly-line of so-called pandemics is planned, precisely as predicted. The WHO failure in Geneva in June 2024 is a setback for them, but it is not over, plans are already afoot to pass the task to the UN. Professor David Hughes is correct; we are in an omni-war on many fronts, not least of all from the flooding of Ireland with non-EU economic refugees, disguised as asylum seekers, robustly supported by the Irish Government and bolstered by its intention to install a surveillance and snitch society through 'Hate Speech' laws.

So, What Can You do?

The first step is awareness. Start asking hard questions, such as "why are we so quick to silence dissenting voices?" "Why is the EU attacking X?" "Who benefits from keeping us divided and afraid?" "What freedoms are we trading away in the name of convenience or safety?"

Awareness alone isn't enough, we also need to do better, to cultivate and to lead locally in critical thinking:

- Don't easily accept what you're told, question everything, especially the things that seem too convenient or align too perfectly with your existing beliefs.
- Engage in real debate: Step away from the screens and have face-to-face discussions with people who think differently than you. You might be surprised at what you learn.
- Support independent journalism: Seek out and support media outlets that aren't beholden to corporate or political interests.
- Protect your privacy: Take steps to safeguard your personal data and digital footprint. Every bit of information you give away is a potential tool of control.
- Engage in local politics: The big picture matters, but real change often starts at the local level. Get involved in your community and make your voice heard.
- Make fun of the situation: see how ridiculous their spectacular science is, how ludicrous the policies are. Laugh and point and jeer, by doing this you take their power away and may wake others up to the lies that are being offered as facts.

Totalitarianism thrives on silence and compliance. By speaking up, asking questions, and refusing to go along with the crowd, we can push back against the creeping tide of control. Remember the words of Aleksandr Solzhenitsyn: "*The line dividing good and evil cuts through the heart of every human being.*" It's up to us to decide on what side of that line we stand.

You've read this book. Once you see this material, it becomes impossible to unsee it in the media headlines, in press releases across the EU and from our own homegrown neo-totalitarians of all political hues. Don't expect conversions from the ranks of the Irish 4th Estate, see Appendix II.

St Augustine was attributed as saying, "*The Truth is like a Lion, just let it loose. There is no need to defend it. It will defend itself.*"

The task now is to release the truth to the *nearly awake*, to reignite their critical thinking function. The more that wake up, the greater chance of sending into the bowels of hell, this foul totalitarian impulse using satire, humour, laughter or prayer, as you please.

Eddie Hobbs

ABOUT THE AUTHOR

Eddie Hobbs is the writer and presenter of *Rip Off Republic,* a landmark satirical polemic that set Irish TV audience records and which joined the dots on how the Ireland was run, before its banking collapse. This time he tells you who, why, and how Totalitarianism is rising across the West to take control and, what you can do to stop it.

He is an Irish writer and activist responsible for the collapse of insurance investment home mortgage sales, the implementation of transparency laws on life and pension products, the collapse of the 1987 Groceries Order which had made it illegal for shops to pass through bulk discounts to consumers and in recent years, assisted in the demise of the mass selling of unregulated loan notes. Since 2020 he campaigned vigorously against vaccinating healthy children and against vaccine passports. He is a former Director of the Consumers Association of Ireland and the National Consumer Agency and runs a private wealth advisory firm based in County Kildare, Ireland. He has written several best sellers and received awards from Trinity Philosophical and UCD Law societies for his contribution to Irish public life. He is aged 62, married for 38 years with four adult children.

MORE BY EDDIE HOBBS

If you enjoyed this book and want to share it with your friends,
or buy the audiobook,
use the Qr code below, or type our web address into a browser:

https://bit.ly/EddieHobbs

BIBLIOGRAPHY

Aaronovitch, David. 2010. *Voodoo Histories: The Role of the Conspiracy Theory in Shaping Modern History*. Vintage.

Arendt, Hannah. 1963. *Eichmann in Jerusalem: A Report on the Banality of Evil.* Viking Press.

—. 1976. *The Origins of Totalitarianism.* London: Harcourt Brace & Company.

Barkun, Michael. 2003. *A Culture of Conspiracy: Apocalyptic Visions in Contemporary America.* University of California Press.

Barton, Alana, and Howard Davis. 2018. *Ignorance, Power and Harm: Agnotology and the Criminological Imagination.* Palgrave Macmillan.

Beck, Ulrich. 1992. *Risk Society: Towards a New Modernity.* London: Sage Publications.

Brotherton, Rob. 2016. *Suspicious Minds: Why We Believe Conspiracy Theories*. Bloomsbury USA.

Byford, Jovan. 2011. *Conspiracy Theories: A Critical Introduction* . Palgrave Macmillan.

Cassam, Quassim. 2019. *Conspiracy Theories.* Polity Press.

Curry, Judith. 2023. *Climate Uncertainty and Risk: Rethinking Our Response.* Anthem Press.

Dentith, M R X. 2024. *The Philosophy of Conspiracy Theories.* Taylor & Francis.

Desmet, Mattias. 2022. *The Psychology of Totalitarianism.* Chelsea Green Publishing.

Dickie, John. 2015. *The Cosa Nostra: A History of the Sicilian Mafia.* St. Martin's Publishing Group.

Douglas, Karen M., Robbie M. Sutton, and Aleksandra Cichocka. 2017. "The Psychology of Conspiracy Theories." *Current Directions in Psychological Science* 538—542.

Fricker, Miranda. 2007. *Epistemic Injustice.* Oxford: Oxford University Press.

Giddens, Anthony. 1991. *Modernity and Self-Identity: Self and Society in the Late Modern Age.* Cambridge: Polity Press.

—. 1990. *The Consequences of Modernity.* Cambridge: Polity Press.

Goldberg, Robert Alan. 2008. *Enemies Within: The Culture of Conspiracy in Modern America.* Yale University Press.

Heidegger, Martin. 2008. *Being and Time*. New York: HarperCollins Publishers.

Hofstadter, Richard. 1996. *The Paranoid Style in American Politics: And Other Essays.* Harvard University Press.

Hughes, David A. 2024. *"Covid-19," Psychological Operations, and the War for Technocracy: Volume 1.* Springer International Publishing.

Huxley, Aldous. 1932. *Brave New World.* Chatto & Windus.

Keeley, Brian L. 1999. "Of Conspiracy Theories." *The Journal of Philosophy* 109—126.

Kennedy, Robert Francis. 2021. *The Real Anthony Fauci: Bill Gates, Big Pharma, and the Global War on Democracy and Public Health.* Skyhorse Publishing.

—. 2023. *The Wuhan Cover-Up: And the Terrifying Bioweapons Arms Race.* Skyhorse.

Kierkegaard, Søren. 1980. *The Concept of Anxiety.* New Jersey: Princeton University Press.

Lanham, Richard A. 2006. *The Economics of Attention: Style and Substance in the Age of Information.* University of Chicago Press.

Lewis, Michael. 2017. *The Undoing Project: A Friendship That Changed Our Minds* . WW Norton.

Marrs, Jim. 2017. *The Illuminati: The Secret Society That Hijacked the World* . Visible Ink Press.

McGoey, Linsey. 2019. *The Unknowers: How Strategic Ignorance Rules the World.* London: Zed Books.

Michels, Robert. 1915. *Political Parties: A Sociological Study of the Oligarchical Tendencies of Modern Democracy.* The Free Press.

Mills, Charles Wright. 1956. *The Power Elite.* Oxford University Press.

—. 1959. *The Sociological Imagination.* Oxford University Press.

—. 1951. *White Collar: The American Middle Classes.* Oxford University Press.

Nietzsche, Friedrich. 1966. *Beyond Good and Evil.* Vintage Random House.

—. 2006. *On the Genealogy of Morality.* Cambridge University Press.

Oliver, Eric J., and Thomas J. Wood. 2014. "Conspiracy Theories and the Paranoid Style(s) of Mass Opinion." *American Journal of Political Science* 952—966.

Orwell, George. 1949. *Nineteen Eighty-Four.* Secker & Warburg.

Pigden, Charles. 2007. "Conspiracy Theories and the Conventional Wisdom." *Episteme* 219—232.

Proctor, Robert N., and Londa Schiebinger. 2008. *Agnotology: The Making and Unmaking of Ignorance.* Stanford, California: Stanford University Press.

Rachman, Stanley. 2004. *Anxiety.* Second Edition. East Sussex: Psychology Press Ltd.

Scheff, Thomas J. 1994. *Bloody Revenge: Emotion, Nationalism and War.* Westview Press.

—. 1991. *Emotion and Violence: Shame and Rage in Destructive Conflicts.* Lexington Books.

Scheff, Thomas J. 2000. "Shame and the Social Bond: A Sociological Theory." *Sociological Theory* 84—99.

Smith, Adam. 1998. *An Inquiry Into the Nature and Causes of the Wealth of Nations.* Oxford University Press.

Turner, Jonathan H. 2007. *Human Emotions: A sociological theory.* London: Rotuledge.

Turner, Jonathan H. 2009. "The Sociology of Emotions: Basic Theoretical Arguments." *Emotion Review* 1 (4): 340–354.

Uscinski, Joseph E., and Joseph M. Parent. 2014. *American Conspiracy Theories.* Oxford University Press.

van Prooijen , Jan-Willem. 2018. *The Psychology of Conspiracy Theories.* Taylor & Francis.

Varoufakis, Yanis. 2024. *Technofeudalism: What Killed Capitalism.* Melville House.

Walker, Jesse. 2014. *The United States of Paranoia: A Conspiracy Theory* . HarperCollins.

Webb, Gary. 2011. *Dark Alliance: The CIA, the Contras, and the Crack Cocaine Explosion* . Seven Stories Press.

Yalom, Irvin D. 2008. *Staring at the Sun: Overcoming the Fear of Death.* San Francisco: Jossey-Bass.

APPENDIX 1 THE KILLARNEY DECLARATION

Delivered at the gates of the Global Economic Summit in Killarney Co Kerry, Republic of Ireland May 20th 2024 wherein the WHO Director General gave the opening keynote speech, within eleven days of the attempt by the WHO to land its plans for a global technocracy in Geneva, Switzerland.

May 20th 2024

The ancient Irish People, who predate the State by centuries and who have long asserted our rights to freedom from tyranny, do so again.

We declare the right of the Irish People to the unfettered control of Irish destinies, to be sovereign and indefeasible. We, the Irish People, demand our legal endowment from the 1987 Supreme Court Crotty ruling to a national referendum on the continuing membership of the World Health Organisation. We do so because the WHO intends to force a Trojan Horse Treaty upon us disguised as a new 'Agreement' and as a complete overhaul of Regulations. We demand, in the first instance, that the Irish Government rejects these manoeuvres as a breach of WHO membership rules and which require a four-month window before any changes are adopted

But we see through and beyond the agency of the WHO, to a multi-front agenda determined to create a bio-digital technocracy which threatens to subvert all liberal democracies and so we reach out to all at home and abroad, now awakening to the real and present danger from it.

Whispered through the sound of silence during the Lockdowns is the stark warning about the banality of evil from Hannah Arendt who studied the Eichmann Trial in Jerusalem in the early 60's and who predicted that 21st century totalitarianism would be led, not by the monsters of the last one but by the banal bureaucrats of the next.

So, we recognise and applaud the intervention of all US Republican Senators to demand a Senate vote on the WHO plans to subvert US sovereignty, the rejection of it by large numbers of State Attorney Generals and the determination of many State legislatures, led by Louisiana to reject the WHO, the UN and the World Economic Forum. We recognise the intentions of the UK, Netherland and the Slovak Republic to reject the WHO and note that these events occur as the first major vaccine is pulled from human health due to the clotting of our human blood.

We muster here outside this Globalist Summit to

remind its participants of our sovereign rights and personal freedom and to say to them;

We see you.

We see the psychological assault and abuse from advanced military grade propaganda across media that crushed informed consent, targeted, delicensed and deplatformed scientific dissent which, together with Government Lockdown fiats, compelled over 5.5bn people to be injected with experimental substances, while inexpensive, repurposed medicines were denigrated,

We See You.

We see the preparation, the lowering of the bar on defining pandemics in 2009, by dropping high mortality and morbidity. We see the abandonment of established science on corona viruses in favour of inflicting even more damaging lockdowns, we see the redefinition of the term vaccine itself to no longer include stopping infection and transmission. We see the rising evidence everywhere, of excess deaths, disablement and harm caused to the human immune system; infertility, stage four turbo cancers, myocarditis, autoimmune disease and death by clotting.

We see in the WHO plans for a doubling down, for the reintroduction of discredited PCR test cycles but this time used in human wastewater to find pathogens, list them as national resources, enhance them in national gain-of-function bioweapon laboratories, to partner with pharmaceutical manufacturers in a repeat of the same model as the Wuhan Institute of Virology which, clearly birthed Covid 19.

We see and recognise the emblems of control and compliance; the ineffective face masks, the social distancing, the abandonment of the elderly to lonely deaths and the alienation of the Irish People from our ancient rites of grieving.

We See You.

We see the instrument of control revealed as you now attempt to double down; ensnaring freedom further through Digital ID surveillance passports that will hold vaccine records, personal carbon limits and spending restrictions controlled by remotely programmable Central Bank Digital Currency. We know these controls are being discussed at this globalist summit.

We see the captivity of social media platforms and search engines to thwart dissenters and send a cold chill through people splintered and divided by the propaganda from cheerleaders who led the vilification and demonisation of those who failed to comply.

We see the intention to roll out an assembly line of unilateral emergency declarations by the WHO Director General, to repeat the abuse, to control and demoralise the human population. He speaks tomorrow, giving a keynote address.

We See You.

We call on all Irish men and women engaged directly or indirectly, knowingly or unknowingly in the silence of this fading Irish political establishment and we call on those engaged at editorial level that led to the abandonment of the Irish People by the 4th Estate, the old media. We call upon you to turn away from your masters and their captive fact-checkers and turn instead towards the Irish People.

We see you through the wider agenda your attempts to subvert the bonds of homogenous society and family itself; the flooding of Ireland through unrestricted refugees advanced by the UN, the attempt to redefine family itself, rejected so emphatically by the Irish People, the proposal to restrict free speech through so-called Hate Speech laws and the distorted sexualisation and misgendering of our young children through UN education ideologies. We see you attempt to shatter the foundations of society, preparing it for its subjugation to your bio-digital technocracy, the very fulcrum of your 21st century totalitarian ambitions.

We see you in the Irish government's continued participation in a globalist enterprise for which it has no mandate from the Irish People, a people who fought long and hard to repel the grip of empire, to which we have no intention of capitulating, no matter how it disguises itself: WHO Pandemic Agreement, Agenda 2030 with its so-called Sustainable Development Goals and the EU Migration Pact.

We see you in the moves to bring representative democracy to an end by replacing it with Stakeholder Capitalism. This is a model of centralised anti-democratic global governance advanced by the unelected World Economic Forum, which craves fusing state power, NGOs and corporate power, to the growing global power of unaccountable and unelected supranational institutions like the WHO and the UN.

We See You.

We see the Irish government cheering on the WHO while operating a hidden shadow programme for government which is largely founded on policies originating from these globalist institutions and whose impact is destroying social cohesion and stripping the Irish people of their rights, freedoms and sovereignty.

We see the perverse influence of the World Economic Forum in Irish affairs and in Irish leadership. We call on the next Government to prohibit membership of the WEF by cabinet members and by senior civil servants and members of our diplomatic corps and to openly declare the State's opposition to that organisation's Neo-Malthusian depopulation agenda, which traces back to an economic philosophy that underpinned the vast human catastrophe and depopulation of Ireland of the 1840's.

We see the continued use by this fading Irish Government of disingenuous language and rhetoric to promote globalist policies to an unsuspecting public under the patently false pretext of safety, compassion, international obligation and climate change

We see the Irish Government's failure to address critical aspects of the pandemic response including vaccine disabilities, harms and excess deaths. The lack of any meaningful investigation into the crisis betrays a fundamental disrespect for the Irish people who shouldered the burden of your policies, while you demonstrated an intolerable lack of accountability on your part

We demand an immediate independent transparent criminal investigation into the vaccines and into the handling of the pandemic response encompassing all clinical aspects including the legitimacy of using uber-magnified PCR tests. We demand fulsome disclosures of all communication with third party institutions and especially with personnel connected with the WHO, the Wellcome Trust, Imperial College London, European Medicines Agency and European Centre for Disease Prevention and Control.

We call on the new political establishment gathering in the wings to enshrine the Nuremberg Code into Irish law and to fight any resistance to doing so, recognising that this resistance can only have one objective; to cover up potential crimes.

To the Globalists here and everywhere, **We See You.**

We see among you the ambition to become transhuman beings, and an intention to convince us that we are not of Spirit and Soul, that we are not of God. We reject, most of all, this dark impulse in its entirety. We see contriving through it a malevolence that is not and never will be in us

Under God, We Sign This Declaration

18

APPENDIX II THE HEADLINES THAT NEVER WERE

By March 2020, the Irish 4th Estate had ceased to function all investigative journalism into the pandemic response, and instead transitioned to become willing and active participants in establishment propaganda, absorbing undisclosed ad revenues from State agencies. Four years later it continues to passively engage in cover up, despite overwhelming data and studies globally that contradict the editorials, headlines and narratives they assigned. These are the front pages banners that you never read:

1. WHO Dramatically Lowered Threshold for Pandemic in 2009
2. Investigation reveals Covid circulating in Sept 2019
3. Gates Foundation invests $55m in BioNTech, Sept 2019
4. WHO Abandons No Lockdown Health Policy Despite Sound Science
5. WEF Davos calls for Chinese Lockdowns Rejected
6. Zoonic Origins Story Exposed as Cover Up in Emails

7. President Refers Vaccine Passport bill to Supreme Court.
8. Supreme Court Rules Covid 'Yellow' Passport Unconstitutional
9. RTE Investigation Reveals US Regulators paid by Pharma
10. Irish Health Scientists Challenge Ferguson Covid Death Data
11. Scientists state 'No Science' supports masks or two metre rules
12. Irish Economists warn Covid Money Printing will fuel Inflation surge.
13. Central Bank of Ireland says FED and ECB 'Transitory Inflation' is propaganda.
14. Irish Excess Deaths among top in Global League
15. New Vaccines will stop Transmission exposed as a lie
16. Vaccines penetrate beyond injection site to all organs.
17. Gates; Vax won't stop transmission, after selling BionTech stake for $1.3bn
18. Health Scientists admit that Unvaccinated are no risk to population
19. RTE exposes attempts to axe organ transplant list of the unvaccinated
20. Beaumont Organ Transplant Clinicians reject ditching of 'anti-vax' patients
21. Unexplained surge in Excess Deaths since 2021 to be investigated.
22. Gardai launches criminal investigation into pandemic response.
23. NPHET Presser Chaos after robust exchange with RTE duo
24. Taoiseach Announces Exit from WHO after review

25. Bar Council Members Group Warn About WHO Pandemic Treaty Proposal
26. Oireachtas Votes on Open Public Enquiry into Covid.
27. Senior Civil Servants, Diplomats and Politicians banned from WEF membership.
28. Irish Times, INM, Newstalk volunteer emails and disclose revenues received from State.
29. Irish health scientists parse excess death causes, Jabs or Lockdown?
30. HSE Announces Ban on Covid Emergency Use Authorisations
31. Gardai commence criminal investigation into Pharma vax claims.
32. Joint Oireachtas Committee Recommends Nuremburg Code adoption into Irish Law
33. Investigation widens into Zero Covid advocacy funding
34. Government announces amnesty for pandemic whistleblowers
35. Top Officials in health establishment lawyer up

19

APPENDIX III – BREAKING OUT OF THE DIGITAL ECHO CHAMBER – AN ESSAY BY EDDIE HOBBS

IN THIS DIGITAL AGE, algorithms act as puppeteers, smoothly controlling the strings of our online encounters. They curate, sort, and display content based on our interests, habits, and preferences. Originally intended to enhance consumer satisfaction through relevant information transmission, these algorithms have unwittingly taken on a more harmful function. They've developed into architects of division, emphasising underlying biases, creating echo chambers, and frequently bypassing serious debate in favour of sensationalism. Cracking the code of these algorithms necessitates a critical examination of the impacts of algorithm-driven content personalisation, as well as an inquiry into the psychology behind its exploitative tactics.

Most digital platforms, whether they are news websites, social media networks, or video streaming services, aim to engage their users. Engaging users keeps them on the site, increasing the possibility of exposure to adverts and, consequently, revenue generation. As a result, algorithms prioritise anything that captures attention, elicits strong emotions, and encourages interaction—likes, shares, comments, or longer viewing. The science of engagement focuses on fundamental features of the human psyche. People are naturally drawn to strong emotional content, such as joy, fury, grief, or excitement. According to a study conducted by the University of Pennsylvania's Wharton School, positive content—particularly content that evoked wonder—is more likely to go viral.[1] Material that makes people furious, shocked, or afraid, on the other hand, tends to generate a lot of interest because individuals feel compelled to share, reply, or remark.

Even more significant than emotion is the novelty component. When confronted with unique, unexpected information or perspectives, the brain's reward centres become activated. Knowing this, algorithms frequently recommend content that is distinctive or offers a fresh perspective. This strategy, however, has two disadvantages. When paired with contentious or extremist perspectives, novelty can worsen divisions and reinforce prejudices, while simultaneously spurring creativity and opening up new possibilities. Personalisation is the next step in the algorithmic toolkit. Algorithms modify each user's digital experience based on their preferences, habits, and previous interactions. From the outside, this appears advantageous. Content tailored to consumers' interests ensures a seamless and enjoyable online experience. However, beneath this surface lies a more worrisome fact. When algorithms provide users content that is relevant to their own interests and viewpoints, they unintentionally create echo chambers. These are closed online groups in which participants are rarely exposed to opposing or

1. https://faculty.wharton.upenn.edu/wp-content/uploads/2011/11/Virality.pdf

divergent points of view in a fair and balanced way. Rather, their prejudices and informational horizons are restricted, and their pre-existing ideas are constantly reinforced.

Consider a user with conservative political leanings. They teach the algorithm to prioritise similar content if they connect with conservative news sites or pundits on a frequent basis. Over time, a single position takes centre stage in the user's feed, whereas moderate or liberal viewpoints are rarely or never presented. This phenomenon transcends political leanings and encompasses a wide range of interests, connections, and viewpoints. The algorithm doesn't care what you actually believe, only that it learns what that thing is so it can provide you with more of it.

Algorithm-driven division has numerous and serious repercussions. The divide between various groups widens as people become increasingly restricted to their echo chambers. Misconceptions proliferate as a result of people's lack of exposure to the nuances and explanations of opposing views. Stereotypes persist, and the complexities of different points of view are frequently reduced to gruesome parodies or simple falsehoods. Furthermore, there is a threat to the fundamental underpinning of informed and deliberative democracy. Reasoned discussion, the sharing of ideas, and respect for opposing viewpoints are all essential components of democracy.

Sensationalism frequently triumphs over nuance, however, when algorithms prioritise interaction above equitable information distribution. Strongly felt, contentious material is brought to the forefront, displacing more measured, detailed debate. The algorithmic emphasis on disputed or extreme topics may unintentionally support fantastical conspiracy theories or fringe beliefs, whilst also undermining critical conspiracy hypotheses. As people interact with such material, whether out of genuine belief or simply curiosity, algorithms interpret this interaction as interest and display more of the same. This feedback loop results in the rapid spread on of erroneous information or extremist ideologies.

Digital platforms should reconsider their performance metrics, shifting from a narrow engagement focus to a more thorough evaluation of user well-being, intelligent conversation, and social cohesiveness. Sadly, there is little social and political pressure to adopt these standards and little talk about the possibility of regulatory action. A more peaceful digital environment can be created by ensuring transparency in algorithmic operations and holding platforms accountable for the impact of their algorithms on society. Users who understand algorithmic biases can be more proactive. They can avoid algorithmic echo chambers by intentionally seeking out a range of information sources, challenging their own preconceptions, and regularly assessing their digital consumption habits.

In the digital world, algorithms have taken centre stage, controlling a wide spectrum of human decisions, interactions, and experiences. They influence search engine results, movie selection, and even purchasing decisions. Even if their skills have improved the personalisation and smoothness of the digital experience, the algorithms' underlying architecture and biases create substantial ethical concerns. Algorithms are fundamentally complicated systems of rules, or formulas for processing data. Despite their essentially mathematical nature, human choices, preferences, and prejudices have a considerable impact on the design and implementation of algorithms in digital platforms. When developers construct algorithms, they integrate specific goals, such as improving customer satisfaction, increasing ad revenue, or increasing engagement. Meanwhile, these aims rarely exist in isolation and are typically intertwined with broader societal standards, beliefs, and prejudices.

Consider a search engine algorithm. Despite its efforts to give the most relevant results, a variety of factors influence how it defines relevance, including user behaviour, public opinion, and even business interests. One seemingly simple choice, prioritising recent material, may unintentionally conceal historical context or established professional judgements. The potential for algorithms to reinforce or even exacerbate prejudices is one of the most pressing ethical challenges. Data is a fundamental input for algorithms, reflecting our society's inherent prejudices, stereotypes, and injustices. Algorithms trained on biased data have a tendency to internalise and perpetuate these prejudices. For example, it has been discovered that underrepresented groups obtain less reliable facial recognition software, which is mostly trained on photographs of people of specific genders or ethnicities, potentially leading to prejudice. The text generated by AI, such as ChatGPT, depends on the data upon which it was trained. Algorithms know only what we feed them. Their *diets* are rarely representative of the whole internet.

The extent to which algorithms can profile, forecast, and analyse user behaviour raises serious privacy concerns. Algorithms can compile massive amounts of data, ranging from social media interactions to internet searches, to generate an astonishingly accurate portrait of a person's interests, habits, and even future behaviours. This capacity raises concerns about monitoring, consent, and the right to privacy, even if it is beneficial for targeted advertising. Many modern algorithms, particularly those that use deep learning, act as "black boxes," with extremely accurate decision-making processes. This lack of transparency impedes accountability, especially in cases when algorithmic decisions have serious real-world consequences, such as criminal sentence or medical diagnosis. Algorithms powering internet advertising and e-commerce, have the potential to exacerbate or sustain economic inequality. Predatory pricing methods can easily arise from dynamic pricing algorithms that change rates based on user data.

The numerous ethical issues surrounding algorithms necessitate a reassessment of the paradigms utilised in their development and use. Ethical considerations should be incorporated into algorithm design at all stages, including data collection, algorithmic training, deployment, and evaluation. Designers should make the detection and correction of biases in training data a major focus. Algorithmic justice frameworks are one way to ensure that algorithms do not discriminate against specific populations. Routine audits and outside evaluations can further improve algorithmic fairness. Transparency should be a fundamental concept rather than one that is added later. Methods such as explainable AI, which aims to make algorithms' decision-making processes understandable to humans, may enable more open and responsible systems.

Setting up ethical review boards including professionals from a variety of fields—philosophy, sociology, and psychology, for example—can ensure that algorithms are thoroughly tested for moral flaws before being utilised. Users deserve more control over their digital experiences, even if they do not notice inherent constrictions and manipulations. This could include informing individuals about how algorithms affect their online experiences and providing tools to amend or influence algorithmic decisions. Governments and regulatory bodies play a vital role in this by ensuring that algorithms obey moral, social, and legal standards by establishing clear rules, criteria, and accountability systems.

All of this will be possible only if the users themselves actually fight for these rights and regulations. It will not be handed to them freely. Governments ought to set a higher standard for digital platforms and search engines however, this does not mean that it is completely up to legislation. Culture must also adapt, and people must be made aware of algorithmic manipulation in their own experiences. As we get closer to an algorithm-powered future, it is vital that we align these powerful tools with human values and interests so that they promote collective growth rather than divide us. The opportunities to create a digital world that is genuinely diverse, just, and reflective of our shared humanistic ideals are as numerous as the challenges.

As we progress further through the artificial intelligence (AI) era, a surprising phenomenon is emerging: AI's dynamic learning capacity from human behaviour. This constant process of collecting data from human interactions and then modifying AI itself has created a unique feedback loop. This loop poses philosophical, ethical, and practical concerns while also having the potential to improve customisation and efficacy. To properly understand the complexity of the feedback loop, we must first understand the underlying synergy between AI and human behaviour.

AI particularly that based on machine learning (ML) paradigms, use a variety of datasets to improve and sharpen their performances. These datasets are often derived from human interactions, such as those occurring through social media interactions, internet searches, e-commerce transactions, or a variety of other digital traces. Underlying AI algorithms collect, assess, and learn from human interactions with digital platforms, constantly adjusting future outputs to better match perceived human preferences. If a user frequently clicks on sensationalist news articles or engages with divisive material on social media, the AI will prioritise analogous information in subsequent interactions to increase user engagement. This seemingly harmless adaptation can have a domino effect, as the AI mirrors and possibly amplifies inherent human preconceptions, preferences, and inclinations.

When artificial intelligence learns to behave like humans, it frequently offers information or solutions that closely fit its users' preexisting tendencies, neglecting alternative, more diverse, or opposing points of view. Because people are continuously exposed to validating information, their preexisting ideas become even more embedded over time.

These are complicated issues involving intricate feedback loop interactions between AI determinism and human agency. They also emphasise the importance of reflection on the design principles that guide AI systems, as well as our own behaviour, which feeds into these systems. To serve as a force of social improvement rather than accidental divisiveness, AI systems must be exposed to a variety of sample datasets that capture the breadth of human experiences, values, and beliefs.

Algorithmic tools designed specifically to detect and battle biases can be combined with this to ensure fair and equal AI outputs. Users should be able to see inside AI systems and how their activities impact and are influenced by them. When visible and explainable AI aids in demystifying the feedback loop, users may make more informed decisions. Instead, AI is often presented as an inhuman, objective and neutral arbiter of truth. It supposedly does not have the same flaws and biases as we do. Its wide database and cold rationality make it a trustworthy source of information. That's how the story goes. In truth, the outputs of artificial intelligence are conditioned on what we put into it and how we program it. It is still all too human and must be subjected to the same scepticism and critical analysis.

In the digital domain, opinions appear to come and go like the swallows in murmuration, seemingly influenced by a plethora of invisible forces. The evolving nature of online opinion is both intriguing and perplexing. The concept of digital persuasion is fundamental to the malleability of online opinion. Rhetoricians, orators, and writers have long dominated persuasion; their ability to argue and convince us has built paths through both our hearts and mind. In the digital realm, however, persuasion takes on a more subtle, data-driven face. Algorithms choose content based on massive volumes of user data that appeals to specific preferences. Every like, share, remark, and search help these algorithms improve their persuasiveness.

Nonetheless, the reality is far more complex than the concept of carefully selected content, which suggests just the amplification of existent preferences. In their pursuit of engagement, online platforms regularly expose people to sensationalist, overblown content that pushes opinions to the limit. When assaulted with algorithmically selected extremist content, a moderate perspective can silently shift, emphasising the division of opinions. Our inherent demand for social approval amplifies algorithmic impact. Upvotes, retweets, likes, and shares are all forms of measurable validation on digital networks. This public declaration of approval or disapproval can have a significant impact on opinion formation and behavioural change.

Algorithmic curation paired with the desire for social acceptability commonly results in echo chambers, in which users are locked in self-reinforcing opinion loops with opposing perspectives conspicuously absent and beliefs—regardless of their validity—constantly reinforced. In these conditions, the malleability of online opinion becomes paradoxical because, while attitudes inside the chamber are firmly reinforced, opinions outside the chamber are fluid and are constantly drawn in the direction of the chamber's essential principles. Influencers—those with large digital followings and disproportionate persuasive power—also dot the landscape of online thought. In today's world of digital stardom, influencers can change opinions about politics, society, health, and other topics. Their endorsements, condemnations, anecdotes, or even hints become powerful triggers that induce waves of change in the brains of their followers. They do all of this with little to no expertise. They are simply influential because they are popular.

Influencers are influential because of their perceived sincerity, as well as their reach. Unlike traditional celebrities, many influencers emerge from grassroots internet movements, establishing their identities through carefully picked moments from their daily lives. This pseudo-intimacy—where followers believe influencers have a personal relationship with them—increases their persuasiveness. Their recommendations or criticisms are regarded as friendly advice rather than mere opinions from random strangers.

One often overlooked, but crucial aspect of online opinion malleability, is its commercial underpinning. Digital platforms, despite their appearance as open forums, are for-profit corporations. Advertisers invest heavily in sophisticated campaigns aimed at changing people's minds because they recognise the value of flexible ideas. The lines between genuine opinion and commercial influence are muddled by everything from sponsored content masquerading as genuine articles to astroturfing, in which well-planned activities are made to appear as grassroots movements. This commercial aspect is overlooked because there is no clear membership fee or required payment on social media. If you want to socialise with the elites in real life, you will have to cough up a lot of cash to attend their yacht parties and exclusive events. On social media, all you have to do is find someone's account or a specific group.

The formation and strengthening of echo chambers are a well-established tendency and these virtual enclaves, which encapsulate individuals in self-reinforcing loops of homogenised thought, exemplify the dialectic contradiction between the promise and risk of online communication. It is critical to investigate their long-term implications for individual cognition, society cohesiveness, and democratic discourse. The mutually beneficial combination of inherent human impulses and algorithmic determinism is essential to echo chamber formation. Large social media firms and news aggregators are only two examples of digital platforms that utilise sophisticated algorithms to curate content based on user preferences. These algorithms prioritise material that corresponds to a person's preexisting interests, viewpoints, and habits, with the primary purpose of enhancing user engagement. This personalised feed gradually narrows the digital experience, systematically excluding various points of view and perspectives.

This automated curation is complemented by the human desire to seek praise and avoid cognitive dissonance. People naturally look for information that supports their beliefs and shun stories that contradict them. Users of the broad digital world unknowingly create walls of confirmation around themselves when they join organisations, follow influencers, and subscribe to channels that match their interests. They might not think that they are entrenching themselves into lasting positions, but the algorithm remembers their likes and dislikes. With this information, the exposure to future content is already planned out.

Echo chambers are dynamic structures that evolve over time due to intense feedback loops. They are not rigid. Instead, they embrace flexibility as a way of maintaining their group cohesiveness and identity. The overwhelming amount of homogenised content in these chambers creates the impression of consensus, reinforcing the illusion that the dominant views are not only popular but also generally accepted. These ideas appear to be ubiquitous, giving them assurance of truth. When people stuck in echo chambers are confronted with radically different ideas, they see them as extremist or undesirable. Since the echo chamber already contains the final truth, anything outside of it suspicious and bizarre. The algorithms magnify the chamber's echoic quality while also limiting the breadth of information by doubling down on content screening after reading these encounters as endorsements of its stories.

In addition to algorithms and clicks, complex socio-psychological factors contribute to the reinforcement of echo chambers. Somewhere in these chambers, a sense of connection and community appears. Because they share similar ideas, individuals usually build a group identity, resulting in a tribal worldview. Members of the chamber dislike outsiders and typically dismiss their opinions without giving them any consideration, exacerbating in-group prejudices. Group solidary ends up being founded on the content individuals consume. Speech in the echo chamber is frequently conveyed in a strong and emotional way. Members frantically express their loyalty and lampoon those who do not belong to the group. Emotionally charged material is thought to have a substantial effect on the human mind, strengthening beliefs and increasing resistance to new ideas. Pride is fostered, whilst shame and anxiety are nullified.

Echo chambers are dangerous, posing severe challenges to modern civilization. Democracies based on educated electorates struggle with citizens trapped in various information bubbles, preventing healthy political discourse. They present a form of modern tribalisation. Because echo chambers exaggerate radical viewpoints and foster hatred and distrust among groups, societal polarisation worsens. Collectively, echo chambers undermine the cohesiveness and unity of the public sphere. This makes it much easier for the elite to divide and conquer the numerically superior population. Individually, echo chambers impair cognitive growth. They stifle critical thinking and perpetuate ignorance by isolating people from different perspectives and narratives.

Platform changes that promote algorithmic openness and diverse content curation are important, but they are only one component of the whole picture. Digital literacy, critical thinking growth, and open communication should be the top priority for education. As individuals, we ought to embrace the intellectual curiosity that leads us to venture outside of our digital comfort zones and engage with the diverse ideas that the internet world has to offer. This sort of modern education is not only for children, teenagers and adolescents. We should all accept the burdens of living in a technologically advancing age and adapt ourselves to the new challenges. Though echo chambers symbolise the challenges of our digital age, they also represent an opportunity—a cry for a digital renaissance in which we reclaim the internet as a venue for genuine communication, education, and progress. The technology itself is neither good nor bad, it is up to us to deal with it accordingly. Individually, we ought to cultivate the right habits. Collectively, we must create a culture that deals with technology in a healthy way.

This is more than just an issue of fatalistic predeterminism; it is plainly a dangerous tool if utilised inappropriately to dominate substantial sectors of public opinion. In its excesses, it is the source of modern authoritarianism. The echo chamber and feedback loops are undoubtedly major contributors to the deafening silence that has greeted counter narrative science and data that, in other circumstances, should have broken the illusion surrounding Covid as a pandemic and revealed the global impact as a mass psychological formation exercise. It is not the only explanation, since trillions of dollars in funding and tireless efforts from social and mainstream media, as well as so-called fact checkers, would not have enabled the effect to linger in the public mind. Even though the influence is waning, the concept that human-caused CO2 emissions are the only explanation for a minor increase in temperatures and that humanity is doomed if we do not reach net zero remains.

Breaking free from algorithmic bonds is more than simply a search for digital autonomy or a holistic digital experience in which platforms serve users rather than the other way around; it is also a defence against manipulation, a foundation for critical thinking, and beneficial to brain and mental health. As we stand at this digital crossroads, the path ahead is apparent. It envisions a future in which algorithms enhance rather than limit human potential and curiosity. Although arduous, the path to an enlightened digital era holds great promise, requiring a harmonious synthesis of technology and the highest attributes of humanity. However, it is also fraught with the siren call of tribalism, as well as the evident threat of centralised authority and a loss in individual freedom, imagination, and free speech.

Printed in Great Britain
by Amazon

4e70c789-e5ab-424a-9b87-8cea63f2cc1aR01